MIND IN THE WATERS

Whales Weep Not

They say the sea is cold, but the sea contains
the hottest blood of all, and the wildest, the most urgent.

All the whales in the wider deeps, hot are they, as they urge
on and on, and dive beneath the icebergs.
The right whales, the sperm-whales, the hammer-heads, the killers
there they blow, there they blow, hot wild white breath out of the sea

And they rock, and they rock, through the sensual ageless ages
on the depths of the seven seas,
and through the salt they reel with drunk delight
and in the tropics tremble they with love
and roll with massive, strong desire, like gods.
Then the great bull lies up against his bride
in the blue deep of the sea.
as mountain pressing on mountain, in the zest of life:
and out of the inward roaring of the inner red ocean of whale blood
the long tip reaches strong, intense, like the maelstrom-tip, and
  comes to rest
in the clasp and the soft, wild clutch of a she-whale's fathomless
  body.

And over the bridge of the whale's strong phallus, linking the
  wonder of whales
the burning archangels under the sea keep passing, back and forth,
keep passing archangels of bliss
from him to her, from her to him, great Cherubim
that wait on whales in mid-ocean, suspended in the waves of the sea
great heaven of whales in the waters, old hierarchies.
And enormous mother whales lie dreaming suckling their whale-
  tender young
and dreaming with strange whale eyes wide open in the waters of
  the beginning and the end.

And bull-whales gather their women and whale-calves in a ring
when danger threatens, on the surface of the ceaseless flood
and range themselves like great fierce Seraphim facing the threat
encircling their huddled monsters of love.
and all this happiness in the sea, in the salt
where God is also love, but without words:
and Aphrodite is the wife of whales
most happy, happy she

and Venus among the fishes skips and is a she-dolphin
she is the gay, delighted porpoise sporting with love and the sea
she is the female tunny-fish, round and happy among the males
and dense with happy blood, dark rainbow bliss in the sea.

D. H. Lawrence

From The Complete Poems of D. H. Lawrence, *Viking Press*

MIND IN THE WATERS

A Book to Celebrate
the Consciousness of Whales and Dolphins

assembled by Joan McIntyre

CHARLES SCRIBNER'S SONS, NEW YORK
SIERRA CLUB BOOKS, SAN FRANCISCO

This book was edited and prepared for publication by The Yolla Bolly Press in collaboration with Project Jonah. The work was done in Sausalito, California, between January and June of 1974.

The Yolla Bolly Press
James Robertson
Queenie Taylor, *Editor*
Catherine Flanders, *Designer*
Sadako McInerney, *Design Assistant*
Bob Gumpertz, *Design Assistant*
Richard Ellis, *Illustrator*
Pamela Cope Vesterby, *Illustrator*

Project Jonah
Joan McIntyre, *President*
Gail Madonia, *Coordinator, International Children's Campaign*
Eugenia McNaughton, *Administrative Coordinator*
Bettina Miller, *Assistant*
Angela Borregaard, *Assistant*

Acknowledgements

To begin, we would like to acknowledge the life and presence of the whales, dolphins, and porpoises, whose being has inspired us to gather together in their defense and explication. Then, there are the many people we would like to thank who helped us in so many ways with the book, whose names do not appear on any of its pages.

David Brower, for first insisting that such a book should be done; Kenneth Norris and Thomas Dohl, for use of unpublished manuscripts and moral support; Georg Pilleri, for use of materials and commitment to the cause of Cetaceans; Peter Matthiessen, Laurens van der Post, Henry Truby, Ken Balcomb, Robert Brownell, Tom Hill, Carl Sagan, Paul Ehrlich, Steve Katona at Allied Whale, Phoebe Wray, Duncan McNaughton, Richard Baker, George Quasha, Ishmael Reed, Donald Finkel, Lewis Hyde, and Edward Mitchell, for valuable material we were not able to include; Donald Patten (Natural History Museum of Los Angeles County), Ernie Rook (California Academy of Sciences, San Francisco), Theodore Walker, Jerome Rothenberg, Robert Bly, Gary Snyder, and Howard Norman, for assistance and understanding; Valerie Cross of General Whale, Malcolm Jones and Maxine McCloskey of Project Jonah, for advice and support; Richard Matthews, for research; Richard Ellis and Pamela Cope Vesterby, for drawings and illustrations; Joe Fay of Marinstat; Othmar Peters of Peter's Typography; Irwin and Florence Welcher of General Graphics Services; Harris Dienstfrey of Scribner's and Jon Beckmann of the Sierra Club, for understanding this book from the beginning; Moses, who was the only non-human animal present during the book's production; Lillian Widder, my mother, and Ian McIntyre, my son, who are my links with the past, the future, and the continuity I cherish; and finally, special thanks to all of the contributors who gave of their material and time, royalty-free, so that the proceeds from this book could be used to help save the whales.

Thank you.
Joan McIntyre

We would also like to thank these sources and people for material used on the following pages in the book: cover and title page: Larry Foster; 2: "Whales Weep Not," from *The Complete Poems of D. H. Lawrence,* edited by Vivian de Sola Pinto and F. Warren Roberts. Copyright © 1964, 1971, by Angelo Ravagli and C. M. Weekley, Executors of the Estate of Frieda Lawrence Ravagli. All Rights reserved. Reprinted by permission of The Viking Press, Inc.; and by permission of Laurence Pollinger, London. 3: Drawing by Larry Foster. "The Trapped Whale," by Farley Mowat, copyright © 1972 by Farley Mowat. Used by permission of Little, Brown and Company in association with The Atlantic Monthly Press; and by permission of the author. Parts of this essay were originally printed in *A Whale for the Killing.* 31: Excerpts from *A Dictionary of Symbols,* by J. E. Cirlot, translated from the Spanish by Jack Sage. Copyright © 1962 by The Philosophical Library, New York. Reprinted by permission of The Philosophical Library; and Routledge & Kegan Paul, Ltd., London. 32: "Magic Words," text by Edward Field from *Songs and Stories of the Netsilik Eskimo,* part of the upper elementary school course *Man: A Course of Study* developed by the Social Studies Program of EDC under a grant from the National Science Foundation. Text copyright © 1967, 1968 Education Development Center, Inc. Used with permission. Haida Indian whale illustration from *Annual Report of the Board of Regents of the Smithsonian Institution, year ending June 30, 1888.* 30 (top): From Cathedral at Rimini. (bottom): Illustrations from *The Gods of the Greeks,* by Carl Kerenyi, Hirmer Verlag, Munich. 36 (top): "Girl Riding Fish," by Jay Lynch. Cover of Roxy Funnies, No. 1, copyright © 1972 Bijou Publishing Empire, Inc. World rights reserved. (bottom): From Conservation Museum, Rome. Published in *Archaeology Magazine,* April 1970, Volume 23, No. 2, p. 91. 39: From State Hermitage Museum, Leningrad. 40 (top): From the British Museum. (bottom): From the Naples Museum, Italy. Published in *Archaeology Magazine,* April 1970, Volume 23, No. 2, p. 94. 41: Illustration from *Sexual Symbolism,* by R. P. Knight and T. Wright. Copyright © 1957 Julian Press, Inc., reprint 1969 Bell Publishing Company. Used by permission of Julian Press. 42: Illustration from *The Gods of the Greeks,* by Carl Kerenyi, Hirmer Verlag, Munich. 43 (top): From the Louvre, Paris. (bottom): Drawing of fresco in the Museum of Nauplia, Greece. Used by courtesy of the German Archaeological Institute, Athens, Greece. 46: Dionysos Cup used by courtesy of the Antikensammlungen, Munich. 47: "News for the Delphic Oracle," reprinted with permission of Macmillan Publishing Co., Inc., from *The Collected Poems of W. B. Yeats,* by William Butler Yeats. Copyright 1940 by Georgie Yeats, renewed 1968 by Bertha Georgie Yeats, Michael Butler Yeats and Anne Yeats; and by permission of M. B. Yeats, Miss Anne Yeats and Macmillan of London and Basingstoke and Macmillan Co. of Canada. 50: Excerpt from *The Kalevala* reprinted by permission of the publisher from *The Kalevala: Or, Poems of the Kaleva District.* Elias Lonnrot, compiler, and Francis P. Magoun, Jr., trans. Harvard University Press, Cambridge. Copyright © 1963 by the President and Fellows of Harvard College. 53: Drawings by Pamela Cope Vesterby. 61: Taxonomy from *Investigations on Cetacea,* edited by G. Pilleri, Institute of Brain Anatomy, University of Berne, Switzerland. Used by kind permission of the editor. 62-66: Illustrations by Richard Ellis. 71: Reprinted by permission from *The Archives of General Psychiatry,* Volume 8, February 1963, pp. 111-116. Copyright © 1963 American Medical Association. Originally published as "Productive and Creative Research with Man and Dolphin." 74, 88: Excerpts from *The Cosmic Connection* (Doubleday, New York, 1973). Copyright © Carl Sagan and Jerome Agel. Used by permission. 78-79: Excerpt from "The Three Brains," from *The Seventies* (The Seventies Press, Odin House, Madison, Minnesota 56356) used by permission of Robert Bly, editor. 80-82: Illustrations courtesy Myron Jacobs. 85-90: Illustrations courtesy Peter Morgane. 92: "Potheads Deform," by Scott McVay. Used by permission. 98-104: Event cards from The Smithsonian Institution Center for Short Lived Phenomena, Cambridge. 105-106: Photographs by Robert Brownell. 107: "Going Out To Meet the Moon Whales," translated from the Creole of Paule Barton by Howard A. Norman. Used by permission. 108: "For A Coming Extinction," by W. S. Merwin, from *The Lice.* Copyright © 1967 W. S. Merwin. Reprinted by permission of Atheneum Publishers. First appeared in *The Southern Review.* 111: Illustration from "The Nature of Oceanic Life," by John D. Isaacs. Copyright © September 1969 by Scientific American, Inc. All rights reserved. 114 (bottom left), 117: *Investigations on Cetacea.* 119: Photograph by William Curtsinger. "Leviathan," by Pablo Neruda, translated by Ben Belitt, reprinted by permission of Grove Press, Inc., from *The Selected Poems of Pablo Neruda.* Copyright © 1961 by Grove Press, Inc., New York. 120 (left): Pamela Cope Vesterby. 121 (bottom): *Investigations on Cetacea.* 122: Illustration from *Marine Mammals of the Northwestern Coast of North America,* by Charles M. Scammon, Dover 1968. 125-128: Pamela Cope Vesterby. 126: "Whales," by Scott Bates. Reprinted from *The Carleton Miscellany,* copyright © June 12, 1962, by Carleton College. Used by permission of the author. 130: Pamela Cope Vesterby. 131 (top): *Investigations on Cetacea.* 134, 137, 138: Pamela Cope Vesterby. 140: Photograph by David K. Caldwell and Melba C. Caldwell. 146: "Observations of a Cetacean Community," by Gregory Bateson. Used by permission of the author. 164: "Six Seri Whale Songs," by Santo Blanco. Copyright 1939, by Dane Coolidge and Mary Roberts Coolidge. Renewal, © 1967 by Coit Coolidge and Mrs. Calvin Gaines Collins. Reprinted by the permission of the publishers, E. P. Dutton & Co., Inc., New York. From *The Last of the Seris.* 165: Photographs by David K. Caldwell and Melba C. Caldwell. 166-168: Edited from No. 70 and No. 95 of *Contributions in Science,* Natural History Museum of Los Angeles County. Used by permission. 167: Photograph by David K. Caldwell and Melba C. Caldwell. 169: "For the Death of 100 Whales," by Michael McClure. Used by permission. 171: "Salamanca A Prophecy," by Jerome Rothenberg. Used by permission. 175-183: Photographs by Paul Spong. 185: "Prayer of a Man Who Found a Dead Killer Whale," from *The Religion of the Kwakiutl Indians,* by Franz Boas, Volume 2, p. 184. Used by permission of Columbia University Press. 186: Photograph by Malcolm Brenner. *Color section photographs by the following:* 193-197: William Curtsinger; 198: Joan McIntyre; 199: Malcolm Brenner; 200-202: William Curtsinger; 203-205: Charles Jurasz; 206, 207: William Curtsinger; 208: Scott McVay. 210-216: Photographs from *Memoirs of the American Museum of Natural History,* "Monographs of the Pacific Cetacea. I—The California Gray Whale," by Roy C. Andrews, March 1914. Excerpts from *Lost Leviathan,* by F. D. Ommaney, copyright © 1971 Dodd, Mead and Company, New York. Used by permission of Dodd, Mead and Company; and by permission of Hutchinson Publishing Group, Ltd., London. 232: "The Great Whales and the International Whaling Commission," by Lee Talbot. By permission of author and Maxine E. McCloskey.

Invitation

For the last six hundred years, men have been going out in small boats and large to hunt down and murder wild whales and dolphins for their meat, bone, oil, and baleen. Yet three thousand years ago, in the ancient Mediterranean, the dolphin, a small whale, was the doorway to profound religious mysteries and the honored guardian of life in the sea. Gemistos Pletho, a fifteenth century Byzantine philosopher, saw the dolphin swimming through the sea as the mind of God in the waters. More recently, Melville reckoned that if God returned to earth in our lifetime, it would be in the guise of the whale.

The whale is a split in our consciousness: on the one hand viewed as product, as resource, as an article, an object to be carved up to satisfy the economic imperative; on the other, a view almost lost now, as the great leviathan, the guardian of the sea's unutterable mysteries. Ever since we discovered the awesome abilities of our hands to fashion the world to our making, we have dishonored the unknown, until instead of inspiring us, it merely seems an inconvenience. Yet in that time when human beings lived a less exploitative life, the earth still held her secrets, and we revered those creatures who could reveal them. Now we find ourselves at the threshold of approaching the sea as we did the land: creating boundaries, carving up territories, dividing—in the name of nations—the waters that still flow in our veins and link each living thing to every other. One of the points of this book is that in so doing we are furthering the annihilation of our spirit.

We have, for too long now, accepted a view of non-human life which denies other creatures feelings, imagination, consciousness, and awareness. It seems that in our craze to justify our exploitation of all non-human life forms, we have stripped from them any attributes which could stay our hand. Try for a moment, if you can, to imagine the imagination of a whale, or the awareness of a dolphin. That we cannot make those leaps of vision is because we are bound to a cultural view which denies their possibility.

Moreover, we are bound to a view that relegates feeling and emotion to inferior functions, that searches in vain for pure objectivity, and in so doing denies the humanity of the investigator and the livingness of the creature under investigation.

We are bound to a vision that leads us further away from nature, and further away from each other.

This book is written by some people who wish to take a second look. Who are as concerned with the death of the planet, and the death of the spirit of the planet, as they are about the current slaughter of the whales. It is our belief that we must take this second look, for we cannot accept the wholesale destruction of life and the alienation and desolation that accompanies it. Whatever the actual living reality of whales and dolphins, the truth of these creatures can be more easily found by people viewing a whole world. This truth is no more·certain in science than it is in religion or in myth. But wherever we may find it, we do know that we have for too long accepted a traditional way of looking at nature, at nature's creatures, which has blinded us to their incredible essence, and which has made us incomparably lonely. It is our loneliness as much as our greed which can destroy us.

So consider yourself now in a living room full of people who have spent some time trying to find out something of the truth of a whole order of creatures: the Cetacea. Imagine us sitting around in a circle; on the leaf-laden floor of a forest clearing; around a round table in your kitchen; on the front porch in the late-day sun; and we are having a conversation about these animals, and ultimately, about what we see and believe of the world—about how we want it to be. There is no beginning and end to this conversation because it takes place in a circle. There is no particular place to start in this book, because all places only start with a single human idea or or experience.

We invite you to join our circle.

Joan McIntyre

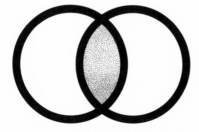

Contents

FARLEY MOWAT
The Trapped Whale

A curiosity about the whale nation has been a part of me for as long as I can remember. When I was a very small child, my grandfather used to sing me a song that began:

> *In the North Sea lived a whale*
> *Big of bone and large of tail . . .*

The song went on to describe how this particular whale was the master of his world until the day when he espied a stranger in his domain: a big, gleaming silver fish who stubbornly refused to acknowledge the whale's mastery. The whale grew angry and slapped the interloper with his tail. That was a fatal error, because the strange fish was actually a torpedo.

The moral of the song must have been that it does not pay to be a bully. I never understood it that way; my sympathy was entirely with the whale—the victim, so it seemed to me, of a very dirty trick.

As I grew older, the whale became a symbol of the ultimate secrets which have not yet been revealed to us by the "other" animals. Whenever anything came to hand about whales, I read it avidly; but the only thing which seemed to emerge with certainty from all my reading was that the whales appeared to be doomed by human greed to disappear and to carry their secrets with them into oblivion.

During the first thirty years of my life I never actually saw one of the great whales, and, knowing how rapidly they were being de-

Farley Mowat is a naturalist, author, and president of the Canadian branch of Project Jonah. This account of his relationship with a trapped seventy-foot female fin whale is excerpted from his book, A Whale for the Killing, *with some new ideas and one old story added. For the last thirty years he has been passionately interested in the combined destiny of human and animal, and has written about that common bond in a number of books, including* The People of the Deer, Never Cry Wolf, *and* The Siberians.

stroyed, I was afraid I would never meet one. And that was strange, because for several years I had been spending more and more time at sea; an insignificant mote moving at the wind's will upon the trackless wastes of the North Atlantic.

Whatever other motives I may have had for sailing my little ship in that grey, sounding void, they were as nothing to the buried hope that one day I would meet one of the Lords Of Ocean.

The day was a long time coming, but it was presaged by an omen that arose from the titanic confusion which is the aftermath of a hurricane. My father and I had been at sea for nearly a week in a thirty-five-foot ketch, lost, lonely and exhausted, for we had been the playthings of the great wind through those interminable days and nights. Now the furious winds had passed, leaving behind such a turmoil of heaving seas that the compass spun in its box like a drunken top. We were filled with a consuming need to escape this alien planet and scrabble back upon the land. Our ship crawled westward, toward Nova Scotia, and when we guessed, by dead-reckoning, that we were closing on those reef-ridden shores, the fog came down. It simply obliterated the world in an almost palpable black shroud. We dared not sail farther westward for fear of the reefs, yet we were desperate to escape the sea.

I was alone on deck. It must have been about 2:00 A.M., and I was weary almost unto death. The night was a muffled sepulchre, soundless except for the uneasy creaking of our booms and gaffs—then, with a heart-stopping violence, a gigantic *voice* broke over our small ship.

It was a sound that thrummed and rumbled through the sea; through the fabric of our vessel; and through the fragile human flesh. It might have been the voice of God for all I knew. Yet, though it transfixed me with awe, it did not fill me with fear.

My father, who had been sleeping so soundly that only the Last Trump itself should have been able to rouse him, came tumbling into the cockpit.

"What in Christ's name was that!" he asked, and was so moved that his voice was only a husky whisper.

I did not *know* what that voice was, and yet I knew.

"A whale," I said. "It has to be a whale."

The mighty reverberation rolled through the water and the fog again; this time a little farther off. I glanced at the moisture-beaded compass. . . . Sou'sou'west. I looked at my father in the hazed beam of a flashlight: and somehow—there is no rational explanation for this—we understood, and knew we understood, that we should follow that sonorous beacon.

Perhaps it was only an instinct that told us the maker of that sound would steer clear of dangers and, since it was apparently moving in the direction we wished to go, that it would be safe to follow after. Perhaps.

We followed where the great voice led for many hours. It never seemed to vary its distance from us very much, and always it led us to the sou'sou'west. Under full sail in an almost windless night we were making no more than two or three knots, and the whale—if indeed such it was—must have had to slow its pace to ours.

Shortly after dawn the next morning, still in impenetrable fog, we heard that voice for the last time—but almost immediately thereafter heard another: the lugubrious grunt of a whistle buoy. It emerged suddenly out of the grey murk, so close aboard we could easily read the legend it bore: Egg Island.

We scrambled for the chart, and there it was: Egg Island buoy, lying less than a mile to seaward of an impenetrable maze of reefs and marking the channel south and west to Halifax, and a safe anchorage.

For many years I wondered about this incident . . . and never told another soul about it. I tell it now because now I believe it was in truth an omen, the forecasting of another day, another time, when I would hear that voice again, and meet the secret face-to-face.

In 1961, my wife Claire and I went to live on the edge of the sea in the little fishing village of Burgeo on the south coast of Newfoundland. I had not been there long before I heard that several pods of fin whales had spent the previous winter amongst the archipelago of rocky little islands which shelters the port. The possibility that they might return again was a prospect that excited me to a pitch I had not known since the passing of childhood. Through three long months I waited—until one cold December day, with a hazed sky and sun dogs circling a half-veiled sun. Claire and I were in our kitchen reading. Uncle Art, a near neighbor, came quietly through the door to tell us that whales were spouting just off nearby Messers Head. And so began my first-hand encounter with whales.

Uncle Art—a fisherman and a keen observer—was fascinated by the whales; fascinated by the sense of mystery that enveloped these mighty beings. Although he may have known as much about living whales as any man, he was aware that this—in total—represented no more than smatterings, intimations, of the truth.

Because fin whales are herring eaters, and because the herring strike inshore every winter along the ice-free southern coast of Newfoundland, there is a period when the great mammals live almost at the portals of our world. And because of men like Uncle Art, who are possessed of that abiding curiosity about other forms of life which is the hallmark of natural man, we know a little more about the great whales than the scientist concedes. At the age of ten, Uncle Art had begun accompanying his father in a four-oared dory to the dangerous offshore fishery at the Penguin Islands. Here, while hand-lining for cod, he met his first whales.

"They was t'ousands of the big whales on the coast them times. Times we'd be the only boat, but the whales made it seem like we was in the middle of a girt big fleet. They whales never hurted we, and we never hurted they. Many's the toime a right girt bull, five times the length of our dory, would spout so close along-side you could have spit tobaccy down his vent. My old Dad claimed they'd do it a-purpose; a kind of a joke, you understand. We never minded none, for we was in our ileskins anyway.

"And I'll tell you a quare thing. So long as they was on the fishing grounds along of we, I never was afeared of anything; no, nor never felt lonely neither. But after times, when the whales was all done to death, I'd be on the Penguin grounds with nothing livin' to be seen, and I'd get a feeling in my belly, like the world was empty. Yiss, me son, I missed them whales when they was gone.

" 'Tis strange. Some folks says as whales is only fish. No, bye! They's too smart for fish. *I* don't say as what they's not the smartest creatures in God's ocean.

"Aye . . . and maybe out of it as well."

It is proper for me to acknowledge my debt to such men as Uncle Art. I have drawn heavily on the observations and on the intuitions of such natural observers. My own subsequent experiences enlarged upon the picture and, when combined with some of science's discoveries about whale sonar, enabled me to come to an understanding —a somewhat awestruck one—of how a finner feeds himself.

The whale locates a herring school either by sight, or by means of a highly sophisticated echo location system, transmitting a pulse of very low-frequency sound through the water. Able to distinguish and identify herring as distinct from other species of fish of similar size, the whale heads for the target at his normal underwater cruising speed, which seems to be about eight knots.

As he closes with the school he accelerates in a burst of speed which may reach twenty knots. Closing with his target, he alters course, and at torpedo velocity begins circling the school, spiraling steadily inward. As he does so, he turns on his side with his belly presented toward the herring. His belly offers a huge expanse of glistening white with a very high light-reflecting value. Encircled by this flashing ring of light, the herring jam tightly in upon one another in much the same manner as if they were surrounded by a seine.

When the circle (the "net" of reflected light) is tight enough and the herring sufficiently concentrated, the whale abruptly charges straight into the mob of little fishes with his enormous mouth agape.

He then brings into play another very special device. The whole underpart of his body, from directly beneath his mighty chin and

16

extending aft to a point near his navel, is slit and pleated like a gigantic accordion. When a finner is traveling at speed and suddenly opens his mouth, the whole gaping forefront of his body promptly inflates to gargantuan size as the accordion pleats open to their fullest extent. Thus, he almost instantaneously ingests many tons of water together with its contents. Smartly now he closes his mouth, contracts the muscles controlling the pleats, and squirts the unwanted water out of apertures set at the corners of his jaws. The herring are trapped against the sieve of baleen plates. When there is nothing left in his mouth but herring, he uses his tongue to sluice them through his surprisingly small gullet into the first of his several holds, or stomachs. The entire operation takes about ten minutes.

Although some of my attempts to gain insight into the lives of the finners were bound to be frustratingly inadequate, I occasionally had a stroke of luck. Lee Frankham, a friend who was the pilot of a Beaver airplane on floats, was responsible for one such happy accident.

On a July day in 1964 we flew off with him to visit the abandoned settlement of Cape La Hune. It was a cloudless afternoon and the cold coastal waters were pellucid and transparent. Suddenly Lee banked the Beaver and put her into a shallow dive. When he leveled out at less than a hundred feet, we were flying parallel to a family of six fin whales.

From our unique vantage point, they were clearly visible, and we could see minute details of their bodies and of their actions. Yet if it had not been that their swift progress underwater was relative to a light wind-popple on the surface, it would have been hard to believe they were progressing at all.

Their mighty tails and flukes swept lazily up and down with what appeared to be a completely effortless beat. Their great, paddle-like flippers barely moved at all. There was no visible turbulence in the water although the whales were moving at a rate of twenty knots. The effect was of six exquisitely streamlined bodies hovering in the green sea and seeming to undulate just perceptibly, as if their bodies were composed of something more subtle and responsive than or- dinary flesh and bones. There was a suggestion of sinuosity, of abso- lute fidelity, to some powerful but unheard aquatic rhythm.

They were supremely beautiful beings.

As we lived out our time in Burgeo, we became increasingly anxious about the fate of these mighty beings. In 1958 a Norwegian- financed and directed whaling operation had begun in Nova Scotia, and year by year we saw a steady decline in the number of finners on our coast. During the winter of 1965–66, only two fin families returned to Burgeo. There were four individuals in one, and only three in the other. In addition there was one lone whale whom I believe to have been the sole survivor of a family which had been destroyed by the whalers.

The "Loner," as we called the single whale, spent part of his time in company with one or other of the two family groups, but even more time by himself. His favorite fishing place seemed to be the restricted waters of Messers Cove, upon whose shores our house stood. Here, apparently oblivious to houses, people, and moored boats which almost surrounded him, he spent many hours eating herring which misguidedly continued to pour into this cul-de-sac. Returning homeward late on winter evenings, I would often hear him blowing in the Cove.

Late one chilly afternoon I was chatting with another neighbor, Sim Spencer, on Messers Bridge, when we both became aware of a deep thrumming sound which seemed to be as much felt as heard. We turned in surprise toward the Cove and saw a fading pillar of vapor hanging over the icy water.

"Was that the whale?" I asked in astonishment.

"Never heard no whale blow like that before. But if 'twarn't he, what do you suppose it were?"

After a minute or two the sound came again, deep and vibrant; but this time the surface of the Cove remained unbroken. It was four or five minutes later before the whale rose and blew, with no more than his normal whooshing exhalation. Although Sim and I continued to stand there, half-frozen, for the better part of an hour, we did not hear that other-worldly sound again.

Nevertheless, I could still hear echoes of it in the caverns of my mind, for I believed I had heard the *voice* before. It was the same voice—I was almost sure of this—I had heard that long-ago day in the foggy seas off Nova Scotia. However, a year was to pass before I would hear it once more and know for certain that this sound was the voice of the fin whale.

In the early winter of 1966–67, we awaited the annual visit of the finners with foreboding. It was common knowledge that 1966 had been a very good year for the whale catchers and that no great whales had been seen "in passage" by any of our local draggers throughout the autumn months. However, during the first week in December, Uncle Art was delighted to discover they had returned. It was a sadly diminished band—a single family numbering five individuals, which soon took up residence in a little fiord called The Ha Ha.

The whales were not alone in The Ha Ha. They shared it with several Burgeo fishermen working cod nets from open boats. When the whales moved in, these men were concerned for the safety of their nets. Two among them, the Hann brothers, Douglas and Kenneth—small quiet men—even considered moving their gear to some safer ground.

" 'Twarn't as we t'ought they'd tear up our gear a-purpose-like," Douglas Hann remembered, "but The Ha Ha is a right small place and not much water at the head of she. We t'ought, what with six fleets of nets scattered round, them whales was bound to run foul of some of them . . . couldn't help theirselves. Well, sorr, they never did. Sometimes when we'd be hauling a net they'd pass right under the boat close enough you could have scratched their backs with a gaff. First off, when they did that, we used to bank the oars on the side of the boat and yell to make them veer away; but after a time we sees they knowed what they was about, and was going to keep clear without no help from we."

The Hanns' experience reminded me of a story I had heard some years earlier from a very old man at Hermitage Bay. One Saturday afternoon he was homeward bound from his work at a whale factory when he saw a pod of finners. There were three of them, and they were behaving in a peculiar fashion. Instead of briefly surfacing and then sounding again, they were cruising on top. Their course converged with his as he was rowing, and as they drew close, my friend saw that they were swimming, as he put it, "shoulder to shoulder." The center whale was blowing much more rapidly than the rest and its spray was pink in color.

" 'Twarn't hard to know what was the trouble," the old man remembered. "Yon middle whale had been harpooned and the iron had drawed and he'd got clear of the catcher boat. The bomb must have fired, but no deep enough for to kill he.

"I laid back on me oars, not wantin' to get too handy to them three, but they never minded I . . . just steamed slow as you please right past me boat, heading down the bay and out to sea. They was close enough so I could near swear the two outside whales was holding up the middle one. I t'inks they done it with their flippers. That's what I t'inks. . . . They two other whales took the sick one off someplace . . . some said 'twas to the whales' burying ground . . . but all I knows is they kept that sick one afloat somehow for five days, and close onto sixty miles."

On Friday, January 20, the weatherman was predicting a sou'-easter—the worst kind of storm on the Burgeo coast—and the Hann brothers were in a hurry to get clear of The Ha Ha. During the previous several days they had noticed that nearby Aldridges Pond had acquired a dense herring population which seemed to surge in and out with the ebb and flow of the tides.

Despite the ominous forecast, it only blew a "moderate breeze" that night. The Hann brothers were early getting out to haul their gear and they entered Aldridges before dawn began to break on Saturday to find their nets.

They had been at work only a few minutes when they were startled by what would have been a familiar enough sound outside the Pond but which was totally unexpected inside its confines. It was the explosive *whoooof* of a spouting finner; and it came from "close aboard." Kenneth described the discovery.

" 'Twas hard to believe a whale that big could get herself into the shoal entrance of the Pond. But there she was, and looking twice as big as life."

It will never be known with certainty how the female whale managed to trap herself, but it is possible to make a reasonable reconstruction of the probable events.

Early Friday afternoon the family of finners in The Ha Ha decided to try a change of ground. They rounded Aldridges Head and entered Short Reach. It was alive with herring and the whales had good fishing while daylight lasted. With the coming of night, most of the whales had gorged and were no longer hungry. Not so the female. She was still ravenous, for she was carrying a calf within her vast womb, a new life growing at such a furious pace as to keep her perpetually hungry. So the female continued fishing in the dark, and it was not long before she discovered that the entrance cove to Aldridges Pond was fairly seething with herring.

The female whale went streaking into the cove like the black shadow of Nemesis—hunting her herring—only to find that the school was fading away before her. She had no way of knowing that it was pouring like a living river through the channel to seek safety in the Pond.

The hungry whale fractionally delayed applying her brakes. When she did decide to stop, momentum carried her into the mouth of the channel where the water abruptly and horrifyingly shoaled until her belly touched the bottom rocks. Propelled by the frenzied thrusting of her flukes, she moved in the only direction open to her— forward through the channel, contorting herself to squeeze over and between the boulders which partially barred her way. Then, miraculously it must have seemed, the water deepened and she was free. Her relief must have been short-lived. It could not have taken her many minutes to realize that she had escaped . . . into a trap: Aldridges Pond.

On Saturday afternoon, the Hann brothers reached the fish plant about 4:30 P.M. and began forking their fish up on the wharf, while an interested audience of plant workers listened to the story of the trapped whale. "But," Kenneth Hann told me later, "if I'd a-

20

knowed what they fellers had in mind, I'd have told they she was gone clear of it already."

Only a few minutes after the Hanns finished unloading and departed for their homes in Muddy Hole, another boat put out from the plant wharf carrying five men. It was already growing dusk when their boat passed the mouth of the cove leading to Aldridges Pond. They ran the boat's nose ashore on a patch of shingle, sprang over the side and raced across the narrow neck separating the cove from the Pond. They reached the crest to see what one of them described as ". . . the biggest goddamn fish that ever swum! It was right into the mouth of the gut and looked to be half out of water."

The five men wasted no time. Some dropped to their knees, levering shells into their rifles as they did so. Others stood where they were and hurriedly took aim. The crash of rifle fire began to echo from the cliffs enclosing the Pond and, as an undertone, there came the flat, satisfying thunk of bullets striking home in living flesh. After an hour the men had exhausted their supply of shells. Reluctantly they returned to Burgeo. But not long after dawn on Sunday, between twenty and twenty-five gunners had ringed Aldridges Pond. This time each man had a good supply of shells. As the day wore on, more and more boats arrived. Most people were content just to watch from the natural rock amphitheater which cradles Aldridges. But not everyone who saw the show that day was happy about it. An elderly fisherman from Muddy Hole, who had brought his daughter and grandchildren to see a live whale, was disconcerted.

"It made me feel right ugly just to watch her. She had no place to go, only down under, and she couldn't stay down forever. I expected her to go right crazy after a couple of hundred bullets had smacked into her, but it was like she knowed that would do her no good. Once or twice she got wild, but for the most of it she war right quiet.

"One thing . . . she warn't alone. I was standing high up on a pick of rock where I could spy into the Pond and out across Short Reach as well. 'Twasn't long afore I sees another whale outside. It blowed first just off Fish Island. And every time the whale in the Pond come up to blow, the one outside blowed too. It happened *every* time they blowed. I could see both of them, but they was no way they could see one t'other. You can say what you likes, but the one outside knowed t'other was in trouble, or I'm a Dutchman's wife."

Because we lived at the opposite end of the strung-out settlement, we did not know about the whale until the following Thursday. By that time she had been under spasmodic rifle fire for five days. When I belatedly heard about her, and what was being done to her, my fury was close to being homicidal. I at once called our local policeman, an R.C.M.P. constable, and insisted he stop the shooting. He was a cooperative fellow and he undertook to do so. Meanwhile Claire and I set off for the Pond in a friend's small long-liner. The account of our first meeting with the great being in the Pond is Claire's.

"We slid into the pretty little Pond under a dash of watery sunlight. It was a beautifully protected natural harbor ringed with rocky cliffs. Little clumps of dwarfed black spruce clung in the hollows here and there along the shore.

"We looked and looked for the whale and finally saw a long, black shape that looked like a giant sea-serpent, curving quietly out of the water, and slipping along from head to fin, and then down again and out of sight.

"We just stared, speechless and unbelieving, at this vast monster. Then we chugged to the middle of the Pond, just as the R.C.M.P. launch entered, and headed for us. Farley called to the police boat and we agreed to anchor the two boats in deep water near the south end of the Pond and stop the engines.

"Then began a long, long watch during which the hours went by like minutes. It was endlessly fascinating to watch the almost serpentine coming and going of this huge beast. She would surface about every four or five minutes as she followed a circular path around and around the Pond. At first the circles took her well away from us but as time passed, and everyone kept perfectly still, the circles narrowed, coming closer and closer to the boats.

"Farley identified her as a fin whale, the second largest animal ever to live on earth. We could see the marks of bullets—holes and slashes—across the back, from the blowhole to the fin.

"The undulations on the surface came closer and closer until the whale was surfacing within twenty feet of the boats. She seemed to deliberately look at us from time to time as if trying to decide whether we were dangerous. Oddly, the thought never crossed my mind that *she* might be dangerous to us. Later on I asked some of the others if they had been afraid of this, the mightiest animal any of us ever likely to meet in all our lives and nobody had felt any fear at all. We were too enthralled to be afraid.

"Apparently the whale decided we were not dangerous. She made another sweep and this time that mighty head passed right under the Mountie's boat. They pointed and waved and we stared down too. Along came the head, like a submarine, but much more beautiful, slipping along under us no more than six feet away. Just then the constable shouted: 'Here's the tail! Here's the tail!'

"The tail was just passing under the police launch while the head was under *our* boat, and the two boats were a good seventy feet apart! The flippers, each as long as a dory, showed green beneath us, then the whole unbelievable length of the body flowed under the boat, silently, with just a faint slick swirl of water on the surface from the flukes. It was almost impossible to believe what we were seeing! This incredibly vast being, perhaps eighty tons in weight, swimming below us with the ease and smoothness of a salmon.''

Once she accepted the fact that our presence boded her no harm, the whale showed a remarkable interest in us, almost as if she took pleasure in being close to our two forty-foot boats. Not only did she pass directly under us several times but she also passed *between* the two boats, carefully threading her way between our anchor cables. We had the distinct impression she was lonely—an impression shared by the Hann brothers when she had hung close to their small boat. Claire went so far as to suggest the whale was seeking help, but how could we know about that?

I was greatly concerned about the effects of the gunning but, apart from a multitude of bullet holes, none of which showed signs of bleeding, she appeared to be in good health. Her movements were sure and powerful and there was no bloody discoloration in her blow. Because I so much wished to believe it, I concluded that the bullets had done no more than superficial damage and that, with luck, the great animal would be none the worse for her ordeal by fire.

At dusk we reluctantly left the Pond. Our communion with the whale had left all of us half hypnotized. We had almost nothing to say to each other until the R.C.M.P. launch pulled alongside and Constable Murdoch shouted:

"There'll be no more shooting. I guarantee you that. We'll patrol every day from now on, and twice a day if we have to."

Murdoch's words brought me my first definite awareness of a decision which I must already have arrived at below—or perhaps above—the limited levels of conscious thought. As we headed back, I knew I was committed to the saving of that whale, as passionately as I had ever been committed to anything in my life. In some incomprehensible way, alien flesh had reached out to alien flesh . . . cried out for help in a wordless and primordial appeal which could not be refused.

During the next few days I moved heaven and earth—or tried to, at any rate—to enlist help for the whale from the "outer world" which was so remote from our isolated fishing village. My demands on the authorities, on science, became increasingly frantic, but I might as well have been howling at the distant moon. Even the local people who might have helped seemed apathetic, if not downright antagonistic. The doctor, who was also a town councilor, expressed the mood when she stated it as her opinion that the local people had every right to kill the whale, for whatever reason or for no reason at all.

Saturday night, a week after the whale had been trapped, we were struck by a furious winter gale. The house shook and shuddered

in its grip, and the telephone—our one link with the outer world—
went dead. As I sat hearing the paeon of wind in the night, the devils
of self-doubt began to assail me. Perhaps I *was* a little mad—deluded
anyway—in thinking I might save the whale. Perhaps the battle
was already lost. Perhaps I *had* no business meddling in a tragedy
which was essentially a natural one . . . but then I saw again the
whale herself, as we had watched her slipping through the green void
beneath our boat. That vision routed the devils instantly. That lost
leviathan was one of the last of a disappearing race, and I knew she
had to be saved if only because contact with her, though it lasted no
more than a few brief weeks, might narrow the immense psychic
gap between our two species; might alter, in some degree, the remote and awesome image which whales have always projected onto
the inner human eye.

What, I wondered, was the whale doing in the bitter darkness of
this raging night? What had she felt during the long days of her
captivity?

Pain, she had surely felt—and fear. Had she felt despair? Did
she have any hope of eventual escape? As she circled the confines of
the prison Pond, did she ponder the horror of her probable fate?
What wordless thoughts were passing between her and the whale
who closely patrolled the entrance to the Pond and whom we had
come to call the Guardian? What did she feel about the two-legged
beasts who had tried to kill her?

No answers . . . none. Her mind was as alien to mine as mine to
hers. Strangers . . . strangers . . . we were *all* aliens, one to the other,
even those of us who were cloaked in the same fleshy shapes. What
did I really know of the innermost feelings even of my Burgeo neighbors . . . or they of mine? Was there any real comprehension or true
communication even between the human actors involved in this
bizarre drama?

Finally I dozed, and dreamed vividly of the whale. She had become a veritable monster and I was fleeing from her . . . drowning
in the unfamiliar element. I woke, sweating, and knew the truth.

The whale was not alone in being trapped. We were all trapped
with her. If the natural patterns of her life had been disrupted, then
so had ours. An awesome mystery had intruded into the closely
circumscribed order of our lives, one that we terrestrial bipeds could
not fathom, and one, therefore, that we would react against with
instinctive fear, violence, and hatred. This impenetrable secret,
which had become the core of our existence in this place, was a mirror
in which we saw our own distempered faces . . . and they were ugly.

During the days that followed it began to appear that my earliest
pessimism was unfounded. Slowly, almost reluctantly, the outside
world was becoming interested in the trapped whale. Scientists were

now talking about visiting her. The government of Newfoundland was talking (alas, it remained all talk) of assisting in feeding her by loaning us the services of a herring seiner. More important, some local people—mainly fishermen—were rallying to her cause. With some of these to assist, we managed to drive schools of herring into the Pond so that I no longer had to worry about the whale starving. On the fourteenth day of her captivity, fisherman Onie Stickland and I went to visit her in his dory.

As we had come to expect, the Guardian was in his usual place, patrolling in front of the cove. Finners seem to be strictly monogamous, and by now we were fairly sure that he was the trapped whale's mate. We had grown so used to his presence—and perhaps he had come to understand us—that, when our courses threatened to meet, Onie did not even slow the engine. The whale sounded easily just in time to avoid collision.

When we entered the Pond it was soon clear that something was amiss with the female whale. Her movements were sluggish, lacking the fluid grace of earlier days. She was blowing at short intervals and the spout seemed low and weak. The full length of her spine now showed clearly in a chain of knobby vertebral projections. Worst of all, great swellings were showing under her gleaming black skin.

On her first circuit she changed course slightly and passed fifty yards away, but on her next she came straight for us. When she was about a hundred feet off, she did something we had seen her do only a few times before and then always at a distance. She rose to blow, but instead of breaking the surface with her hump, she thrust her whole head high out of the calm waters. That gigantic head appeared to rear directly over us, like a moving, living cliff.

It might have been a moment of terror, but it was not. I felt no fear even when her eyes came out of water and she swung her head slightly so that one eye looked directly at us. She had emerged from her own element as far as she could in order to see us in ours.

Then she sank forward and her head went under. The blowhole/hump appeared, she blew and sounded and, a few seconds later, was passing directly under the dory; so smoothly and gently did she pass that we felt no motion except when the vast flukes went under us and the dory bobbed a little.

It was then I heard the voice of the fin whale again and knew it with absolute certainty for what it was. It was a long, low, sonorous moan with unearthly overtones in a higher pitch. It was unbelievably weird and bore no affinity with any sound I have heard from any other living thing. It was a voice not of the world we know.

When the whale had passed on, Onie sat as if paralyzed. Slowly he relaxed. He turned and looked at me with an anxious and questioning expression.

25

"That whale . . . she spoke to we! I t'inks she *spoke* to we!"

I nodded in agreement, for I will always believe she deliberately tried to span the chasm between our species—between our distant worlds. She failed, yet it was not total failure. So long as I live I shall hear the echoes of that haunting cry. And they will remind me that life itself—not *human* life—is the ultimate miracle upon this earth. I will hear those echoes even if the day should come when none of her nation is left alive in the desecrated seas, and the voices of the great whales have been silenced forever.

Early afternoon of the following day, Onie and I set off through the grey storm scud for Aldridges Pond.

As we bucketed into the cove, visibility was so bad we did not realize we were not alone until we nearly rammed a whale, head-on. The whale was so deep inside the cove that there was hardly enough room for it to swim, let alone submerge. I glimpsed the gleaming mass of its head surging toward us when it was less than twenty feet away and, at my startled yell, Onie swung the tiller hard over and cut the engine. The whale also went into a hard turn, but in the opposite direction, and with such acceleration that the boil from its flukes heeled the dory far over on her side. Then another snow flurry swept down, obliterating everything from view. When the flurry passed, the whale had disappeared.

The wild thought flashed into my mind that, aided by a high tide raised higher still by the sou'wester, the prisoner had escaped!

In jubilation, I yelled at Onie to start the engine.

"I think that's her! I think she's *out*, Onie! Head into the Pond. Quick, man, quick!"

Obediently he put the tiller over and we puttered through the driving scud. As I stood in the bow peering about, I was vaguely aware that my initial surge of jubilation was fading and in its place was a growing and aching sense of anxiety; but I had no time to dwell on that. For then I saw her.

She was on the surface and moving very slowly. Almost all of her great length was exposed. She could easily have been mistaken for one of those colossal sea monsters which decorate ancient charts. The illusion was intensified by the vagueness given to her outlines by the drifting snow.

She stayed on the surface an unnaturally long time. Onie kept the dory running close alongside so we would not lose sight of her in the snow flurries, and I was horrified by the difference a single day had made in her appearance. Not only had her back become steeply and ominously V-shaped, but the inexplicable bulges under her skin had grown much larger. There was no longer an aura of almost supernatural vitality about her—an aura which had strangely affected everyone who had seen her, including those who wished her dead.

26

At length she sounded, but slowly, as if with great effort or reluctance. The snow scud streamed down over the surface of the Pond, obliterating the last faint swirl from her flukes.

When I awoke on Monday morning it was to the imperious demands of the telephone. A fisherman was on the other end of the line.

"Skipper Mowat? We was out to The Ha Ha to see was our gear carried away by the starm, and the whale is beached. Aye, hard aground just inside the gut. 'Tis bleeding bad. . . ."

Frantically I called Curt Bangay and that good man agreed to chance the voyage to Aldridges in his decked motorboat in spite of the growing storm.

The harbor waters were "feather white," but Curt was undismayed. He pushed his boat at full throttle until I thought he would drive her under. When Curt grounded the bow of the boat on the shore of the cove, I ran recklessly across the intervening ridge. As I cleared the crest I saw her. She was lying directly below me. Her vast white chin was resting on the shore but most of her immense body was still afloat.

As I plunged down the slope toward her, I became aware of a foul stench. I also saw that the beach near where her head was resting was white with the partially digested bodies of herring. However, I saw these things without really seeing them, for I was totally engrossed in the urgency of getting her off that beach before the falling tide doomed her to die from her own great weight.

My memory of the next few minutes is hazy, but Curt, stumbling along behind me, remembered the scene vividly.

"When I cleared the crest you was already on the beach. I could hear you yelling your head off before I even see you. '*Get off, you crazy bitch*,' you was yelling.

"Then, next thing I sees you pounding on the head of her with your fists. You was acting like some fellow what's drunk too much white lightning."

It was insane, a hundred and sixty pounds of puny human flesh pitting itself against the inertia of eighty tons of leviathan. Nevertheless, I pushed and kicked and I yelled, and I may also have wept out of sheer frustration.

Then, almost imperceptibly, she began to move! I saw the flippers, big as dories, shimmer as they turned like hands on wrists. Slowly, so very slowly, she backed herself off the shore, turned, and cruised on the surface to mid-Pond.

Curt stumbled down the slope to join me.

"You done it, bye, you saved her, sure!" he cried.

But I knew better. The scales were off my eyes, and now I saw the truth. She had not grounded by accident. She had *deliberately* gone ashore because she was too sick to keep herself afloat any longer. I had misread the evidence, but now it was unmistakable. As she moved slowly away from us she left thin ribbons of dark swellings which had formed beneath her skin. I could see one of them pulsing out a dark flow of blood; and I realized that those swellings were reservoirs of pus and infection, some of which were breaking open to discharge their contents into the cold sea water.

As I watched, stunned and sickened, the whale continued to move across the Pond. She did not submerge. I doubt if she had sufficient strength to do so. Almost drifting, she reached the opposite shore and there she again rested her mighty head upon the rocks.

"Lard Jasus, she's beached again!" Curt shouted in alarm.

"No," I replied dully. "She's sick, Curt. She's too sick to even swim. If she stays in deep water she knows she'll sink, and then she'll drown."

Curt could not take that in. It seemed incredible to him that any beast which lived its life in the sea could drown. He shook his head in bewilderment.

And then I heard the voice of the fin whale again. It was the same muffled, disembodied, and unearthly sound, seeming to come from an immense distance: out of the sea, out of the rocks around us, out of the air itself. It was a deep vibration, low-pitched and throbbing, moaning beneath the wail of the wind in the cliffs of Richards Head.

It was the most desolate cry that I have ever heard.

And I knew, for she spoke to me—*to me*—and I knew, and know today, that this was her leave-taking.

The following day word came that she had vanished. Some thought, and it was the wishful thinking born of guilt, that she had somehow escaped. But I knew otherwise. The Guardian still remained at his post at the mouth of the cove. His mate was still inside —lying silent now, forever silent, on the hard granite bed of the Pond five fathoms down. She had returned to the heart of mystery from whence she came.

We turned back then, and made our way out to Messers Head from whose lonely summit I had watched the fin whales fishing only a few weeks earlier. I became fully aware of a rending sense of loss. It was dark, and there was none to know that I was weeping . . . weeping not just for the whale that died, but because the fragile link between her race and mine was severed.

PART ONE

MYTHS
AND
BEGINNINGS

DOLPHIN

When two dolphins—or even figures representing an indeterminate fish—are pointing in the same direction, the duplication may be obeying the dictates of the law of bilateral symmetry for merely ornamental reasons, or it may be a simple symbol of equipose. But the inverted arrangement, that is, with one dolphin pointing upwards and the other downwards, always symbolizes the dual cosmic streams of involution and evolution; this is what seventeenth century Spanish writer Saavedra y Fajardo meant by "either up or down." The dolphin by itself is an allegory of salvation, inspired in the ancient legends which show it as the friend of man. Its figure is associated with that of the anchor (another symbol of salvation), with pagan, erotic deities, and other symbols. The ancients held that the dolphin was the swiftest of marine animals, and hence, when it is shown twined round an anchor, it comes to signify arrested speed, that is, prudence.

WHALE

Symbolic of the world, the body, and the grave, and also regarded as an essential symbol of containing (and concealing). Nowadays, however, the whale seems to have acquired more independence as a symbolic equivalent of the mystic mandorla, or the area of intersection of the circles of heaven and earth, comprising and embracing the opposites of existence.

MANDORLA

Although the geometric symbol of the earth is the square (or the cube) and the symbol of heaven is the circle, two circles are sometimes used to symbolize the Upper and the Lower worlds, that is, heaven and earth. The union of the two worlds, or the zone of intersection and interpretation (the world of appearances), is represented by the mandorla, an almond-shaped figure formed by two intersecting circles. In order that, for the purposes of iconography, the mandorla might be drawn vertically, the two circles have come to be regarded as the left (matter) and the right (spirit). The zone of existence symbolized by the mandorla, like the twin peaked Mountain of Mars, embraces the opposing poles of all dualism. Hence it is a symbol also of the perpetual sacrifice that regenerates creative force through the dual streams of ascent and descent (appearance and disappearance, life and death, evolution and involution). Morphologically it is cognate with the spindle of the *Magna Mater* and with the magical spinners of thread.

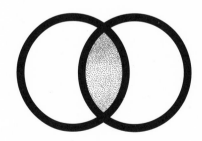

From A Dictionary of Symbols, *by J. E. Cirlot, Philosophical Library*

MAGIC WORDS (*after Nalungiaq*)

In the very earliest time,
when both people and animals lived on earth,
a person could become an animal if he wanted to
and an animal could become a human being.
Sometimes they were people
and sometimes animals
and there was no difference.
All spoke the same language.
That was the time when words were like magic.
The human mind had mysterious powers.
A word spoken by chance
might have strange consequences.
It would suddenly come alive
and what people wanted to happen could happen—
all you had to do was say it.
Nobody can explain this:
That's the way it was.

From Shaking the Pumpkin, *by Jerome Rothenberg, Doubleday Anchor*

CHARLES DORIA
The Dolphin Rider

The ancients believed the dolphin represented the vital power of the sea: water—*thalassa*—as the source of life. *Delphys*, the Greek word for dolphin, is related to *Delphis* which means womb. The dolphin, then, is the living womb of the sea of creation. The ancients could, through words and images, experience their gods' endless shifts in sex, body, and character without too much difficulty. This was in a time before reductive logic became fashionable and attempted to explain and confuse matters by forcing shapes and identities on what did not require them. So the dolphin can partake of such mythic forms as sea fish mother, womb monster, boy lover, and hermaphrodite, and can also become through Triton the aggressive phallos, through Aphrodite/Isis the marine love goddess, and through Dionysos part of the wheel dance of birth and rebirth.

To return to the image of the sea as the source of life, the Mildenhall, England, Okeanos (Figure 1), for example, portrays the sea as a vigorous old man with four dolphins radiating out of his wavy/leafy hair and beard, while around him dance Nereids and Sea Satyrs. Homer made Okeanos, the sea father, the "genesis of gods and everything else," and Thales, the sixth century sage, took the world as an island afloat on the sea, which he considered the "material cause/beginning of all things." Both of these stories depend on the still more ancient view of creation as flowing from the womb of a fish or whale woman: Leviathan or Tiamat.

The oldest known versions of this creation story embody the sea

Charles Doria is a poet and former professor of Classics and Comparative Literature at the University of Texas. He is editing and translating creation myths from the ancient Near East with Harris Lenowitz and Jerome Rothenberg for an anthology called Origins. *This paper, with its original translations, was written in response to a question: What do you know about Greek dolphin mythology?*

Figure 1. Okeanos, the "genesis of gods and everything else," according to Homer (*Iliad,* 14, 201, 246). The Nereids—marine Venuses—using their clothes as sails, dance with Sea Satyrs. From Mildenhall, England. Now in the British Museum.

33

as a whale/serpent/fish woman locked in combat/making love with a god of light/sperm, being defeated/impregnated, cut open/giving birth, to the various orders of the universe. We find this story in the Bible (the god Jahweh and Leviathan) and the *Enuma Elish* (Baal and the goddess Tiamat). Perhaps the clearest account of this myth— of the birth of the beings of the world—is given in the *Babylonian History* of Berosos, a priest of Baal in Babylon around 300 B.C. There the whale/fish woman is called Omorka.

(in the beginning)
many born and living there (in Omorka)
marvelous their holding their self-born form

men two wings
or four and double-faced

one body two heads maybe
both sexes
a man a woman?
or goat-footed goat-horned

or horse-footed
horse behind
man in front
hippocentaur
Jusparik
Siren

born and lived (in her)
bulls men-headed
dogs four-bodied fish-tailed
horses dog-headed horse-bodied fish-tailed

all kinds
plus swimmers creepers snakers
plus many more
you'd be surprised

they kept borrowing from each other

. . .

they all lived inside a woman
she was their mistress
Omorka/Um-ruk
in Chaldean Thalath/Tiamat
in Greek Thalassa [sea]
equaling in number Selene [moon]

. . .

things were like that
when Bel/Marduk came rushing in
and cut the woman in half
the lower slice he made earth
the upper the sky . . .

Bel/Marduk cut off his head
the other gods mixed his blood with earth
and made figures/people
that's how we get minds
and share in gods' thoughts

. . .

Bel/Marduk in
Greek Dios *the light/Zeus*
cut open the darkness (of the woman)
he sliced sky and earth apart
put everything where it belongs
*this the Greeks call order/*cosmos

everything that lived
that could not bear
the power of his light
checked out

Figure 2. The boy Apollo sprouting from his mother Leto's stomach/womb shoots arrows at Delphyne, the Womb Monster, at Delphi ("dolphin town") while his virgin sister, Artemis, looks on.

This story occurs in various guises among the Greeks. The best known tale pits Apollo the Sun God against Delphyne, the dolphin/womb monster (Figure 2). At Delphi (Dolphin Town), where he defeats her, he builds his famous oracular shrine and assumes the title *Delphinios*—"dolphin-god." He institutes a festival called *Delphinia* to commemorate his victory.

What's more, Apollo then becomes a dolphin. Whoever or whatever a god defeats/eats he can turn himself into at will, for it is part of his god-body now. As a giant dolphin, Apollo commandeers a boat full of Cretan merchants and re-directs their craft to Delphi where he reveals himself as a god and orders them to serve from now on as his priests in the new shrine. So Apollo, a male, now becomes in effect the director of the living womb of the world.

An encounter between a strong god or hero and a snake/dolphin/woman/etc. crops up in so many places I am beginning to suspect this must have been an integral part of a once-universal Mediterranean creation story. (Examples are Egyptian Horus, son of Osiris, who fights Seth the crocodile; Zeus, Kronos' son, who fights Typhon, a sea serpent; Kronos, Uranos' son, who fights Ophion the Snake; Herakles, Zeus' son, who makes love to the Scythian Snake Woman; Baruch, Elohim's son, who duels with Serpent Naas; St. Michael Archangel of the Lord, who drives the Serpent Lucifer out of heaven.) As Carl Kerenyi observes in *The Gods of the Greeks*, "It is always difficult to make out whether the deity concerned was believed to resemble in the parts below the hips a serpent, a dolphin or a fish" (Figures 3 and 4).

Figure 3. Zeus about to hurl lightning at Typhon.

In other stories the woman and the snake/fish/dolphin are separate creatures, or rather the human form is elaborated out of and then at times imposed as a "rider" on the original beast. This leads to the figure of the dolphin rider, whose relationship to the dol-

Figure 4. Echidna, the Sea Mother, swirling in a bed of ocean flowers.

phin the Greeks could never unambiguously determine. Was the Rider male and hostile (Apollo and Delphyne)? female and loving (Aphrodite and the dolphin)? male and loving (Eros and the dolphin)? male and homosexual (Boy of Iassos)? Did dolphin and god share a common divinity? Was the dolphin part of the god's own nature or vice versa? Such questions are impossible to answer; by posing them, however, we are brought nearer the shifting currents of identity, change, and renewal that the sea has always been emblematic of. And, as we will see, these variform polarities are reflected in the very words of the myths themselves.

Jay Lynch's cartoon of a woman riding a fish (Figure 5) is a good modern interpretation of the myth form, showing the imminence of the eternal in the commonplace. The girl, rising up out of the bath tub, proclaims, "Respect yourself!"—respect your origins, don't spit in the waters of your birth. But these words, as befits a sea creature, are also somewhat mysterious: they can also mean, "Take another look at yourself; you may not be who you think you are." Her body nicely articulates reconcilable polarities of light and sexuality, a convergence we will examine in more detail later on. The star on her thigh (*femur*) allies her to Aphrodite Urania (The Heavenly), another goddess who rose from the sea and rode the dolphin/fish. Her face and skin radiate light not simply because she is freshly covered with shining water. She is turned on from within, participating in and revealing the special illumination that the ancient gods of love, light, and (re) creation brought, and which is still preserved in hidden fashion in the words and images of the ancient myths.

The words the fish thinks recall an old tune of the 1950s, "Duke of Earl." In themselves they summon up the overwhelming power of water—"Nothing can stop the Duke of Earl"—how in flood time water sweeps away all that is dead, worn out, and in need of a rest so that new life will have a chance. Yet these are words to dance to; they bring to mind the close association dancing as creation/mime has always had with the gods and goddesses of genesis—Okeanos and his Nereids and sea sprites (Figure 1); Triton and his dolphin satyrs (Figure 12); Dionysos and his Maenad nurses. (These linkages, between dancing and creation, are preserved for us in the word "ball," as we shall see.)

The face and posture of the old man register extreme shock. He is about to undergo the trials of renewal, the birth trauma. He lets go the duck made of plastic, that imitation flesh, by way of preparation. The towel, brush, and soap suddenly convert into the implements of his baptism. With them he will scrub off the skin of age and death and reveal/put on the pink baby flesh the water woman will provide him with. The shock seizing him is the panic spread by old gods

Figure 5. Girl riding fish: a recent impersonation of the ancient dolphin rider.

Figure 12. Detail of a sixth century Etruscan black-figured amphora in the Conservation Museum in Rome. The bearded men with dolphins attached to their backs may represent the chorus of a satyr play.

36

like Pan (whence the word), Triton, and Dionysos' Maenads, heralding the difficult moment of passage from birth to rebirth, creation to recreation—and this is the whole burden of the stories of genesis.

Keeping this birth-to-rebirth element in mind, let us examine dolphin and riders more closely.

The image of a bright god riding/making love to/destroying the dolphin womb of the sea, which the Greeks originally assigned to Apollo, was later transferred to his servant: the poet. The most famous of such stories concerns Arion, who lived in the seventh century B.C. Returning to Greece from Southern Italy, he took passage on a ship manned by Corinthian sailors. They decided to rob and kill him once they reached the open sea. Arion made one last request of them: Could he sing once more to his lyre and then throw himself into the sea? His music was so beautiful it brought the dolphins; when he jumped off the boat one of them, to show appreciation, carried Arion safely to the Cliffs of Taenarum. (Later he erected there a bronze statue of a dolphin rider to thank Poseidon.)

The Hymn to Poseidon which celebrates his rescue is a fifth or fourth century recreation of Arion's original poem (which no longer exists). The epithets used for the sea—"child-swollen," "swellings" —are very old. They enfossilize the old belief that the waves of the sea were wombs, each filled with a child who in the fullness of time the breakers would deliver safe and sound on the beach.

"ARION": HYMN TO POSEIDON

                        sea lord Poseidon
                            golden trident
biding earth
    in the child-swollen salt sea
                        you most high
                            whom fish encircle
                            dance about lightly
                                fins up down
                                    back forward
snub nose manes rippling
    running hard   sea pups
        dolphins music lovers
    briny kids
        the Girl goddesses
                            Amphitrite's
                            Nereids
                                milk breast feed
whose hump backs I rode
        to Taenarum Cliffs
        in Pelop's Land
    furrowing the flat sea plains
                            a trackless way
the time the trickers
    threw me off their smooth ship
    into the swellings of salt purple sea

The emblem of a Young God/Poet Holding Lyre/Boy Riding a Dolphin, then, is a picture of the beginning of the world, a fusion of the creative and destructive personalities of the sea, and of the ambiguities of the human sexual relation.

In another example, the tale of the Dolphin Rider at Iassos, a powerful evocation of Love/Death, we see the dolphin's personality as a male. So the relationship between people and sea can be homosexual as well as maternal. But the old creation imagery is still present. All that has happened is that the story has become localized and secular—transferred from the boundless world of the mythic past to a cozy little fishing town in Asia Minor.

Yet to call this a story is not to say that dolphin-riding never happened. Brunilde Sismondo Ridgeway in her article, "Dolphins and Dolphin-Riders," discusses the evidence that real boys (and possibly girls) rode gentle but not domesticated dolphins in just about every bay, harbor, and inlet of the ancient Mediterranean. This bespeaks a time when enough mutuality existed between people and the animate world that neither was afraid to entrust wholeheartedly and cooperatively, even lovingly, their bodies and souls to each other.

This event raises another issue: Were these young riders imitating the act of the first creation? Were the stories told just to explain this pleasant past-time? It is probably foolish to attempt any final answer to this problem, which is almost central to any mythologem: Does present condition justify the story or does story bring it into being? I would say that dolphin riding records the inescapable fact of the sea as eternal abundance, unfailing genesis. The youngsters who rode the dolphins, I think, re-experienced the sea through mimesis as their immortal lover—it doesn't matter whether as man or woman, father or mother. They would have learned how exciting and precarious, provident and passionate, the sea is; that it can provide good as well as bad luck; and that the best way to find this out comes from natural and open confrontations between ourselves and the sources of ourselves—and not by manipulating the world through the dead ego of the machine.

Here is the story of the Dolphin Rider at Iassos, as told by Aelian in the second century A.D.

AELIAN: THE DOLPHIN OF IASSOS

A dolphin's love for a beautiful boy at Iassos: a famous story:
here it is

Iassos' gymnasium is near the sea
after running and wrestling all afternoon
the boys went down there and washed
a custom from way back when

38

one day a dolphin fell in love
with the loveliest boy of the time
at first when he paddled near the beach
the boy ran away in fear
but soon by staying close by and being kind
the dolphin taught the boy to love

they were inseparable
they played games
   swam side by side
     raced
       sometimes the boy would get up on top
         and ride the dolphin like a horse
he was so proud his lover carried him around on his back

so were the townspeople
visitors were amazed

the dolphin used to take his sweetheart out to sea
   far as he liked
     then turn around
       back to the beach
         say goodbye and return to the sea
           the boy went home

when school was out
there'd be the dolphin waiting
   which made the boy so happy

everyone loved to look at him
he was so handsome
   men and women
     even (and that was the best part) the dumb animals
for he was the loveliest flower of boy ever was

but envy destroyed their love
one day the boy played too hard
tired he threw himself down belly first
   on the dolphin's back
     whose back spike happened to be pointing straight up
it stuck him in the navel
veins split blood spilled
   the boy died
the dolphin felt him riding heavier than usual
(the dead boy couldn't lighten himself by breathing)
saw the sea turning purple from blood
knowing what had happened
   he chose to throw himself on their beach by the gymnasium
     like a ship rushing through the waves
       carrying the boy's body with him

they both lay there in the sand
   one dead
   the other gasping out life's breath

Figure 6. Dead boy on a dolphin, provenance unknown.
It could possibly have illustrated the story of the Rider of
Iassos. In the State Hermitage Museum, Leningrad.

Figure 7. An Egyptian sculpture of Eros riding a dolphin, showing the sharp dorsal fin erect which killed the Boy of Iassos. Now in the British Museum.

Figure 8. Eros riding a dolphin. The blending of their bodies is remarkable. Fountain ornament from Capua, now in the Naples Museum.

Iassos built them both a tomb
to requite their great love
they also set up a stele
which shows a boy riding a dolphin
and put out silver and bronze coins
stamped with the story of their love death

on the beach
they honor Eros the god who lead boy and dolphin here

The most popular dolphin rider in antiquity was Eros, and I think it would be right to say that his identity lurks behind most of the other dolphin-loving youngsters we hear of, either as local boy gods of love or as real boys whose stories assimilate the mythic event (Figures 7 and 8).

Eros is a very powerful god, not to be confused with the later Roman Cupid we see on Valentine's Day cards. The Orphics (who observed a religion that pre-dated by three hundred years Homer's Olympians) had a teaching about Eros. The story went something like this: Eros is another name for bright *Phanes*, who hatched from the World Egg which in turn was produced by Flying Dragon Kronos the Mixer and his wife, known either as Lady Hyle (the Matter-mother) or Mother Rhea (Queen Flow). After quitting the Egg, Phanes/Eros makes Sky out of the top half of the shell and Earth out of the bottom.

So Phanes/Eros created the world.

Later, his great-grandson Zeus swallows Phanes (and with him, his creation, the world), but out of love for a beautiful woman, Semele, Zeus returns him to us, now safely tucked away in Zeus' womb—as Dionysos.

Here it is worth pausing for a moment. The word "belly womb" comes from the original tale and probably dates back to a time when one did not distinguish between the belly and the womb, when the men equally with the women could be mothers; e.g., Zeus gave birth to both Dionysos and Athene. The hermaphrodite condition is crucial to understanding the ancient view of the dolphin. What is at its source?

Let me explain by etymology, starting with a common word for father.

The word "papa" is related to "pap," meaning both "teat" and "baby food" —cf. the following series of Latin words: *papa*, father; *paparium*, pap, baby food; *papilla*, nipple, breast, rosebud; *pappo*, to eat pap, to eat; *papaver*, poppy, a kernel, seed; *pappus* (also Greek), old man, grandfather, the woolly, hairy seed of certain plants, the first down on the chin. But the meaning of the word *papa* equals Greek and Latin *mamma*, breast, mother (Latin *mammatus*, teated; *mammo*, give suck, suckle; Greek *mammao*, cry for the breast, for food; *mammai*, mother; English "mammal").

For *pap* Greek supplies: *papias*, janitor of the palace; *pappazo*, to call anyone papa; *pappas, pas, pa, papa; pappizo*, to coax, wheedle one's father, to seduce, etc. The etymologists Liddell and Scott, and Lewis and Short refer *pater* (Greek) and *pater* (Latin) to the root *pa* which means *to feed*.

This root gives us an astonishing variety of words: father, pasta, pabulum, pasture, pastor (shepherd), palace, food, feed. The same root turns up in (Latin) *Pales*, the shepherds' goddess; *Penas*, Guardian of the Inner House; *penes*, in the possession, power, presence, or house of someone; *penus*, food; *penetro*, to pierce; *penetralia*, inner place, secret space; *penis* (Greek *peos*), tail, penis. This root is related to others which yield such words as: (Latin) *femina*, female; *feminal*, the pudenda; *femur* (plural *femina*), upper thigh; *follis*, a pair of bellows, inflated ball, cushion, pillow, purse, stomach; *felix*, happy, fertile; *faenus*, interest on loaned capital; *fello*, to suck either nipple or penis; *flo*, blow; *folium*, leaf; *flos*, flower, *futuo*, to fuck; *fui, futurus*, etc., parts of the verb "to be"; *fetus* (noun), embryo (adjective), pregnant; and in Greek, *pallas*, strong young man or woman; *ballantion*, bag, pouch, purse; possibly *balanos*, acorn (Latin *glans*), balsam nut, glans penis, iron peg, suppository, pessary; *thao*, to suckle; *thelys*, female, refreshing, fruitful, tender, soft, yielding, weak; *tithene*, wet-nurse, mother; *tithenos*, foster-father (cf. tit, teat); *thalamos*, women's quarters, inner part of the house, bed-room, bride-chamber, store room for food; possibly *thalassa*, sea; *thalame*, den, hole (mostly of fish that live in rocks), grave, body cavity; *phyo*, to give birth; *phallos*, penis, images of which served as emblems of the generative power of nature; *Phallen*, name for Dionysos as Penis God and *phalle, phale, phallaina* (Latin *balena*), whale, any (a Delphyne) (belly womb) devouring monster (cf. Latin *papilio*, moth, English mouth? and mother?). This base is related to the one for light, *pha*, from which we get *phallo*, to see, and perhaps most importantly for this study, to Phanes, the hermaphroditic creator we have already encountered.

Greco-Roman Flying Phallus. The cushion-like objects below the cock-bird are vaginal-shaped wombs. Notice the bells: an invitation to "dance?"

These etymologies indicate how such vital functions as love-making, begetting, eating, and drinking all spring out of a common sea of words that denote acts reciprocated and shared by all those they involve and affect. That the words "suckle" and "drink," for example, are related means that at one time people thought of drinking by linking it to what they did on their mother's breast. But sucking is also fucking (as in the "modern" "dick/lick" and "tit for tat"). These associations are based on more than sound; rather, they go to the heart of how people think about themselves in words. To take another example: given its roots, "ball" is indeed an appropriate word for (1) making love (2) dancing, and (3) throwing a baby into the womb—cf. Greek *ballo*, throw, and *pallo*, shake, rattle, and roll; Latin *ballo*, dance; *follis*, inflated ball, stomach; and English "balloon," "bag." In Orphic and other creation stories, a cosmic egg, womb or sphere is the first "mattermother" which the flame/ sperm/father as a penis or windspirit seeds/feeds/fires/pierces/ blows. This can be taken as an abstract re-statement of the Baal/ Tiamat love/war we considered earlier. And as for the links between eating and baby-making, Texas women when they become obviously pregnant often say they swallowed a watermelon seed.

I think we can understand now why words for boy and girl, male and female, father and mother, are often so close in sound and etymology: because they each name and describe the same acts as performed in much the same way only by different (but complementary) agents for different (but complementary) reasons. Active and passive, strong and weak—other sexually based dichotomies are unnecessary and are not even part of the ancients' universe of discourse. Who is really "blowing/eating/fucking" whom? Who's really got the ball(s)? The mama or the papa or both? How sad that this knowledge no longer acts in the mind and is only latent in the words, and that most dictionaries offer such timid "scientific" etymologies if they offer them at all—symptomatic of the morbid and professional withdrawal of information from life. But perhaps in this state of affairs lies the real value of the study of mythology: to bring us, our words, and world, back to source.

But to finish the discussion about Eros/Phanes as the hermaphroditic god of creation.

The choice of the hermaphrodite as dolphin rider brings with it certain advantages. These advantages perhaps explain why the Greeks, like so many other ancient people, liked to find and elaborate the hermaphroditic character in their gods. Even Christ, according to some of the Gnostics, was a hermaphrodite. And to the Orphics of course the hermaphrodite came first; sexuality they saw as part of the strife and contradiction of everyday experience, as the small change of a world which had fallen away through division and multiplicity from its once-resourceful simplicity.

For heshe can resolve in hisher person the dichotomies caused by the willful separation of male and female, phallos and womb, father and mother, penis and breast (*pappa, mamma*). In the old language of Pythagorean numbers, the hermaphrodite is a three. Heshe wears three names (Phanes-Metis-Protogonos) to tell us this. Phanes the first is one, the male and indivisible, the number of origin and unity. Metis the second is two, the female and, like all other even numbers, she breaks the one in two. Protogonos ("First-Born") the third is the three who (re)creates the one and the two by joining them. For all creation then was joining, a mixing and mingling of what was there already but unresolved and uncommunicating—and this joining was an art: Latin *ars*, skill in combining; Greek *ararisko*, to fit together snugly, as in making love. There was no other way: *nihil ex nihilo fit*, Lucretius said, repeating the tradition—"Nothing comes of nothing."

The dolphin is a good embodiment of the triadic hermaphrodite. Its bland, round, apparently self-contained body shows no obvious sexual differences; its genital organs are kept snugly withdrawn in a pouch below the belly until needed. Yet her billowing curves and graceful swells that recall the waves of the sea and statues of pre-Greek wom(b)man goddesses earned her the name *delphys*. His blunt snub nose, strong snout, flashing speed, the smooth, bulging head

Figure 9. Triton, the male Aphrodite, with a scaly serpent body and dolphin tail, holding an erect dolphin phallus in his left hand.

42

white with water, and generally cylindrical shape lend him a phallic character which is more fully realized in the hands of Triton (Figure 9). So in a sense, all the hermaphrodite is recorded in the dolphin.

Let us look at our remaining dolphin gods, starting with Aphrodite. She was born inside the ball of bloody foam her father's severed testicles created when they hit the sea. Then she was met by a dolphin who carried her on his (her?) back to Cypris. So afterwards, whenever this goddess (who is really, I think, a later refiguration of the Sea Mother: Tiamat or Echidna) went out to sea, she rode a dolphin. Next to Eros, Aphrodite was the most popular dolphin rider. And by keeping her so close to a dolphin, the myth is not only placing her by her source, but also explaining her to us (Figure 10): Aphrodite as dolphin womb mother in human form, given kindred shape in the playful beast who carries her briskly over the seas of our genesis. (Yet we should also remember, as many Minoan and Mycenean cult pictures show [Figure 11], the dolphin once swam alone—was once seen as the integral whole.)

Figure 10. Aphrodite riding a dolphin using her dress as a sail. From Tunis. Now in the Louvre, Paris.

Through Aphrodite we can find a link between the dolphin and the cosmic egg we talked about earlier. Eunice Stebbins in her book *The Dolphin in the Art and Literature of Greece and Rome* offers this explanation for the presence of ostrich eggs with dolphins appliqued on them in Mycenean Shaft Graves from the Second Millennium, B.C.: "The egg is a symbol of future life, its surface representing the water over which the dolphins convey the dead, and at the same time the symbol of the universe from which springs the goddess who is carried ashore by the dolphin after her birth from the sea-foam." So in Stebbins the egg-born Phanes reappears as female only—as Aphrodite.

The reference earlier to dolphins as conveyors of the dead, in the story of the Iassos rider, brings us to the stories connected with Apollo and Leucas. Apollo, in his dolphin body, used to take the souls of the departed to the Land of the Dead. Apollo himself was probably originally a death god, as his name shows: from *apollymi*, to destroy utterly. In the story the disembodied soul waits on top of the Rock at Leucas, near a temple of Apollo for a ship, later a pair of dolphins (i.e., "Apollo"), who will ferry it to the Islands of the Blest. When the dolphins appear, the soul leaps from the Rock; they catch it and swim away. The giver of life can also take it away, as we recognize in the common reversal, womb/tomb, where Prolific and Devouring meet. I should also point out that during the month *Delphinios*, the Greeks customarily honored the dead.

Now let us examine Triton, the phallic dolphin. Triton, whom Hesiod calls *eurybias*, "wide-ranging and violent," was a son of Poseidon and Amphitrite. He is usually represented (like Typhon or

Figure 11. One of a series of panel frescoes from Tiryns illustrating sea life in the Mediterranean of the Second Millennium, B.C. Now in the Museum of Nauplia, Greece.

Echidna) as half man/half snake with a dolphin, holding in his left hand an upright dolphin in a manner that suggests an erect penis (Figure 9). Helped by the Fish-Horses (the Ichthyocentaurs), he roamed the shore and raped anyone, girl or boy, who took his fancy. So possibly the Boy of Iassos had good reason to fear when the dolphin first swam up. Yet through his name, Triton, which means "three," "third," he is connected with the triune hermaphrodite of the first creation.

Like Aphrodite, he has a connection with the wind. When he "winds his horn," the giant cockleshell, he creates—like Pan—a panic among all those on the sea. He was known as the Sea Satyr or Silenos; men used to wear dolphin tails and dance in his honor, turning themselves by mimesis into him (Figure 12). So the female powers of dolphin and sea snake reappear in Triton, the water-borne phallos, yet still functioning in the same way.

The last story I am going to present concerns Dionysos. As Eros and as Phanes returned, he was a popular choice to ride the dolphin. Under the name *Phalanthros* he was honored as the dolphin rider of Italian Tarentum and was linked to its legendary founder, Taras, a son of Poseidon. An oracle from Delphi (!) later identified this Phalanthos as Dionysos *Phallen* (of the Phallos).

The important story about Dionysos and dolphins, however, concerns his Epiphany—his first public appearance in the world. The version I give below is found in Homeric Hymn Number 7.

HOMERIC HYMN 7

the story of Dionysos and the Pirates

once showed himself on a beach of the barren sea
on a rock stuck out over the water
young boy in a purple robe
the first hair soft on his face
black and lovely waving   in the wind

the pirates from Tyrrhenenia
sailed up in a nice ship
skidding over the wine face sea
                    black luck for them

saw him
      looked at each other
            "yes do it"
jumped off
grabbed
threw him aboard
            boy were they happy

"you must be a prince"
                  "a lot of money for you"

44

"tie him up"
the ropes fell off
                    willow twigs didn't hold
                              his hands and feet
he smiled
sat down
eyes black

the tillerman knew
"you fools
that's a god you're trying to string up
strong huh?
don't think this big ship can carry him
Zeus? Archer Apollo? Poseidon?
not one of us a Dier
more like a god with a House on Olympus

come on
let him go
back to dark endless earth
right now
hands off or else trouble
bad wind hard storms"

the captain said
"get to work you
none of that god shout and shake
point us to the wind
help raise the mast
set sail

we'll take care of the boy
he's gonna go to Egypt   Cypris
or the people up north   maybe further
unless he speaks up and   tells us
who his people are
where he's got his money
            we've struck it rich"

up went the sail
a belly full of wind
the sailors made tight

suddenly strange
sweet wine the scent of ambrosia
bubbled up through the black ship

surprise surprise

a vine curled along the sailyard
clustered with grapes

in flower in dainty berry
dark ivy whirled around the mast

"helmsman   to shore"

the boy turned into a lion
roared amidships
made a bear with rough shaggy neck
hulking grinding teeth

lion on the benches bent eyebrow over eye
                                        staring at them
the sailors ran to the stern
crowding round the tillerman
out of their heads
        he kept his
the lion leapt on the captain
o captain

the sailors jumped overboard
                                "don't want to die like that"
into the god sea
they were born dolphins

for the steersman
mercy
"stop
I will make you happy
don't be afraid

in my heart
I honor you
I am Dionysos the Screamer

Semele Cadmos' daughter
gave me life
blended in love and friendship with Zeus"

hello good-bye
son of Semele Pretty Face
don't give up the ship

forget him you
might as well forget sweet song

Figure 13. The newly instated Dionysos riding his she-boat. It is also a dolphin, as its shape—as well as the two tiny dolphins it wears stem and stern—testify. Boat *(naus* in Greek, *navis* in Latin, from the common base *gign,* "to give birth") is maternal and, like whale and dolphin, replicates the Sea Mother. Now in the Antikensammlungen, Munich.

    The story is depicted on the Dionysos Cup by Exekias (Figure 13). It can also be read as a map of the world under Dionysos. The god reclines on the ship of the world. The dolphins wheel and dance in a circle around him. This recalls the choral patterns of those who perform the Tragedies and Satyr Mimes. It also recreates the cycling interchange between life and death, the seasons' passage from and return to winter/sleep and spring/renewal. The mast of the ship changed into a huge vine with clustering grapes enrooted and sprouting from Dionysos' organs of generation, a Tree of Life, a World Tree on the model of Ygdrasil, a hermaphrodite which provides food, place, and the energies of the sexual light to all who dwell there. ("I am the vine, you are the branches.")

I would like to close out this study with a poem by Yeats, a writer deeply attentive to the ancient world. It is entitled appropriately:

NEWS FOR THE DELPHIC ORACLE

I

There all the golden codgers lay,
There the silver dew,
And the great water sighed for love,
And the wind sighed too.
Man-picker Niamh leant and sighed
By Oisin on the grass;
There sighed amid his choir of love
Tall Pythagoras.
Plotinus came and looked about,
The salt-flakes on his breast,
And having stretched and yawned awhile
Lay sighing like the rest.

II

Straddling each a dolphin's back
And steadied by a fin,
Those Innocents re-live their death,
Their wounds open again.
The ecstatic waters laugh because
Their cries are sweet and strange,
Through their ancestral patterns dance,
And the brute dolphins plunge
Until, in some cliff-sheltered bay
Where wades the choir of love
Proffering its sacred laurel crowns,
They pitch their burdens off.

III

Slim adolescence that a nymph has stripped
Peleus on Thetis stares.
Her limbs are delicate as an eyelid,
Love has blinded him with tears;
But Thetis' belly listens.
Down the mountain walls
From where Pan's cavern is
Intolerable music falls.
Foul goat-herd, brutal arm appear,
Belly, shoulder, bum,
Flash fishlike; nymphs and satyrs
copulate in the foam.

Creation myths tell us not only of origins, they tell us of relationships. The mythology which depicts humans and animals and spirits acting in concert to create life—order—out of chaos, reveals the basic thought process of the society that invented it. Since creation is not something that occurs once, and then is forever accomplished, but is something which is constantly being renewed and recapitulated, the creation mythology of a culture reveals perhaps its most fundamental sense of itself.

The widespread belief that the world was created from watery beginnings may be a symbolic statement of understanding that our own life issues forth from water. We are born of the water of life—the amniotic fluid that suspends and protects the embryo is the same fluid that forms the primeval matter of all life on the planet. Realizing and honoring this connection is a step toward the unification of the spirit of humans with the spirit of the natural world.

The following fragments can be viewed as a creation play, wherein each culture stands on the stage of its own history and recites its particular understanding of its—and our—beginnings.

MAIDU: *In the beginning there was no sun, no moon, no stars. All was dark, and everywhere there was only water.*

HINDU: *This world was water, a single flood; only Prajapati could be seen, sitting on a lotus-leaf.*

HEBREW: *And the spirit of God brooded upon the waters.*

ARUNTA: *The Ungambikula, the Self-existent Spirits, came down from the sky with long stone knives. They caught embryonic forms of life which swam in the salt water, in the sea shallows of the shore, and with the knives shaped them into complete human forms.*

OCCIDENTAL: *Light stony silicates were the first substances precipitated from the primeval dust cloud, and became the cores of the Earth and its moon. The Earth was not yet solid, but fairly cool and unstable, with a center of light rock around which was a thick layer of relatively heavy stone mixed with iron. Over this was another very thin stratum of stone. The entire surface was covered with ocean, in whose depths life began a billion and a half years ago or earlier. These ancient creatures have left no trace, because all were pelagic, swimming at or near the top of the sea. They deposited no heavy shells or skeletons as fossil remains; they did not develop any, since there were still no shores or shallows for non-floating things to live on.*

ZUNI: *Before the beginning of the new-making, Awonawilone (the Maker and Container of All, the All-father Father), solely had being. There was nothing else whatsoever throughout the great space of the ages save everywhere black darkness in it, and everywhere void desolation.*
In the beginning of the new-made, Awonawilone conceived within

himself and thought outward in space, whereby mists of increase, steams potent of growth, were evolved and uplifted. Thus, by means of his innate knowledge, the All-container made himself in person and form of the Sun whom we hold to be our father and who thus came to exist and appear. With his appearance came the brightening of the spaces with light, and with the brightening of the spaces the great mist-clouds were thickened together and fell, whereby was evolved water in water; yea, and the worldholding sea.

With his substance of flesh outdrawn from the surface of his person, the Sun-father formed the seed-stuff of twain worlds, impregnating therewith the great waters, and lo! in the heat of his light these waters of the sea grew green and scums rose upon them, waxing wide and weighty until, behold! they became Awitelin Tsita, the "Four-fold Containing Mother-earth," and Apoyan Ta'chu, the "All-covering Father-sky."

GERMAN: *The first man must have developed in a uterus much larger than the human one. This uterus is the sea. That all living things have come from the sea is a truth nobody will dispute who has occupied himself with natural history and philosophy. Contemporary science disregards every other doctrine. The sea has nourishment for the foetus; slime to be absorbed through its membranes, oxygen for these membranes to breathe; the foetus is not confined, so that it can move its membranes at will even though it should remain swimming about for more than two years. Such foetuses arise in the sea by the thousands.*

SIBERIAN: *In the beginning when there was nothing but water, God and the "First Man" moved about in the shape of two black geese over the waters of the primordial ocean.*

OCEANIC: *In the lowest depth of Avaiki, where the sides of the imaginary shell meet, lives a woman—a demon, of flesh and blood—named Vari-ma-te-takere, or The-very-beginning. Such is the narrowness of her territory that her knees and chin touch, no other position being possible. Vari-me-te-takere was very anxious for progeny. One day she plucked off a bit of her right side, and it became a human being—the first man Avatea, or Vatea.*

Now Vatea, the father of gods and men, was half man and half fish, the division being like the two halves of the human body. The species of fish to which this great divinity was allied being the taairangi (Cetacea), or great sea monsters, i.e., porpoises, whose sides are covered with pure fat, and whose home is the boundless ocean. Thus one eye of Vatea was human, the other a fish-eye. His right side was furnished with an arm; the left with a fin. He had one proper foot, and half a fish-tail.

HEBREW: *And God said, "Let the waters bring forth swarms of living creatures, and let birds fly above the earth across the firmament of the heavens." So God created sea whales and every living creature that moves, with which the waters swarm, according to their kinds, and every winged bird according to its kind. And God saw that it was good. And God blessed them, saying, "Be fruitful and multiply and fill the waters in the seas, and let birds multiply on the earth."*

Excerpts and fragments give, at best, an incomplete sense of the sweep and meaning of a culture's mythology. To reach more deeply into the richness and complexity of the poetic metaphor of the watery birth, here is a section from the epic poem of Finland, *The Kalevala*

—the history and actions of the great hero Väinämöinen and the virgin sea mother who bore him.

There was a virgin, maiden of the air,   lovely woman, a spirit of nature.
Long she kept her purity,   ever her virginity
in the spacious farmyards,   on the smooth fields of the air.
In time she got bored,   her life seemed strange
in always being alone,   living as a virgin
in the spacious farmyards,   in the vast wastes of the air.
Now indeed she comes lower down,   settled down on the billows,
on the broad expanse of the sea,   on the wide open sea.
There came a great blast of wind,   severe weather from the east;
it raised the sea up into foam,   splashed it into billows.

The wind kept rocking the girl,   a wave kept driving the virgin
around about on the blue sea,   on the whitecapped billows.
The wind blew her pregnant,   the sea made her thick through.
She carried a hard womb,   a stiff bellyful
for seven hundred years,   for nine ages of man.
Nothing is born,   the self-begotten fetus does not come free.

As mother of the water the virgin went hither and yon. She swims east, swims west,
swims northwest, south,   swims along the whole horizon
in the agonies of her burning gestation,   with severe labor pains.
Nothing is born,   the self-begotten fetus does not come free.

She keeps weeping softly and unceasingly,   uttered a word, spoke thus:
"Woe are my days, poor me,   woe is my wandering, wretched child!
Now I have got into trouble: ever to be under the sky,
to be rocked by the wind,   to be driven by the waves
on these extensive waters, boundless billows! It would have been better   to
*   live as a virgin of the air*
than it is nowadays   to keep floating about as the mother of the water.
It is cold for me to be here,   painful for me to be adrift,
to dwell in the waves,   to be going hither and yon in the water.
O Ukko, god on high,   supporter of the whole sky!
Come here, since there is need,   come here, since you are summoned.
Deliver the maiden from her predicament,   the woman from her labor pains!
Come soon, get here without delay;   you are needed without any delay at all."

A little time passed,   a little bit passed quickly.
A goldeneye came, a straight-flying bird;   it fluttered about
seeking a place for its nest,   considering a place to live.
It flew east, it flew west,   flew northwest, south.
It does not find such a place,   not even the poorest kind of place,
in which it might build its nest,   take up its dwelling place.
It flits about, soars about,   it ponders, it reflects:
"Shall I build my house in the wind,   my dwelling place on the waves?
The wind will tip the house over,   a wave will carry off my dwelling place."

So then the mother of the water,   mother of the water, virgin of the air,
raised her knee from the sea,   her shoulder blade from a billow,
for the goldeneye as a place for a nest,   as an agreeable dwelling place.
That goldeneye, graceful bird,   flits about, soars about.

She discovered the knee of the mother of the water   on the bluish open sea;
she thought it a grass-grown tussock,   fresh turf.
She soars about, flits about,   settles down on the knee.

On it she builds her nest,   laid her golden eggs,
six golden eggs,   the seventh an iron egg.
She began to brood the eggs,   to warm the top of the knee.
She brooded one day, brooded a second,   then brooded a third, too.

Now because of that the mother of the water,   mother of the water, virgin of the air,
feels burning hot,   her skin scorched;
she thought her knee was burning,   all her sinews melting.
Suddenly she twitched her knee,   made her limbs tremble;
the eggs tumbled into the water,   are sent into the waves of the sea;
the eggs cracked to pieces,   broke to bits.
The eggs do not get into the ooze,   the bits not get mixed up with the water.
The bits were turned into fine things,   the pieces into beautiful things:
the lower half of one egg   into the earth beneath,
the top half of another egg   into the heavens above.
The top half of one yolk   gets to glow like the sun,
the top half of one white   gets to gleam palely as the moon;
any mottled things on an egg,   those become stars in heaven,
anything black on an egg,   those indeed become clouds in the sky.

The ages go on,   the years go by still longer
while the new sun is glowing,   the new moon gleaming palely.
The mother of the water, the mother of the water,   virgin of the air, keeps on swimming
on those gentle waves,   on the misty billows,
before her the flowing water,   behind her the clear heavens.

Now in the ninth year,   in the tenth summer
she raised her head from the sea,   lifts up the crown of her head.
She began to perform her acts of creation,   to accomplish her works
on the wide expanse of the sea,   on the wide open sea.
Where she swung her hand,   there she arranged headlands;
where she touched bottom with her foot,   she hollowed out deep spots for fish;
where, moreover, bubbles came up,   there she deepened deep places.
She turned her side against the land;   there she made the coasts smooth;
she turned her feet against the land;   there she formed places to seine for salmon;
she came with her head against the land;   there she fashioned bays.
Then she swam farther out from land,   lingered on the open sea.
She forms little islands in the sea,   produced hidden reefs
for a ship to run aground on,   to destroy seamen.
Now the islands were arranged,   little islands created in the sea,

the pillars of the sky erected,   lands and continents sung into being,
patterns marbled in rocks,   designs drawn on crags.
Väinämöinen is not yet born,   the eternal singer has not appeared.

Sterling Bunnell, M.D., is a psychiatrist and ecologist who combines an encyclopedic understanding of ecosystems with an understanding of the ways of the human mind. He has studied two endangered species of the West: the San Joaquin kit fox and the desert pup fish, and has raised a variety of wild animals, from falcons to coyotes. In addition to his medical practice, he teaches evolutionary ecology at the California College of Arts and Crafts, and is developing an experimental school of ecological land management.

STERLING BUNNELL
The Evolution of Cetacean Intelligence

We have only in recent years begun to wonder if, in their way, dolphins and whales might be as intelligent as ourselves. This idea has had to penetrate a heavy barrier of anthropocentric prejudice, for most human traditions have assumed that we are the apex of animate creation due to our presumably exclusive possession of rational intelligence. However, behavioral work with captive dolphins and observations of wild Cetaceans have often documented actions explainable only by assuming high intelligence, and anatomical evidence backs this up. Many Cetacean species have brains that much exceed ours in cortical surface area, which is what we use for thinking, and are perhaps our equal in neuronal complexity. Though some might argue that whales have very large bodies in relation to their brain size, it should be remembered that only a minor percentage of the cerebral cortex is directly concerned with control of the body, and that the Cetacean brain is larger than the human brain in the general association cortex, which in us is known to function in memory and conceptual thought.

From the standpoint of brain size and complexity, our planet is shared by three animal types with comparable mental equipment: humans, elephants, and Cetaceans. The human beings' superiority in manipulating the physical world is shown by our present ability to exterminate the other two types. However, intelligence has many possible dimensions, and in some of these we may be less advanced than certain big-brained non-manipulators.

While elephants have very large brains (thirteen pounds as compared to three pounds of *Homo sapiens*) and give evidence of considerable rational and conceptual ability, their communication systems appear to be much less elaborate than the ones which Cetaceans use. So dolphins and whales seem the most likely local candidates for the intelligent non-human life that we occasionally seek to communicate with in space projects or speculate about in science fiction fantasies.

Since the human being is thought to have acquired its large brain and intelligence by a rather unique series of evolutionary circumstances, we might wonder how so different a creature as the whale also evolved a large brain.

The Environment of Evolution

Natural selection favors only those attributes which have survival value in a given environment. Humans more than doubled their brain capacity when they came out of the sheltering forest and began to live as hunters and scavengers in the dangerous and challenging savannah. There they had to outwit alert, fleet-footed prey and protect themselves from such predators as lions, sabertooths, and other hominids. There was heavy selection pressure for certain kinds of intelligence, especially those related to strategy, defense of the group, and goal-oriented communication, and the hominid brain capacity increased very rapidly, from 450cc five million years ago to

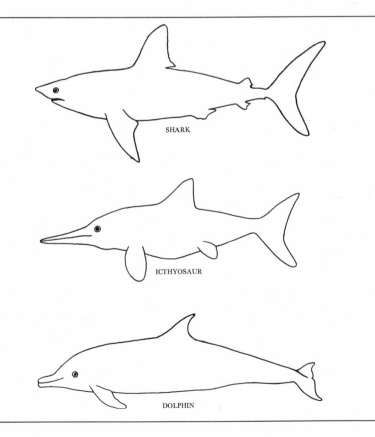

SHARK

ICTHYOSAUR

DOLPHIN

To move easily in the sea involves reducing the turbulence and resistance of the water. The sea shaped the body for these fast, easy movers, no matter what the order of animals. The shark is a fish; the icthyosaur is a reptile; the dolphin is a mammal.

about 1300cc half a million years ago. Speech, tool- and weapon-use proliferated rapidly when brain size became greater than about 700cc.

In contrast to our abrupt and recent evolution to intelligent status, whales appear to have developed their large, domed brains much earlier and more gradually.

The most ancient known fossil whales, from the Eocene period (about fifty million years ago), were already completely aquatic but had rather small and primitive brains. Their tooth structure indicates that they may have evolved from primitive mammalian carnivores which prowled the shores of Africa and gradually became adapted to life in the seas. These earliest whales—the Archaeocetes (*Zeuglodon* is a well-known example)—had large eyes, numerous long, pointed teeth, and nostrils located at the end of their snouts, an arrangement rather similar to crocodiles. By the late Eocene, perhaps forty million years ago, *Agorophius* shows telescoping of the skull and the nostrils have moved above the eyes. In the upper Oligocene, about thirty million years ago, the first fossil squalodonts appeared. These are much like the present-day river dolphins of South America, the Ganges and China. *Delphinidae*, the modern dolphins, began to appear in the early Miocene, about twenty-five million years ago,

A chronology of whale history showing the extinction and survival of various families of Cetaceans. Today, almost all families are barely surviving. The thickness of each area represents the size of the population believed to have existed on earth during earlier geological eras.

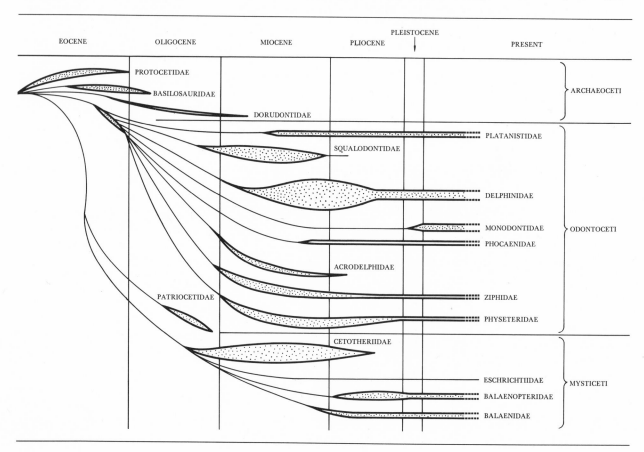

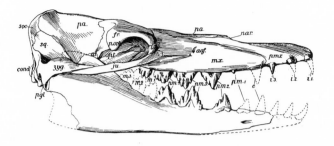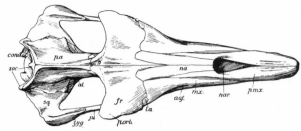

and became common in the seas within the next ten million years. Sperm whales appeared about the same time. The Mysticeti (baleen whales) are first found in the Oligocene and appear to have evolved directly from the Archaeocetes, since skull telescoping in baleen whales occurs in a different way than in toothed whales. Skull telescoping in both Cetacean groups (toothed and baleen) seems to have accompanied increasing brain size, posterior migration of the nostrils, and the modification of the forehead as a bony reflector for the sound production system.

We might wonder, therefore, what environment could exert selection pressures to bring the Cetacean brain to a size comparable with ours.

The present life pattern of the river dolphins may offer some clues to that evolutionary transition. These animals depend mainly on echolocation and their tactile sense to find their way around. Their eyes are small and one species is blind. During the tropical rainy seasons the rivers flood and spread muddy water far over the land. At such times the dolphins range miles from the river bed in pursuit of fish, threading their way among tree trunks and roots in the flooded forest and traveling easily in very turbid water only a few feet deep. (An American expedition found them difficult to capture because of their skill at swimming between the legs of wading Hindu crowds.) During these long semi-terrestrial excursions they must be able to form and retain detailed topographic maps in order not to be trapped by the receding waters. Under such conditions the auditory and tactile senses would become highly developed (the trigeminal nerve, which supplies tactile sensation to the face, is enormously developed in toothed Cetaceans), as would the general association areas of the brain in which concrete memories are stored. Brains of South American river dolphins of the genera *Inia* and *Sotalia* measured around 670 to 690cc, which is larger than *Australopithecus* and close to *Homo erectus*, the first real human. It is interesting to reflect that Cetaceans reached this point in the evolution of brain size perhaps thirty million years ago, while we got there only a million years ago, which in turn leads to the issue of whether this indicates anything as to the

Lateral and top views of the skull of a primitive whale, *Prozeuglodon.*

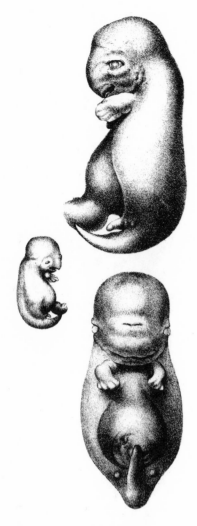

The whales have a long and distinguished evolutionary history, and much of it is recapitulated in embryonic growth. These drawings of the foetus of a white-sided dolphin bear evidence of earlier stages in the evolution of the creature: the neck is constricted, the cranium domed, and the head perpendicular to the spine; nasal opening is located in the facial region; rudimentary hind limbs and external ear pavilions are visible. At this point in its development, the resemblance of the foetus to that of a human is startling.

relative subtlety, complexity, and balance of mind in these two life forms.

If large Cetacean brains did evolve in the rivers and estuaries, the Cetaceans so favored could have returned to the sea, as appears to have happened in the Oligocene, and replaced their more primitive relatives there. In the sea, then, the Cetacean brain continued to increase in size (at present, 1600cc for *Tursiops*, 6000cc for the orca, 9000cc for the sperm whale, and 6000cc for the larger baleen whales). The most likely explanation for this continuing increase seems to be social and sexual selection—that is, the society of the whales— since the sea does not seem to be a demanding enough habitat to require such an increase in brain size. The senses derived for navigation in muddy water seem ideally pre-adapted for social and personal communication. With echolocation, for example, a dolphin gets a three-dimensional, detailed cognition of the physical and emotional state of another dolphin's entire body and it appears that the eroticism of dolphins is related to group organization and hierarchy as well as reproductive functions. The marine Cetaceans make considerable use of their eyes, but vision is third in importance—after the auditory and tactile senses. It is the general association areas or the cerebral cortex which account for most of the increase in Cetacean brain size. In short, the brains of whales and dolphins may have continued to enlarge as an adaptation to intelligent societies, instead of simply being a result of large body size or specialized behavior.

The Architecture of the Brain

The neuronal architecture of whale brains seems constructed in very different patterns from those of humans, perhaps because of the whales' very different life conditions and long standing independent evolution. The lamination and regional differentiation of the cerebral cortex, thought to be related to intellectual acuity and detail of perception, are considered by most investigators to be as developed in Cetaceans as in humans, although differently arranged. The sense projection areas of the Cetacean cortex, especially those receiving information from ears and face, are quite large, while motor control takes up less area than in us, since in Cetaceans it is mainly concerned with swimming and vocalization. This lends support to the assumption that the Cetacean mind is oriented toward perception and intra- and interpersonal relationships more than is the human mind, which emphasizes expression through action and the elaboration of motor skills which the hand makes possible.

The neocortex forms perceptions, memories, and thoughts, but its motivation comes from the emotional activity of the so-called limbic system, or primitive core brain. Evidence from cases of brain damage in humans indicates that a high ratio of neocortical associa-

56

tion neurons to limbic system-brain stem neurons is necessary for such qualities as reality orientation, objectivity, humor, emotional self-control, and the capacity for logically consistent abstract thought, as well as the higher forms of creativity, while a decreased neocortical-limbic ratio is associated with impulsiveness, emotional instability, and irritability, impaired memory, loss of objectivity and humor, marked egocentricity, stereotyped behavior, and sometimes obsessions, mania, delusions, or hallucinations. Dolphins have a higher neocortical-limbic ratio than even healthy, intelligent humans, and captive dolphins and orcas have often shown humor, empathy, and self-control that few of us could match under comparable circumstances. As Fichtelius and Sjölander have suggested, we humans depend on highly adaptive cultures in which most of the mental capacity lies outside the individual and in the traditional knowledge of the culture. As regards our brain and our capacities as individual, conscious beings, we may actually be inferior to some other kinds of large-brained animals.

The paralimbic lobe is a unique feature of the Cetacean cerebral cortex not found in other mammals. It is a specialized region in which all specific sensory (hearing, touch, vision, taste) and motor areas are represented together. In man, the projection areas for different senses are widely separated from one another and the motor area is adjacent only to the touch area. For us to make an integrated perception from sight, sound and touch, the impulses must travel by long fiber tracts with a great loss of time and information. The Cetaceans' paralimbic lobe makes possible the very rapid formation of integrated perceptions with a richness of information unimaginable to us. Motor expression of perceived patterns through vocalization could be especially subtle.

The Range of the Senses

The scattering of sense projection areas which we humans inherit appears to have evolved from conditions of extreme danger orientation. Sight, sound, touch, smell are each bordered by interpretation areas which deal only with one sense modality. When hearing registers a danger sound it does not wait for visual information before signaling alarm. Nor does vision, on seeing the form of a predator, wait for sound or touch. Our intellectual functions have arisen from separate sense modality interpretation areas. Perhaps this may contribute to the ease with which our mental processes become isolated from one another.

Our physical structure which is predominantly eye- and hand-oriented and our long evolutionary history of tool-using, danger preoccupation, and group aggression (all of which are reflected in our inherent neuronal organization) makes it difficult for us to un-

You see, what I found after twelve years of work with dolphins is that the limits are not in them, the limits are in us. So I had to go away and find out, who am I? What's this all about?
John Lilly

derstand intelligent and non-manipulative beings which are so well adapted to their habitat that the survival considerations of finding food and avoiding danger have been much less of a problem for them than they have been for us.

These differences in our sensory modalities have made it very difficult for men and Cetaceans to learn one another's communication systems. Eyesight in humans is a space-oriented distance-sense, which gives us complex simultaneous information in the form of analog pictures but has poor time discrimination. Our auditory sense, however, has poor space perception but good time discrimination. Human languages are therefore comprised of fairly simple sounds arranged in elaborate temporal sequences. The Cetacean auditory system is predominantly spatial, like our eyesight, with much simultaneous information and poor time resolution. So dolphin language apparently consists of extremely complex sounds which are perceived as a unit. A whole paragraph's worth of information might be conveyed in one elaborate instantaneous hieroglyph. For them to follow our pattern of speech might be almost as difficult as for us to study the individual picture frames in a movie being run at ordinary speed. It is not surprising that captive dolphins at first seem more interested in music than in the human voice. Our music is more similar to their voices than our speech is.

Since their echolocation system gives them detailed images of objects in their world, they might even be able to recreate these sounds in their speech and thus directly project images to one another. The possible existence of digital language among dolphins is supported by instances where we know that complex information was transmitted among Cetaceans and also, as Bateson pointed out, by the incomprehensibility of their language to us. Analog emotional communication crosses species barriers fairly easily, while digital communication usually doesn't pass between different linguistic groups of the same species. Dolphin language may in some ways be similar to written Chinese characters, in which analog pictures are given digital functions. Perhaps future computer studies will make their linguistic patterns more recognizable to us.

Extreme playfulness and humor are conspicuous in dolphins and may be found in whales also, although they are harder to observe. Despite its low status in puritanical value systems, play is a hallmark of intelligence and is indispensable for creativity and flexibility. Its marked development in Cetaceans makes it likely that they will frolic with their minds as much as with their bodies.

The Diversity of the Species

The great diversity of present Cetacean species implies the intriguing possibility of a corresponding mental diversity. There would

Both man and Cetacean seem to have a tremendous capacity for digital information exchange (information understood on the basis of its sequence in time and space, like written words or the Morse Code) using variations in pitch and frequency. Cetaceans may also have analog communications systems which are so different from our own that we may not be able to perceive them. (Analog information is information you understand because the data itself is like what you are talking about. For example, the word "loud" spoken loudly.) It seems, too, that digital speech is used mainly to refer to manipulable objects, while analog communication deals with more subjective items like emotions. In this sense, it may be that Cetaceans have the ability (using their clicking apparatus) to communicate digitally as well as analogously.
Peter Warshall

be a variety of contemporary human species as well if our ancestors had not been so zealous in killing off their competition. We know that in the Pliocene there were several hominid genera and a variety of species. During the Pleistocene, beginning about one million years ago, competition became more severe. Finally *Homo sapiens*, the master weapon maker, eliminated his last rival, *Homo neanderthalensis*, about forty thousand years ago, and went on to exterminate most of the species of elephants, as well as many other large mammals. In the present century he has been applying his talents to the extermination of whales. With the knowledge that his civilization has been able to accumulate, the process can be completed in less than a decade instead of millennia, as when he was getting started on his career.

We are beginning to realize that the analytical and manipulative skills by which we have gained a dominant position on our planet have their limitations and that we very much need to develop other mental directions so that we will be less lopsided as intelligent beings. Could it be that some of the undiscovered possibilities which would be most valuable to us have long been known to our fellow mammals of the sea, the whales and dolphins?

So far our efforts to understand the minds of Cetaceans have been sporadic and feeble, almost as if even the investigators did not take them seriously. There are certainly strong psychological pressures toward continuing to regard the whales as lower animals. Whatever tentative research is done can then justify its funding by claiming that it will help us build better sonar equipment or more efficiently manage the whaling industry.

Though we know very little about what Cetaceans do with their large brains, we can be sure that such impressive structures would not have evolved if they were not being used. They are highly organized and well-maintained systems, clearly not vestigial structures or non-adaptive features.

The Cetacean system appears to be a more integrated and contemplative one, evolved in conditions where immediate danger was not so likely as it was for most mammals. It is ironic that our technology, which developed as an adaptation to danger, has now presented the whales with dangers for which their own evolutionary history leaves them quite unprepared.

The gray whale can actually "hide" or avoid detection by what is called "evasive swimming." In this evasion, the whale comes to the surface cautiously, exposing only the nostrils. It exhales slowly without sound or visibly condensed vapor, then sinks silently and quickly to continue underwater until far enough away to safely resume its usual conspicuous surfacing with spout, exposure of head and back, and eventual throw of flukes.

This evasive swimming is one of the unusual habits of the gray whale. One wonders how it ever learned such a trick, with no enemies in its evolutionary history coming either from the surface or from the air.
Raymond Gilmore, The California Gray Whale

MYSTECETI (Baleen Whales)

BALAENOPTERIDAE
Rorqual Whales

BALAENOPTERA
B. acutorostrata
Minke Whale

B. borealis
Sei Whale

B. edeni
Bryde's Whale

B. musculus
Blue Whale

B. physalus
Fin Whale

MEGAPTERA
M. novaeangliae
Humpback Whale

BALAENIDAE
Right Whales

BALAENA
B. mysticetus
Bowhead Whale

EUBALAENA
E. glacialis
Right Whale

CAPEREA
C. marginata
Pygmy Right Whale

ESCHRICHTIDAE
Gray Whales

ESCHRICHTIUS
E. gibbosus
Gray Whale

PLATANISTIDAE
River Dolphins

PLATANISTA
P. gangetica
Ganges River Dolphin

P. indi
Indus River Dolphin

INIA
I. geoffrensis
Amazon River Dolphin

LIPOTES
L. vexillifer
Chinese Lake Dolphin

PONTOPORIA
P. blainvillei
La Plata Dolphin

ZIPHIIDAE
Beaked Whales

MESOPLODON
M. bidens
North Sea Beaked Whale

M. layardi
Strap-toothed Whale

M. europaeus
Antillean Beaked Whale

M. mirus
True's Beaked Whale

M. grayi
Camperdown Whale

M. densirostris
Blainville's Beaked Whale

M. stejnegeri
Stejneger's Beaked Whale

M. ginkgodens
Japanese Beaked Whale

M. bowdoini
Andrew's Beaked Whale

M. carlhubbsi
Hubb's Beaked Whale

M. hectori
Hector's Beaked Whale

M. pacificus
Pacific Beaked Whale

ZIPHIUS
Z. cavirostris
Cuvier's Beaked Whale

BERARDIUS
B. arnouxi
Arnoux' Beaked Whale

B. bairdi
Baird's Beaked Whale

TASMACETUS
T. shepherdi
Tasmanian Beaked Whale

HYPEROODON
H. ampullatus
Northern Bottlenose Whale

H. planiforms
Southern Bottlenose Whale

The Order Cetacea: Whales, Dolphins, and Porpoises. The order of mammals called Cetacea is comprised of wholly aquatic mammals of three groups: *Archaeoceti,* extinct Cetaceans; *Mysticeti,* or baleen whales, living creatures who have baleen plates in their mouths, no teeth, symmetrical skulls, and two blowholes; and *Odontoceti,* or toothed whales, living creatures who have one type of conical tooth that is either visible or buried in the gums, and who have a telescoped, asymmetrical skull with a single blowhole.

Cetaceans have several distinguishable features in common: front feet that have modified into flippers: no hind limbs, external ears, sweat, or tear glands; blubber; bones filled with oil; and a free-floating pelvis that is incredibly small by mammalian standards. Cetacean tail flukes are horizontal. Whales and dolphins must come to the surface to breathe air (although some can remain underwater for several hours).

Baleen or Whalebone Whales

The baleen whales form one of the two great groupings of whales. The Greeks called them *Mysticetes,* meaning "moustached whales." The "moustache" refers to the fringes on the slats that emerge from the gums of the adult baleen whale. These slats are called baleen, or whalebone (although they are really modified mucous membrane, not bone). Baleen whales use the baleen plates to strain plankton from the sea water. Most of these whales have flabby tongues that push the water from their mouths through the baleen, leaving the plankton.

There are ten living species of baleen whales. They are bigger than the toothed whales. The smallest baleen whale is the minke—30 feet long (9 meters). The smallest toothed whale is under 8 feet long (2.4 meters). The largest baleen whale, the blue whale, is the largest animal ever to have lived on our planet.

Toothed Whales

The second of the two great groupings of living whales are the toothed whales—the *Odontoceti.* They have diversified and entered many more niches, or rivers, estuaries, coasts, and oceans of the world, than have the baleen whales. There are sixty-seven species of toothed whales, as compared to only ten of baleen whales. The toothed whales all have the same feeding style. They catch fish or squid individually, rather than scooping up many small organisms as do the baleen whales.

Toothed whales also differ from baleen whales in size, speed, diving abilities, use of sonar-sight and eyesight, body shape, gregariousness, and the form of their skulls and teeth. The jaws and teeth only grasp; they do not chew. Toothed whales chew with their stomachs, which range from four to nine in number.

ODONTOCETI (Toothed Whales)

PHYSETERIDAE
Sperm Whales

PHYSETER
P. catodon
Sperm Whale

KOGIA
K. breviceps/K. simus
Pygmy Sperm Whale

MONODONTIDAE
White Whales

DELPHINAPTERUS
D. leucas
Beluga Whale

MONODON
M. monoceros
Narwhal

STENIDAE
Dolphins

STENO
S. brerdanensis
Rough-toothed Dolphin

SOTALIA
S. fluviatilis
Bouto Dolphin

S. guianensis
Guiana River Dolphin

S. chinensis
Chinese White Dolphin

S. borneensis
Borneo White Dolphin

S. centiginosa
Speckled Dolphin

S. plumbea
Plumbeous Dolphin

S. teuszi
Cameroon Dolphin

S. brasiliensis
Rio de Janeiro Dolphin

STENELLA
S. coeruleoalba
Blue Dolphin

S. longirostris
Spinning Dolphin

S. dubia/S. graffmani
Narrow-snouted Dolphin

S. frontalis
Bridled Dolphin

DELPHINIDAE
Dolphins

DELPHINUS
D. delphis
Common Dolphin

GRAMPUS
G. griseus
Risso's Dolphin

TURSIOPS
T. truncatus/T. gilli
Bottlenose Dolphin

LAGENORHYNCHUS
L. obliquidens
White-sided Dolphin

L. albirostris
White-beaked Dolphin

L. obscuras
Dusky Dolphin

L. acutus
White-sided Dolphin

L. thicolea
Falkland Island Dolphin

L. cruciger
Hour-glass Dolphin

LAGENODELPHIS
L. hosei
Sarawak Dolphin

FERESA
F. attenuata
Pygmy Killer Whale

CEPHALORHYNCUS
C. commersoni
Commerson's Dolphin

C. hectori
Hector's Dolphin

C. heavisidei
Heaviside's Dolphin

C. eutropia
White-bellied Dolphin

ORCINUS
O. orca
Orca (Killer Whale)

PSEUDORCA
P. crassidens
False Killer Whale

ORCAELLA
O. brevirostris
Irrawaddy River Dolphin

GLOBICEPHALA
G. melaena
Pilot Whale

PEPONOCEPHALA
P. electra
Broad-beaked Dolphin

LISSODELPHIS
L. peroni borealis
Right Whale Dolphin

PHOCOENIDAE
Porpoises

PHOCAENA
P. phocoena
Harbor Porpoise

P. dioptrica
Spectacled Porpoise

P. spinipinnis
Black Porpoise

NEOMERIS
N. phocaenoides
Black Finless Porpoise

PHOCAENOIDES
P. dalli
Dall's Porpoise

P. truei
True's Porpoise

The taxonomy—classification in established categories—of the order Cetacea varies from cetologist to cetologist. Some are "lumpers" and prefer to work with a few inclusive categories; others are "splitters" and work with more specific and numerous categories. We have chosen the taxonomy found in the journal Investigations on Cetacea, *edited by Georg Pilleri, from the Institute of Brain Anatomy in Berne, Switzerland.*

There are ten families of Cetacea, thirty-eight genera, and anywhere from ninety to a hundred species. Many of the species are near-total mysteries. One— Iagenodelphis—*has been identified only from a skull found on shore. In the chart above, we provide the Latin family, genus, and species name, and the common names for the families and species. Divisions within species exist but are not included here. In the following pages, more information is provided on most genera.*

Example: **Bottlenose Dolphin; Kingdom: Animal; Class: Back-boned Vertebrate; Order: CETACEA; Suborder: ODONTOCETI (Toothed Whales); Family: DELPHINIDAE (Dolphins); Genus:** *TURSIOPS;* **Species:** *T. truncatus* **(Bottlenose Dolphin);** *(Race or Subspecies: Pacific Form).*

Family: *Balaenopteridae*
Rorqual Whales
"Rorqual" means "whales with folded throats." All the members of this family have grooves on their throats and distinct dorsal fins. Their baleens are short, and more numerous than in the other families. Their heads are torpedo-shaped.

Minke Whale (lesser rorqual, piked whale)
The minke whale is the smallest rorqual, growing to no more than 30 feet (9 meters). It is easily recognized by the white patch across its flippers and the yellow-white baleen plate. Although found worldwide, minke whales are only rarely seen in tropical waters. Along the British Isles, females remain close to the coast, while the males head out to the open sea. Genus: *Balaenoptera*; Species: *B. acutorostrata.*

Sei Whale
The sei whale is the only rorqual both to skim and swallow its food. Unlike the closely related blue and fin whales (who inhabit cold waters), the sei is never seen north of the Aleutians, and rarely penetrates the ice-pack in the Antarctic. The sei whale's ability to skim and swallow has given it a very eclectic diet—equal amounts of copepods, amphipods, and euphausiids, and smaller quantities of swarming fish and squids. This varied diet and manner of obtaining food has made sei whale migrations rather unpredictable compared to other species. The sei is smaller than the fin; it grows to about 60 feet (18 meters). Genus: *Balaenoptera*; Species: *B. borealis.*

Bryde's Whale
This whale is a rare species of rorqual, about 50 feet (15 meters) in size. It is easily confused with the sei whale. Bryde's whale has ventral grooves which reach the navel, while the sei whale's stop before the navel. Bryde's whale has a smaller dorsal fin and much thicker,

stiffer fingers on the baleen plate. Its habit of eating gregarious fish often keeps it close to shore. The Bryde's whale occupies the tropical and subtropical waters (40°N to 40°S), while the other fish-eating rorqual, the minke whale, occupies the sub-Antarctic and Arctic seas. Genus: *Balaenoptera*; Species: *B. edeni.*

Blue Whale (sulphur-bottom whale)
The blue whale is the largest animal ever to exist. Some have been caught weighing 150 tons, and measuring over 100 feet (30 meters) in length. The blue whale keeps to the open oceans throughout the world. It migrates yearly: to the tropics and subtropical waters to breed and calve; and to the polar waters to feed on krill. The stomach of a large blue whale can contain 5 million, or 2 tons, of krill. The animal is near extinction. Genus: *Balaenoptera*; Species: *B. musculus.*

Fin Whale
The whaling industry likes to think of the fin whale as a smaller version of the blue whale, because at present it is the second largest whale in the world (up to 80 feet or 24 meters). After the industry depleted the blue whale stock, it turned to the fins. Actually, there are many differences between the two species. The fin whale is more cosmopolitan. Although it migrates towards the equator—as does the blue whale—it avoids tropical waters. It migrates as far as the ice-pack in the polar summers, but it does not penetrate the ice-packs as does the blue whale. The fin whale can be recognized by its asymmetrical color pattern—blue gray left lower jaw, white right lower jaw. Genus: *Balaenoptera*; Species: *B. physalus.*

Humpback Whale
The humpback whale is the only member of the genus *Megaptera,* and it differs markedly from the other rorquals.

The humpback is black on top (rather than blue or blue gray), with a white throat and belly. Irregular knobs and protuberances appear on its head and flippers. It is frequently covered with whale lice and barnacles. The humpback's outstanding feature is a long flipper with irregular edges. This stocky whale averages about 40 feet (12.5 meters) in length. It is known for its beautiful songs that may continue for three to four hours. The humpback winters in tropical waters near islands or the coast, and summers in temperate and subpolar waters. There are two major populations—one in the Northern Hemisphere and one in the Southern. They are not known to mix. Genus: *Megaptera*; Species: *M. novaeangliae.*

Family: *Balaenidae*
Right Whales
Right whales have long baleen plates that are narrow, elastic, and densely packed with fringes. They have no dorsal fin and no throat grooves. The whole family is endangered.

Bowhead Whale (Greenland right whale)
The bowhead has an enormous head—one-third the total length of the animal. This stocky whale grows to 45 to 60 feet (14 to 18 meters) and may weigh 46,000 pounds (about 23 metric tons). Its enormous mouth contains the longest baleen—up to 14 feet (4 meters) in length—of any of the baleen whales. It is adapted for taking scattered patches of copepods in huge quantities by skimming through swarms of them with an open mouth, head partially above water, at about 9 mph (6kmph). The bowhead lives only in the Arctic, in regions of floating ice. It makes short migrations in rhythm with the melting and freezing of the ice. The bowhead was considered exterminated by humans until 1932, when four males were sighted. Subsequently, one was sighted off the coast of Norway in 1958 and again in 1963. A small herd presently exists in the Pacific Arctic. Genus: *Balaena*; Species: *B. mysticetus.*

Black Right Whale
The black right whale is similar to the bowhead, but smaller. It is easily distinguished by a horny "hat" that caps the top of the blowhole, and by its unique color pattern on the belly. The spout is double, V-shaped, and angled frontwards. There are three subspecies of the black right whale: one in the North Atlantic, one in the North Pacific, and one in the southern Arctic waters. Genus: *Eubalaena;* Species: *E. glacialis.*

Family: *Eschrichtidae*
Gray Whales
The gray whales differ from the other baleen families because the baleen is short and coarse—there are only two to four short grooves on the throat—and they have no distinct fin. They have a dorsal hump. They have the smallest number of baleen plates and the lowest density of fringes on the plates.

Gray Whale (hard-head, mussel digger, rip sack)
This gray whale is between 33 and 50 feet long (10 to 15 meters). It is black or slate colored, with many white spots and blotches. The gray whale is the only baleen whale that enters shallow water to breed and calve. It lives most of its life in coastal waters, migrating south from the Arctic Seas—the longest migration of any known mammal, up to 16,000 miles (11,000 kilometers). Genus: *Eschrichtius;* Species: *E. gibbosus.*

Family: *Platanistidae*
Fresh Water River Dolphins
This family is a conglomerate of five species of fresh water dolphins. They are considered "primitive" dolphins because their skeletons closely approximate some dolphin fossils. Their place in the taxonomy is in a state of flux because the fossil sequence tends to place the La Plata River dolphin (*Pontoporia*) with the oceanic dolphins; to separate

the Ganges and Indus River dolphins (*Platanista*) into an independent family; and to put the Chinese Lake dolphin (*Lipotes*) and the Amazon dolphin (*Inia*) into yet a third family. At present, the family is characterized by a long, thin beak with teeth ranging from 100 to 250 and a symmetrical skull.

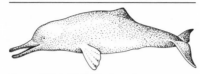

Ganges River Dolphin (susu)
This pure black dolphin travels up the Ganges, Indus, and Brahmaputra rivers. Although it has diminutive eyes, the Ganges dolphin is really sightless. It relies totally on its echolocation capacities to steer its way through the muddy rivers to find fish and shrimp to eat. It is curious and inoffensive around humans. Ganges dolphins travel in schools of ten or more. The largest recorded Ganges dolphin was over 10 feet long (3 meters), but most appear to be about 8 feet (2.4 meters) long. Genus: *Platanista;* Species: *P. gangetica.*

Chinese Lake Dolphin (white flag dolphin, peh ch'i)
Very little is known about this dolphin. It lives only in the Tung ting Hu Lake and the Yangtze Kiang River. It never approaches estuaries or ocean waters. The largest grow to 7 or 8 feet long (2 to 2.4 meters). When the lakes rise in spring, the Chinese Lake dolphin is said to travel up small, clear rivers to breed. It appears to feed on catfish and other bottom-dwelling animals. Its low dorsal fin resembles a flag when seen above water. Genus: *Lipotes;* Species: *L. vexillifer.*

Family: *Ziphiidae*
Beaked Whales
These medium-sized Cetaceans grow to 15 to 30 feet (5 to 9 meters). They are open sea whales of little commercial value. Consequently, little is known of their food and social habits. Their unique identifiable features are: no

teeth in the upper jaw; teeth reduced to one or two pairs in the lower jaw; fin placed far back on the body; a pair of throat furrows which form a V; and no tail notch.

Japanese Beaked Whales
The Japanese beaked whale—and the other nine species of the genus *Mesoplodon*—are believed to live in deep cold ocean water and to eat squid, cuttlefish, and some fish. The two teeth of this genus do not chew or grasp. When the mouth is closed, they appear as small tusks outside the mouth. Since they appear in males earlier and more often than in females, they may be sex significators, or are perhaps used in fighting. Genus: *Mesoplodon;* Species: *M. ginkgodens.*

Cuvier's Beaked Whale (goose-beaked whale)
This species averages about 26 feet (7.2 meters) in size. Its body is similar to that of other beaked whales, but its head is less narrow, and pointed. The beak is also relatively short. It is found in all oceans, but is rare in polar waters. It eats squid and other cephalopods in the the open oceans, and undertakes long migrations. Nothing is known of the social habits of this genus. Genus: *Ziphius;* Species: *Z. cavirostris.*

Baird's Beaked Whale (giant bottlenose whale)
This is the largest beaked whale, and the second largest toothed whale (after the sperm whale). The male attains lengths of up to 39 feet (12 meters), and the female up to 42 feet (13 meters). The Baird's whale is powerfully built and robust. It is dark colored—gray or black with lighter blotches sometimes appearing on the belly. A prominent forehead rises abruptly from the beak. The lower jaw contains two pairs of triangularly

shaped teeth that are exposed only in the mature male. The whale travels in schools of ten to twenty. The species is said to be very alert and hard to capture although some have been taken by Japanese whalers. Genus: *Berardius*; Species: *B. bairdi*.

Northern Bottlenose Whale

This whale grows to about 30 feet (9 meters). It becomes lighter in color as it matures. The calf is grayish to black; the immature whale is spotted with buff and white; and the old bottlenose whale may be completely yellow white. The head rises abruptly from the beak, giving the "bottlenose" appearance. This forehead contains fat in the male and dense oil (spermaceti) in the female. The forehead is believed to be a lens which focuses sound during echolocation. The bottlenose whale is a migratory species. In summer, the whale is found in the Arctic circumpolar region. In winter, it may migrate from the North Atlantic all the way to the Mediterranean. Schools of from four to twelve have been sighted. No member of this genus will desert an injured member. Genus: *Hyperoodon*; Species: *H. ampullatus*.

Family: *Physeteridae*
Sperm Whales

This family contains two genera and three species—a giant sperm whale and two pygmy forms. They can be identified by the blowhole on the left side of the head; the upper jaw which extends beyond the bottom jaw; and numerous teeth, very prominent in the lower jaw.

Sperm Whale (cachalot)

This "Moby Dick" of the whales is the largest toothed Cetacean. A large male can grow to 60 feet (18 meters); the female is usually about half that size. The sperm whale is very distinctive in appearance, with its huge box-like head and underslung lower jaw. In place of a dorsal fin, there are a series of hump-

like ridges along the midline of the back. The animal is purplish brown or dark gray on its back, and gray or white underneath. Albino "white whales" have also been sighted. Gregarious and polygamous, the sperm whale usually travels in herds of fifteen to twenty, but herds of several hundred have been seen. The skull of the sperm whale is the most asymmetrical in the animal kingdom. The blowhole rises on the top left side of the tip of the snout. It is called the *museau de singe* and gives the sperm whale its unique, oblique blow. The sperm whale is the only producer of ambergris, a substance containing feces plus undigestible material. It has historically been used in medicines, as a perfume fixative, and as an aphrodisiac. It is waxy with a sweet, musky smell when warmed. Although ambergris has been less valuable since the advent of synthetic perfume fixatives, the sperm whale is still heavily hunted for its spermaceti oil—a substance misnamed because whalers thought it to be part of the reproductive system. Genus: *Physeter*; Species: *P. catodon*.

Pygmy Sperm Whale

This whale grows to only 13 feet (4 meters), but it resembles the giant sperm whale in the location of its teeth and blowhole, and the presence of the spermaceti reservoir. The pygmy sperm differs from the giant in having a blunted, pointed snout, recurved sharp teeth, and a very short lower jaw. There are some indications that it migrates, but its distribution is confusing. Genus: *Kogia*; Species: *K. breviceps*.

Family: *Monodontidae*
White Whales

This family is somewhat arbitrarily defined as the Arctic dolphins. They have no dorsal fin, no beak, and a blunt head. Their true relationship to the other dolphins and porpoises will only become clear when more genetic information is available. There are only two species: the beluga and the narwhal.

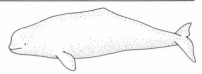

Beluga Whale (white whale)

The beluga may grow up to 18 feet (5.5 meters) in length. The young are gray, but the adults are pure white. The beluga lives in Arctic waters, but sometimes travels south in the western Atlantic as far as the St. Lawrence River. It likes coastal waters and penetrates rivers inland for miles. The animal follows the Arctic cod which is its favorite food. If cod is not available, the beluga eats the most varied diet recorded for any Cetacean: worms, molluscs, crabs, plaice, squid, and more. It is very gregarious and is sometimes seen in groups of hundreds. It vocalizes so much that sailors have dubbed it the "sea canary." The beluga is hunted extensively for oil from its blubber (for oil and human and dog food), hide (for boots), and flesh (for mink food). There are no controls on beluga whaling. Genus: *Delphinapterus*; Species: *D. leucus*.

Narwhal (narwhale, narwal)

The largest narwhal is about 15 feet (4.6 meters) long, not including the distinctive tusk. The tusk itself may be 8 to 10 feet long (2.4 to 3 meters). The adult has a brownish upper part, and a whitish lower part, with "leopard spots" all over the body. The narwhal has only two teeth in the upper jaw. In the female, these rarely grow into tusks. In the male, the left tooth spirals forward to become the tusk. This tusk is not used to break ice, for combat, or for feeding. Some scientists have speculated that it is used in thermo-regulation. The narwhal often travels in groups of six to ten—all the same sex. It migrates with the ice pack in large numbers, ahead of the ice in the fall, following the ice in spring. It eats cuttlefish, crustaceans, and fish. The tusks of the narwhal were regarded as the horn of the unicorn in medieval times. They were highly treasured for their medicinal properties. Genus: *Monodon*; Species: *M. monoceros*.

Family: *Stenidae*
Dolphins
This family of dolphins was recently established, and as yet has no common name. Its members have teeth in both jaws, no grooves on the throat, and a notched tail like other dolphins. However, the arrangement of the air sacs and passages between the lungs and the blowhole is unique. The taxonomy of this family is confusing: there are anywhere from fourteen to nineteen species depending on the human analyst.

Rough-toothed Dolphin
The rough-toothed dolphin grows to 6 or 7 feet long (1.8 to 2.1 meters). It inhabits the deep and warm waters of the Atlantic, Pacific, and Indian oceans; the Bay of Bengal; and the Mediterranean and Caribbean seas. It is characterized by its long, evenly curved snout that rises smoothly to meet its head; the roughened and furrowed surfaces of its teeth; and its gray top, white bottom, and blotchy body. In captivity, the rough-toothed dolphin is very bold and curious. It has a long attention span, loves puzzles, and is the favorite dolphin for complex and prolonged tasks. Genus: *Steno;* Species: *S. brerdanensis.*

Ocean Dolphins
These dolphins have a great range of color patternings. The animals resemble the common dolphin *(Delphinus delphis)* in shape, but are longer. Color pattern varies from light spots on a dark background *(S. graffmani)* to typically countershaded with strong black bands running from eye to flippers *(S. frontalis)* and/or from eye to anus *(S. coeruleoalba).* This genus can work in precision groups and some species are magnificent aerial acrobats. Genus: *Stenella;* Species: *S. coeruleoalba* (blue dolphin), *S. longirostris* (long-beaked or spinning dolphin), *S. dubia, S. graffmani* (narrow-snouted dolphin), *S. frontalis* (bridled dolphin).

Family: *Delphinidae*
Dolphins
These are "typical" dolphins. They are mainly oceanic, although a few species enter estuaries or live near the coast. They have teeth (10 to 150) in the upper and lower jaws. There are no grooves on their throats and their tails are notched. Usually there is a beak that is sharply separated from the forehead. There are a few exceptions, where the melon produces a bulge over the beak. These dolphins show the characteristic triangular dorsal fin.

Common Dolphin (saddle-back dolphin)
The common dolphin is one of the most beautifully patterned of all dolphins. It has a black ring around its eye, and yellow and gray side markings that tend to form an hour glass. It rarely grows longer than 8 feet (2.4 meters). The common dolphin is found in all the warm and temperate seas. There are at least three subspecies which have distinctive color patterns. Thousands of common dolphins have been known to approach a ship and cavort around its bow. In captivity it is an excellent jumper. Genus: *Delphinus;* Species: *D. delphis.*

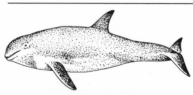

Risso's Dolphin (gray grampus)
This dolphin looks much like the pilot whale. It can be distinguished from the pilot whale in that it has only a few teeth in the lower jaw, a deep groove in the forehead, and numerous scratch marks all over the body. These marks are so predictable that they were formerly thought of as natural coloring. The adult Risso's dolphin is about 13 feet (4 meters) long. It inhabits all except polar seas, and is usually seen in groups of less than a dozen. Genus: *Grampus;* Species: *G. griseus.*

Bottlenose Dolphin
The bottlenose dolphin is the most widely recognized dolphin for many humans. It has appeared as Flipper on television, and has been in many movies. Both the Pacific and the Atlantic bottlenose dolphins are well suited to captivity. Either will adapt readily to new conditions. They are bold, curious, and enjoy variety. The Atlantic bottlenose has a very mobile neck and can catch and throw objects with great accuracy. It can easily grow bored if required to perform unchallenging, monotonous work, and may rebel or invent its own variety of game. Genus: *Tursiops;* Species: *T. gilli* (Pacific bottlenose), *T. truncatus* (Atlantic bottlenose).

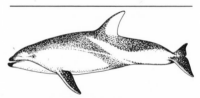

Pacific White-sided Dolphin
This species of white-sided dolphin resides in the North Pacific. The body form is streamlined, the fin is high and recurved, and the beak is short and poorly defined. The color is dark on the back, with shades of gray and white on the sides. It can grow to between 4 and 10 feet (1.2 to 3 meters). In captivity, this dolphin is known for its high jumps. Genus: *Lagenorhynchus;* Species: *L. obliquidens.*

Pygmy Killer Whale
This is one of the rarest of the large mammals on earth. It is similar to the false killer whale but much smaller— 6 feet (1.8 meters). The few sightings and captures have been made in warm seas. It is dark gray except for white bands around the lips and another small white area near the genitals. Genus: *Feresa;* Species: *F. attenuata.*

Orca (killer whale)
The orca is the largest of the dolphins. It is one of the most beautiful Cetaceans, and one of the most docile when in oceanaria with humans. (It will let people ride on its back.) The orca is found wild in all seas, from the coldest to the warmest, and is chiefly coastal. The male grows to about 30 feet (9 meters) with a tall, almost straight dorsal fin. The female is several feet shorter with a dorsal fin about half as tall, and hooked. Its bold black and white markings disruptively color the orca's body. The orca is the only dolphin to eat warm-blooded sea mammals (seals and smaller porpoises). It may also attack larger baleen whales. The orca hunts in packs (three to thirty) and coordinates attacks on larger prey. Genus: *Orcinus;* Species: *O. orca.*

False Killer Whale (lesser killer whale)
This whale is so-named because its teeth are large and sharply pointed, like the orca's. Actually, the teeth have a different shape and form, and the false killer whale resembles a pilot whale more than an orca. All three are actually large dolphins. The false killer whale grows to 18 feet (5.5 meters) for the male and 12 feet (3.6 meters) for the female. The false killer whale does not eat marine mammals. It eats very large fish and tears them apart much like the orca. The false killer whale can be distinguished from the pilot or orca by its all-black coloration, tapering head and flippers, and the small dorsal fin. False killer whales kept in captivity are the best trained species of any dolphin. A female at Marineland of the Pacific learned the tricks of its tank mates without instruction, simply by watching. Genus: *Pseudorca;* Species: *P. crassidens.*

Pilot Whale (pothead, blackfish)
The pilot whale is actually a large dolphin. The male seldom exceeds 20 feet (6.1 meters), and the female rarely grows longer than 16 feet (5 meters). The color is entirely black, though other subspecies have white on the chest and belly. The bulbous forehead and the triangular dorsal fin are easily recognized. The pilot whale lives in the warm and temperate seas, but it may penetrate sub-polar waters in summer. It migrates seasonally in schools of hundreds, often accompanied by bottlenose dolphins. The pilot whale seems to follow one leader and swim in incredibly geometrical formations. The pilot whale is the major Cetacean hunted by the Newfoundland whaling industry. From three to four thousand are annually taken. Genus: *Globicephala;* Species: *G. melaena.*

Broad-beaked Dolphin
This equatorial species is found in the Atlantic, Indian, and Pacific oceans. It is considered to be closely related to the white-sided and white-beaked dolphins (*Lagenorhynchus*). Genus: *Peponocephala;* Species: *P. electra.*

Right Whale Dolphin
This little-known dolphin is characterized by its lack of dorsal fin. It is the only dolphin without one. The North Pacific species measures about 8 feet (2.5 meters). A smaller right whale dolphin (*L. peroni peroni*) inhabits the temperate waters of the South Atlantic and Pacific. This dolphin is quick, active, and frequently leaps from the ocean. It travels in small schools. Genus: *Lissodelphis;* Species: *L. peroni borealis.*

Family: *Phocoenidae*
Porpoises
Porpoises are very similar to the true dolphin in general appearance and bone structure. Some taxonomists place porpoises and dolphins in the same family. Technically, "porpoise" is a word used only for small Cetaceans that lack a prominent beak and have laterally compressed, spade-like teeth. The dorsal fin, if there is one, is low and triangular in shape.

Harbor Porpoise (common porpoise)
The harbor porpoise is one of the smallest Cetaceans. The male reaches a maximum of 5½ feet (1.7 meters). Its life cycle is unique. Weaning is very rapid (about five months) and sexual maturity is attained quickly (fourteen months as opposed to two years for most Cetaceans). The coloration is countershaded: black above and white below, though some individuals are all black. It is coastal, and sometimes ascends rivers. It inhabits the coasts of the North Atlantic and Pacific up to the Arctic. Its southern limits are the north coast of Africa and the Black Sea. Genus: *Phocaena;* Species: *P. phocoena.*

White-flanked Porpoise (Dall's porpoise, True's porpoise)
These two porpoises are considered to be the same species by some cetologists. They differ only in the amount of white on the belly, throat, and flippers. Both are oceanic. Dall's is found mostly in the eastern North Pacific, and True's in Japanese waters. The males grow to be about 7 feet long (2.1 meters). The spade-shaped teeth number 19 to 27 on each side. These white-flanked porpoises have horny protuberances of the gums between the teeth which are thought to be useful in gripping squid. Genus: *Phocaenoides;* Species: *P. dalli* (Dall's porpoise), *P. truei* (True's).

PART TWO

BRAINS
AND
CONSCIOUSNESS

My object here is simply to project the draught of a systematization of Cetology. I am the architect, not the builder. But it is a ponderous task; no ordinary letter-sorter in the Post-office is equal to it. To grope down into the bottom of the sea after them; to have one's hands among the unspeakable foundations, ribs, and very pelvis of the world; this is a fearful thing. What am I that I should essay to hook the nose of this Leviathan!

From Moby Dick, *by Herman Melville.*

JOAN MCINTYRE
On Awareness

We are always looking for correspondences. Looking for something that is like us in other creatures. We believe that if we can prove that an animal has human characteristics it is more valuable, more deserving of life. If we wish to save the whales from slaughter, part of our effort goes to proving that they are worthy—that is, that they are similar to us. I think we do this as much to confirm our own value, to reassure ourselves that we are indeed the crown of creation, as to find out anything about what is out there. So when we look at whales, when we try to get close to them, or close to what we think they might be, some extraordinary qualities come to our attention. For want of a better concept we call it *intelligence*, because that's what we think *we* have.

Intelligence may in fact be the wrong way of looking at it. We have a terrible time defining or clarifying it, even in ourselves. We give intelligence tests, only to find out that what we are testing is experience and manipulation; the use of language; the ability to relate to a commonly perceived set of symbols; the ability to share a common cultural configuration. If, for example, you show a photograph of himself to a person from a culture that does not use or recognize photographs, there is simply no image there for him to recognize as his own. What we test and recognize is limited by the questions we can devise and our ability to conceive of a system in which those questions are meaningful.

So even though the word *intelligence* will appear and reappear in these pages, it may be better to think of the quality we are trying to describe as *awareness*.

Whales and dolphins have very large and complex brains. Since we equate large and complex brains with humans, and equate humans with intelligence, we easily slip into extrapolating that large and complex brains must indicate high levels of intelligence.

Often, the people who study Cetacean brains do not study the living animal. The people who work with the living animal do not have the specific expertise to understand the physical intricacies of

Now, you can use fish if you feel you have to, as a signal to say, "I approve of what you've just done." Sometimes we would feed the dolphins to satiation and then still use fish, and they would very politely take the fish away and pile them on the bottom of the tank. Then when they wanted the experiment to stop, they would lift the last fish on the pile up and hand it to the experimenter. I think that's all the Pavlovian system can do with big brains.
John Lilly

the brain. So then understand that the material you are about to read —and the understanding of that material—is at best fragmentary; and that this is the very beginning of our inquiry rather than the definition of it. And also understand that there is real information about these creatures—the whales and dolphins—in the countless stories told throughout the centuries by people who simply watched them, who came in contact with the wild living animal and noticed something—something that gave them pause.

If you look for what might be the common thread in any number of stories about Cetaceans, you are struck with the recurring idea that it appears as if the animals are intensely conscious of what they are doing. Conscious in an exquisitely specific and finely detailed way. This business of being conscious of what you do may seem a simple one, but it is one we commonly do not grant to other animals. We tend to accept the idea that all animals other than humans behave like wind-up clocks of stimulus-response, that their lives are regulated only by instinct, and that the ability to be flexible, to react in a subtle changing way to changing circumstances, is an ability given only unto man—a kind of divine intercession.

But if it is the great right whale that gently lifted up Katy Payne on her enormous flukes; the orca that killed the same logger that tried to kill him; or the right whale that signaled his awesome intentions to Bill Curtsinger by thrashing his head to and fro in the water—all these actions show a very specific awareness. An awareness of the event, the exact placement of each individual in the event, an awareness of consequence, and a clear intent.

It is very hard for us to accept that the actions of the monster might be specific. Or to relate to the intricate and detailed way a mountain of flesh and bone can act. But it may be that our difficulty has as much to do with our own bias and culture as it does with the creature we wish to understand. We expect that anything that big would of course be wild and random, and anything that big and random would of course be dangerous. We reveal our cultural bias even further when we assume that anything big and wild enough to hurt us, *would* indeed hurt us. As if the only deterrent to power is power.

But if we comb through our stories and our encounters with wild whales and dolphins, we find that they seem to hang together along a shining thread—that whales and dolphins know what they are doing, that their actions are purposeful, and stunningly specific to the occasion, that they intend us no harm, that they are *aware*.

Much of what is in this book represents a part of our effort to understand the process of that awareness. We turn the light of our knowledge on these creatures to try to use our intelligence to illuminate theirs. It is the beginning of a long process.

JOHN LILLY
A Feeling of Weirdness

John Lilly, M.D., Ph.D., first delivered this paper at the Fifth Annual Lasker Lecture at the Michael Reese Hospital in April of 1962. At that time, Dr. Lilly was involved in his early pioneering studies of dolphin behavior and communication which he conducted from 1955 through 1963. He then left dolphin research to investigate his own mind, on the theory that the study of the self and the universe are one. His decision to concentrate on himself was prompted by the dolphins who, he feels, taught him a lot about being a human. Dr. Lilly is the author of a number of books, including Man and Dolphin, The Mind of the Dolphin, Programming and Metaprogramming in the Human Biocomputer, and The Center of the Cyclone.

In this paper I would like to discuss a very peculiar effect which we have noticed in the laboratory while working with the bottlenose dolphin (*Tursiops truncatus*). This effect is an example of the peculiarities of a creative process which occurs in this particular kind of scientific research but which may also occur more widely than just here. To state it tersely: if one works with a bottlenose dolphin day in and day out for many hours, days, and weeks, one is struck with the fact that one's current basic assumptions and even one's current expectations determine, within certain limits, the results attained with a particular animal at that particular time.

This effect was first noticed in our work in 1955, 1957, and 1958. As I became more convinced of the neuroanatomical size and complexity of the dolphin brain, I noticed a subtle change in my own attitude in regard to possible performances on the parts of these animals. To one like myself, trained in neurology, neurophysiology, and psychoanalysis, a large complex brain implies large complex capabilities and great mental sensitivity. Such capabilities and sensitivities can exist of course in forms we have not yet recognized.

The working hypothesis of an advanced capability raised our index of suspicion and in turn sensitized us to new sources of information. It was this subtle preparation of the mental climate which allowed us to listen to some rather queer noises that the dolphin was producing in the laboratory and to review them very carefully on the tapes. Because of the possibility of a very large brain capacity and because of musings about the possible areas of achievement already realized in this species but as yet undiscovered by us, our minds began to open.

This opening of our minds was a subtle and yet a painful process. We began to have feelings which I believe are best described by the word "weirdness." The feeling was that we were up against the edge of a vast uncharted region in which we were about to embark with a good deal of mistrust concerning the appropriateness of our own equipment. The feeling of weirdness came on us as the sounds of this small whale seemed more and more to be forming words in our own language. We felt we were in the presence of Something, or Someone, who was on the other side of a transparent barrier which up to this point we hadn't even seen. The dim outlines of a Someone began to appear. We began to look at this small whale's body with newly opened eyes and began to think in terms of its possible "mental processes," rather than in terms of the classical view of a conditionable, instinctually functioning "animal." We began to apologize to one another for slips of the tongue in which we would call dolphins "persons" and in which we began to use their names as if they *were* persons. This seemed to be as much a way of grasping at straws of security in a rough sea of the unknown as of committing the sin of Science of anthropomorphizing. Also, if these "animals" had "higher mental processes," then they in turn must have been thinking of us as very peculiar (even stupid) beings indeed.

About this time we began to be exposed to what I would call the dedicated, opposed skepticism of some scientific workers. These people were for several years in close contact with dolphins in the oceanaria and did not and do not share our views of the possibilities resident in this huge and complex brain. Their view is not incomprehensible to those of us who are in the new area we have opened up. This group of scientists has denied publicly that mimicry of human speech was possible for these animals ("No vocal cords," is typical). When we demonstrated that mimicry existed, they changed their tack, and now say, "Mimicry, so what? Parrots do it, mynah birds do it." If anyone had said to me in 1947 that a whale could mimic human words, I would not have believed him. But in 1957 I was forced to believe—through the experience of hearing a whale do it. The "mimicry, so what" group may have lost their sense of wonder and surprise; we have not.

However, I do not wish to discuss opposing points of view, nor to dwell too long on the effect of such vociferous opposition on one's thinking. As to the latter, all I can say is that at one time it slowed us down a bit, but the dolphins continue to renew our confidence and make us eager to push on.

We first obtained the mimicry effect in 1957 by the use of electrodes implanted deep within the rewarding sites in the brain structures in these animals. These results, therefore, may have been caused by the peculiar way that the brain was being stimulated. We considered that possibly the animals did not have this ability when stimulated naturally through their normal inputs and outputs.

In 1961, Miss Alice Miller and I once again examined the 1957 results. We decided to pay close attention to the tapes of the previous year (1960–61) and look at them from the viewpoint that there might be evidence of a complex mental activity going on in our resident dolphins.

In March 1960 a dolphin named Lizzie had produced a sequence of humanoid noises underwater. This was the first and last time that

We are very superstitious about killer whales up here. We know from our ancestors from way back that they once tried to kill a whale like that, a killer whale, and they hardly wounded it. It is known that the whale capsized the boat and chewed up both human beings who were in the boat. It is said that these whales have a good memory and even after many numbers of years pass, they always know which human being had been shooting at them.
Raymond T. Aguvlak, American Scientist, *January 1973*

72

Lizzie or Baby, the two dolphins whom we were working with during that period, produced any sounds of this type. In the pool together in St. Thomas they had produced whistles and clicks almost exclusively. The language they were using was strictly "delphinese." However, the night before she died, Lizzie (freshly isolated from Baby) said something underwater which sounded suspiciously like, "It's six o'clock," which I had just shouted to her over the water of the tank. Miss Miller and I reviewed that tape many times and each time the uncanny feeling of 1957 was evoked.

After the Lizzie episode we obtained an animal which we named Elvar. During his first year, Elvar had begun to develop a new series of voices over and above his "delphinese" one. These new emissions covered such a vast range of vocalization capabilities that we were hard put to analyze them all. His whistles and clicks were interpolated among a series of barks, wails, moans, buzzings, trumpetings, banjo-like sounds, quacking, etc. All of these sounds first occurred underwater, but later more and more of them were emitted in air from his now-opened blowhole. Some of his "quacking" noises had become similar but not identical with those of human speech. In reviewing these records, Miss Miller and I saw some changes from the native delphinese, to noises which we felt were beginning to bridge the vast gap between delphinese and human sounds. We gradually became convinced that this was evidence of beginning primitive mimicry, not quite as advanced as we had found in 1957, but far enough along to be disturbing and exciting.

During this phase of our scientific development we were moving from one set of laboratory quarters to another; Elvar moved with us. We established a laboratory in Miami in January 1961, and finally had a more stable environment in which to observe Elvar. We began to obtain higher quality recordings of his emissions. In September 1961 we were convinced that it was time to attempt to elicit straightforward and direct production of human speech sounds by Elvar without the use of brain electrodes or even of food reward.

Our reasoning was as follows: It was already known these animals could be trained to do all sorts of circus tricks in a very well-timed and precise way by means of food reward. It was also known that such training could be obtained from other kinds of animals with food reward. We decided to test the hypothesis that possibly the dolphins were rewarded by participating in activities directly with the human, especially vocal activities. At that time we suspected that a human must also be willing to establish a close contact with a given animal and that the animal must also be kept separated from its own species.

Elvar was isolated in a shallow small tank. Alice started an intensive effort to induce him to vocalize in response to her vocalizations and activities. Within a few hours of the time that she started this activity, Elvar responded by beginning to mimic her voice. The unearthly feeling was once again evoked. Why?

Here was an animal who from the viewpoint of evolutionary theory is in a group of mammals who have developed for the last thirty million years in the sea, completely separated from the evolution of the primates which gave rise to *Homo sapiens*. His anatomy and physiology, though strictly mammalian, were of a strange and different form than ours, including his vocalization apparatus. Despite our careful mental preparations, it was literally a shock and a surprise to hear him say so soon after Alice, "More, Elvar."

The repeatedly painful and humbling part of this experience was that we, as human beings, had felt that man was at the top; we were alone; yet here was an "animal" which was entering into that which was peculiarly human, i.e., human speech. At no matter how primitive level, he was entering into it. He was taking step number one. To convey to you our sense of wonder, and yet the sense of the uncomfortable necessity of continuously reorganizing our basic assumptions, is difficult. We gambled on Elvar's taking the first step, and he did. (We still haven't done as well with his delphinese language.) He impressed us with the fact that he took the first step towards repairing a gap of at least thirty million years in a few weeks. He may be skipping some of the belabored efforts of the human race for the last forty thousand years to achieve our present degree of articulate speech among ourselves. Maybe he is not skipping. Maybe he is just beginning what *Homo sapiens* went through forty thousand years ago. *And he first did it when and only when we believed he could do it and somehow demonstrated our belief to him.*

We now are taking a very close look at his processes of acquisition of these words. We are impressed with his amazing ability to analyze our sounds and emit the products of his analysis. He does not reproduce a word in a "tape-recorder" fashion or in the fashion of a talking bird. In one's presence he literally analyzes the acoustic components of our words and reproduces various aspects in sequence and separately.

One of our clearest examples occurred when he started saying, "More, Elvar." In one session he started out with, "More, Var," slowing down his natural pace and lowering his natural frequency well into the human range. He then took Alice's whole transmission, "More, Elvar," speeded it up, took it back into his natural frequency region around 4–12 kc per second and repeated it. He then slowed it down, and lowered his frequencies down near those that Alice was producing, and reproduced, "More, Elvar" on the human scale and in the human frequency region.

In another session in which I was working on the word "squirt"

74

with him, he took the word and reproduced it at a high frequency and in a very short abrupt fashion. It was so high-pitched and so fast that one could not recognize it at all unless it was slowed down several times in playback. Next he went through at least five different variations of the word, each of which he produced in response to my repeating the word "squirt." His productions sounded like "irt," "squir," "ir," to something which sounded very close to "squirt" in a Donald Duck–like voice. The latest studied voice that he uses resembles that of a very small child; it is very high-pitched and thin in quality, and yet of such an intensity in air that it is sometimes painful to listen to when one is closer than three or four feet from his blowhole.

When one is doing such vocalizations experiments with Elvar, one sometimes has the feeling that he is very impatient with our slow and laborious methods. He acts as if he wishes we would hurry up and understand him. He apparently is pushing points we as yet cannot imagine. For example, he sometimes inserts long passages of delphinese alternating with our words as if to translate for us.

This peculiar feeling of "as if a person or a personality or a being" who somehow reaches out towards us, who comes as far as we believe he can come at a particular time, and who seems to be waiting to proceed to the next as yet unknown step are some of the elements in the feeling that I above called "weirdness."

I do not wish to give the impression that every new thing we try with Elvar works. We have done several new things with him which turned out to be inappropriate. For example, we expected that when he was sick he would come and volunteer for an antibiotic shot with a hypodermic needle. (We had seen another dolphin do this in the hands of Adolph Frohn.) Elvar would have none of it. As a consequence of several such injections, he singled me out as the villain of the piece and expressed great dissatisfaction with my presence for literally weeks.

At first I found this inconvenient, but it led to another episode in which we learned something. Dolphins not only discipline their young somewhat the way humans do, but the young ones learn proper manners very rapidly. Elvar was expressing his dissatisfaction with me and his injections in the presence of Chee-Chee, an older female. I was attempting to induce him to approach me at the side of his shallow tank. He had been avoiding me assiduously by swimming to the far side. Suddenly, he whirled about in the water, opened his mouth and barked (underwater) as he charged towards my arm in the pool. Chee-Chee intercepted him at right angles to his course and slammed the bottom of her beak down on the top of his head so hard that I could feel the resulting jar at the side of the tank. She

We have never seen a porpoise "go berserk" and attack a human with persistence as a dog or a horse may do. One gains the subjective impression that the porpoise is a firm, fair disciplinarian, exhibiting just as much aggression as will serve its purpose and no more. A female rough-toothed porpoise, mother of a hybrid calf, was kept in a tank alone with her calf and frequently solicited stroking from her trainer. The calf occasionally situated itself between mother and trainer while the mother was being stroked. When the calf was approximately a month old, the trainer in this situation one day stroked the calf. The mother swung her tail from the water, reached up and out, and struck the trainer a sharp, but not damaging, blow across the shoulders, and then with no further apparent fear or anger continued to solicit stroking for herself. *Karen W. Pryor,* Behavior and Learning in Porpoises and Whales, *Naturwissenschaften 1973*

Dave and Melba Caldwell, of Los Angeles County Museum, have summarized care-giving behavior in killer whales. A mortally wounded mother stood by her dead calf, circling the body for an hour until she died, though she never attacked the collector's boat. Another female lingered three days near Hat Island, Puget Sound, after her calf was killed. A crew from Marineland of the Pacific captured a large female near Bellingham, but the lasso caught in the ship's propeller. As she struggled in the water, she emitted a high-pitched, penetrating vocalization. After twenty minutes the high dorsal fin of a male killer whale appeared and the animal zeroed in on the female as if by radar. The two animals together charged toward the boat at high speed, veering only when they had approached to within five to eight feet; then together charged again. This time they struck the boat. The crew killed both whales to save the boat.

Pacific Search *1967*

did this just before his jaws reached my arm. Since that episode Elvar has not attempted to charge me. (In general, our dolphins now tend to express their dissatisfaction with someone who is putting an arm or a leg, or an entire body into the pool by pushing the person gently out again by a series of rapid bumpings with their closed jaws against the arm or leg.)

In such maneuverings, and in such non-vocal signals to us, they are amazingly silent in the humanoid sphere. Yet they emit whistles, clicks, and their sonar, ultrasonic creakings as if signalling to one another. However, I doubt that this silence will continue. There are times when they make valiant attempts during their maneuverings with us to use humanoid sounds, apparently in (to them) an appropriate fashion. They apparently become discouraged by our inappropriate responses. The semantics of their language and their thinking is probably so different from ours that we sometimes become enamored of the differences and fail to see simple similarities right in front of our noses.

Since September 1961 we have been working every day with Elvar's enunciation and his vocabulary. We are now eliciting words with food rewards. He has been working in a tank immediately adjacent to that of Chee-Chee. In general they tend to communicate from one tank to the other underwater in natural delphinese clicks and whistles. During weekends they are allowed to be together for courtship and sexual play. Elvar apparently has been practicing his humanoid sounds when we are not there. We had not attempted to elicit these sounds from Chee-Chee until about two weeks ago. She was not giving them to us except at peculiarly odd intervals. Every so often, however, we would detect a humanoid exchange going on in air between Chee-Chee and Elvar, so we suspected that she was getting some practice in private.

About two weeks ago it was decided that Miss Nadell (a psychologist working with Elvar) would attempt to elicit humanoid sounds and a humanoid vocabulary from Chee-Chee. Chee-Chee shifted from delphinese (clicks and whistles) in air to fully formed humanoid word-like sounds on the first try. Miss Nadell held a fish up and said "speak" to Chee-Chee. Chee-Chee came back and said something that sounded like "speak" and was given the fish. Miss Nadell then said "louder," and Chee-Chee came back with something that was like "louder" plus a lot of other completely nonunderstood emissions.

One gets the impression during such experiences that the dolphin has been waiting for the day when he or she would be treated in the same way that another dolphin has been treated. When the day comes, if the "proper" gesture and language are used with that particular animal he responds in the way that the previous one did.

A third animal, Sissy, has been kept in isolation from Elvar and

76

Chee-Chee on another floor of the same building. Sissy is a much younger animal than either Elvar or Chee-Chee and is relatively undisciplined in comparison to the others. Sissy, about a week ago, was asked to vocalize for a food reward. In the first session she replied and demanded the food reward with a very peculiar delphinese emission in air: with the vocalization apparatus on the right side (inside her blowhole) she whistled in air and on the left side simultaneously she clicked in air. One could see the right side opening fairly widely and steadily and the exit pulsing only with the modulations of the whistles; on the left side it was vibrating with each of the very loud "clapping-like" clicks that were emitted into the air. After a week's experience with these noises she suddenly began a series of humanoid noises mixed with the clicks and the whistles. However, the clocks and the whistles are predominant. It is almost as if she is an uneducated dolphin who has barely had enough time to get a toe hold on her own language and has had no opportunity yet to get a good toe hold on ours. (Various reports are coming in from the staff that she has been hitting their hands rather abruptly and suddenly with her beak and opening her mouth at them. It is possible that she needs the teaching and the discipline of an older animal to teach her proper manners at this point.)

These experiences illustrate the thesis that one can protect one's self and maintain one's ignorance by belittling disturbing experiences, or one can newly recapture sensitivity and be open-minded (even painfully so) and *discover* new facts. Discovery, in my experience, requires disillusionment first as well as later. One must be shaken in one's basic beliefs before the discovery can penetrate one's mind sufficiently to be detected. A certain willingness to face censure, to be a maverick, to question one's beliefs, to revise them, are obviously necessary. But what is not obvious is how to prepare one's own mind to receive the transmissions from the far side of the protective transparent wall separating each of us from the dark gulf of the unknown. Maybe we must realize that we are still babies in the universe, taking steps never before taken. Sometimes we reach out from our aloneness for someone else who may or may not exist. But at least we reach out, and it is gratifying to see our dolphins reach also, however primitively. They reach toward those of us who are willing to reach toward them. It may be that some day not too far distant we both can draw to an end the "long loneliness," as Loren Eiseley called it.

I think all animals think. But that again becomes a matter of definition. Some people who would want to put animals into a separate category feel they think, but not on the level of humans. But man is pretty egocentric about these things. He doesn't think anything corresponds to or thinks like him, and that's probably true. That doesn't make them a lower form necessarily. Maybe they haven't been able to conquer the earth and overcome environmental difficulties and fly airplanes, and all that sort of thing, but in another sort of way they seem to do very well. They are free.
Peter Morgane

Myron Jacobs, Ph.D., is a neuroanat-
omist and the former director of the
Cetacean Brain Laboratory of the Os-
borne Laboratories of Marine Science of
the New York Aquarium. He is the co-
author (with Peter Morgane) of A Dolphin Brain Atlas *(in press). Drs. Jacobs,*
Morgane, and Lilly share a ten year
professional association and interest in
the potential of the Cetacean brain. At
present, Dr. Jacobs is a professor of
Pathology at the New York University
College of Dentistry.

In an essay on "The Three Brains,"
Robert Bly refers to the ideas of the
American neurologist Paul McLean.

**During evolution, the body often re-
shaped the body—fins, for example, in
us, turned utterly into arms, but the
forward momentum in evolution was
apparently so great that the brain could
not allow itself the time to reform—it
simply added.**

**The reptile brain is still intact in the
head. Known medically as limbic node,**

MYRON JACOBS
The Whale Brain: Input and Behavior

Human beings have been fascinated by whales for thousands of years. Yet despite this fascination, our understanding of the neural mechanisms underlying the behavior of these animals is slight, and has lagged far behind the knowledge we have accumulated about land animals. The principal reason for this stems from the practical problems that surround the study of these large mammals. One of the most difficult and commonly frustrating of the problems is the task of making long-term observations of animals in the field. Here, the basic obstacle—and one which may never be overcome—is that of trying to bridge the great environmental chasm separating man and whale.

Our knowledge of whale behavior is, thus, very superficial, and much of what is known is based on observations either of animals that have been hunted or harassed at sea, or of captured animals maintained in the unnatural and restrictive confines of the display facilities of public or private oceanaria.

In terms of body structure, Cetacea—both the great whales and the lesser whales, dolphins and porpoises—represent the order of mammals that is the furthest removed from its distant relatives living on land. The long period of adaptation to, and specialization in, the aquatic environment—an evolution lasting approximately twenty-five million years—has produced a unique group of animals that differs radically in shape from that of land mammals. Yet the Cetaceans have retained, in modified form, almost all of the behavioral patterns present in land animals.

The precise progenitors of present-day Cetaceans, and the exact times at which these ancestors gradually moved into a purely aquatic environment, are uncertain, though there appear to have been several ancestral forms that managed to cope successfully with the many obstacles inherent in the vastly different ambient medium of their new environment. Here, they were enveloped by a fluid that was more dense, more optically opaque, more vibration-rich, thermostable, homeostatic, and more buoyant than the air surrounding land animals.

In addition, their new environment lacked the formerly ever-present sensory input provided through gravity by constant physical contact with the surface of the earth. This sensory input is of the utmost importance to land animals, for it serves to signal states of muscle contractility in progressive movements.

A serious gap in our knowledge of the history of whales is the relative absence of fossil records of the progenitors of the now-extinct suborder of early Cetaceans, the Archeocetes. Because of fossil gaps in the early natural history of whales, it is not possible to say just how they evolved from terrestrial antecedents, and it can only be surmised that the reasons for the drastic changes in body configuration that occurred over a long, early period of time most likely had to do with fundamental behaviors related to feeding, individual survival, and reproduction. Out of sheer necessity, therefore, given the available evidence, today's Cetaceans must be considered as a population of mammals isolated both in time and space from unknown ancestors and isolated similarly from all of the animal groups with which man is most familiar.

The brains of modern Cetaceans reflect this complete separation from terrestrial lines of mammalian evolution and differ in many ways from the brains of land mammals. Grossly, the typical Cetacean brain is globular in shape and is both higher and wider than it is long; in these features it contrasts rather sharply with the brains of most terrestrial mammals. The peculiar compressed appearance and foreshortening of the Cetacean brain apparently developed in conjunction with drastic structural reorganizations of the bones of the face and cranium. Comparing skulls of Archeocete whales with skulls of modern whales indicates that this reorganization was the consequence of gradual modifications in the shapes of the individual bones. These alterations contributed to the gradual movement of the external nasal openings to the forehead region, where they became the Cetacean blowhole, and also served to increase the height and shorten the length of the cranial cavity.

In all vertebrates, the brain must be considered the single most important mediator of the patterned sequences of motor and sensory activities constituting behavior. The brain organizes and modifies, in almost instantaneous fashion, the constant and ever-changing stream of bioelectric sensory inputs that reach it from the environ-

it is a horseshoe shaped organ located in the base of the skull. The job of the reptile brain appears to be the physical survival of the organism in which it finds itself. Should danger or enemies come near, an alarm system comes into play, and the reptile brain takes over from the other brains. In great danger it might hold that power exclusively. The presence of fear produces a higher energy input to the reptile brain. The increasing fear in this century means that more and more energy, as a result, is going to the reptile brain.

When the change to mammal life occurred, a second brain was simply folded around the limbic node. This "cortex," which I will call here the mammal brain, fills most of the skull. The mammal brain has quite different functions. When we come to the mammal brain we find for the first time a sense of community: love of women, of children, of the neighbor, the idea of brotherhood, care for the community, or for the country. Evidently in the mammal brain there are two nodes of energy: sexual love and ferocity. (The reptile brain has no ferocity: it simply fights coldly for survival.) Women have strong mammal brains, and probably a correspondingly smaller energy channel to the reptile brain. They are more interested in love than war.

In late mammal times, the body evidently added a third brain. This third brain takes the form of an outer eighth-inch of brain tissue laid over the surface of the mammal brain. It is known medically as the neocortex. Brain tissue of the neocortex is incredibly complicated, more so than the other brains, having millions of neurons per square inch. Curiously, the third brain seems to have been created for problems more complicated than those it is now being used for. Some neurologists speculate that an intelligent man today uses 1/100 of its power. Einstein may have been using 1/50 of it.
Robert Bly, The Seventies, *Odin Press*

ment via the peripheral nerves of the head and the spinal cord. It then rechannels this modified information to motor regions of the central nervous system for the initiation of responses. The various types of information monitored and acted upon by the brain may be considered as arising (1) from the environment outside the body, or *extra-somatic* sources; (2) at the interface between the body and the external environment, or *somatic* sources; and (3) from the environment within the body, or *visceral* sources.

While this generalized overview of sensory inputs applies equally to all animals, the substitution of water for air as an environmental medium greatly alters the types of sensory information that can be received most *effectively* by Cetaceans. The two most uncomplicated examples of this difference have to do with light and sound. Thus, in water, visual stimuli become less effective with the rapid fall-off of incident light at increasing depths below the surface. On the other hand, sound waves are far more effective stimuli, owing to the approximately threefold increase in speed at which sound travels in water.

A less obvious example, but one which probably has had an even greater influence on the gradual adaptive changes of body configuration and behavior in Cetaceans to water, has to do with gravity. In land mammals, the downward force of gravity is opposed by muscular contractions, tonic in nature during static posture or phasic during movement. The conditions are quite different for whales. The buoyancy of water constantly acts against gravity so that at any depth the forces acting everywhere over the body's surface are fairly uniform, and muscle contraction serves chiefly for body motility. In such an environment, appendages as they exist in land mammals would be useless. It is interesting to speculate that the uniformly neutral physical nature of the surrounding medium has contributed in Cetacean evolution to the development of a body form which is

The white whale (left), *Delphinapterus leucas,* in reality a large dolphin, also engages in complex play patterns which have their structural basis in this mammal's relatively large brain. (Their brain weight is about 1500 grams.) Few mammals equal dolphins in their complex patterns of play, a behavior which seems related to large-brained mammals only. The Pacific white-sided dolphin shown here (right), *Lagenorhynchus obliquidens),* has a brain weighing about 1500 grams, almost as large as that of the bottlenose dolphin.

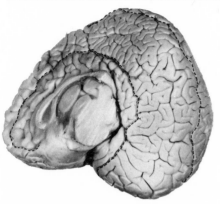

In whales and dolphins, the areas of cerebral cortex receiving sensory inputs and initiating motor responses are distributed along the medial wall of each hemisphere. This mediobasal view of the right hemisphere of the bottlenose dolphin shows the highly folded and continuous nature of this sensorimotor cortex.

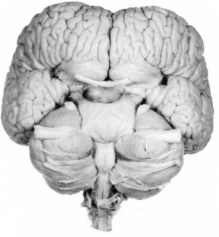

Basal view of the brain of the bottlenose dolphin *(Tursiops truncatus)* which, in the adult, weighs about 1600 grams. Emphasized is the cerebellum which, in Cetaceans, may comrpise up to 20 percent of total brain weight, considerably more than most other mammals, including man (about 12 percent). The intact pituitary gland is also shown in position, near the middle of the brain in this picture.

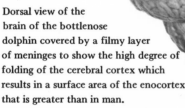
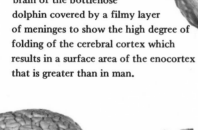

Dorsal view of the brain of the bottlenose dolphin covered by a filmy layer of meninges to show the high degree of folding of the cerebral cortex which results in a surface area of the enocortex that is greater than in man.

Lateral view of brain of the bottlenose dolphin *(Tursiops truncatus)* emphasizing the richness of cortical folding and showing the characteristic foreshortening and increased height of the Cetacean brain.

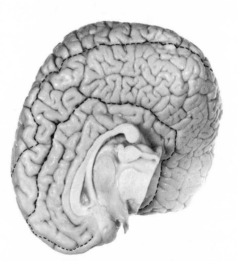

This medial view of the right half of the brain of the bottlenose dolphin shows clearly the continuity of sensorimotor areas of the paralimbic lobe. The dashed lines are superimposed over deep clefts that demarcate this lobe sharply from the rest of the hemisphere.

strongly dominated by the head and in which the remainder of the body surface is used primarily for movement. Because of the nature of the environment, the head region of whales appears to be of relatively greater importance as a receptor of sensory influences from the world that surrounds them than is the case for land mammals.

This view receives strong support from our studies of the Cetacean brain and the cranial nerves that are connected to it in the head region. These nerves convey to the brain impulses relating to the different types of sensory modalities. The number of nerve fibers that they contain (along with the extent of direct or indirect distribution and the regions of the brain receiving the fibers) may provide a clue to the relative importance of each modality to whale behavior. The attempt to use the quality and quantity of the neural substratum to interpret behavior depends very heavily on comparisons with mammalian forms that have been studied in much greater detail. Such comparisons assume, of course, that even though whales developed in isolation from the land along very specialized lines, they are nevertheless mammals, and it is to be expected that their nervous systems would be organized in the general mammalian fashion.

The most striking change in the brain that has occurred during mammalian phylogeny in the line leading to man is the great increase in size of the cerebral hemisphere in comparison to the remaining portions of the brain. Each hemisphere of the human brain may be subdivided into three concentric lobar formations, arching from front to back, that reflect different stages of brain evolution. The innermost and most ancient lobe, lying closest to the midline, is very poorly developed and has been termed the *rhinic* lobe (from the Greek *rhinos*, the nose) because it was once thought to be that part of the brain having to do with smell. The next lobe, modest in extent, has been termed the *limbic* lobe (from the Latin *limbus*, border) because it is disposed along the border, or limbus, of the hemisphere. The third and by far the largest of the lobar formations lies superimposed on top of the limbic lobe and hence has been termed the *supralimbic* lobe. It represents the most recently acquired part of the hemisphere and makes up the bulk of the medial and dorsolateral portions of each hemisphere. Further, each hemisphere has a cellular covering or cortex and well over ninety percent of this surface lies over the phylogenetically newer portions, and hence is referred to as *neocortex*.

When comparing the patterns of brain organization present in several of the smaller species of toothed whales to those described above for man, several significant differences have been uncovered. Rather than three lobes, each hemisphere is organized into four distinct arching lobes. A well-developed extra lobar formation is insinuated between the limbic and supralimbic lobes and has been designated the *paralimbic* lobe. Based on neurohistological criteria, the paralimbic lobe has turned out to be a continuum of all of the specific sensory and motor areas which, in man, are distributed throughout the supralimbic lobe. Although the functional significance of this unique sensori-motor cortical platform is unknown, it is reasonably certain that it has resulted from the special lines along which Cetaceans have evolved.

While adequate means for studying the role of the nervous system in mediating whale behavior have not as yet been developed, our years of surveying the structural organization of the Cetacean brain have prompted much speculative thinking about the level of cortical activity of which the brains of Cetaceans are capable. "Cortical activity" here is not used in place of "intelligence" since the latter term is applied properly only to man. Our impression is, however, that whales are capable of quite high levels of cerebral activity.

The Cetacean brain receives an unusually rich sensory input. The sensory systems that are lacking (e.g., toothed whales lack the sense of smell), reduced (e.g., visual and tactile senses), or modified (e.g., vestibular and gustatory senses) are more than made up for by the unusually well-innervated ears, face, and body viscera. Thus, it is reasonable to assume that strong and rather sophisticated sensory impressions register on the cerebral neocortex. That this may be the case is borne out by the wide expanse of the hemispheric paralimbic lobes which receive such information. It is thus possible that whales experience a broad range of strong cerebral impressions which would be classified as subjective mental images if applied to human beings.

How whales use such cortical activities to bring about meaningful behaviors remains as much a mystery as ever. The sensory portions of their brains seem to be well-developed, whereas the motor portions are quite limited in extent. All of the non-visceral motor responses are channeled into only two directions, body movement and sound generation. The high degree of social behavior among Cetaceans, however, suggests that they may have developed ways of using their two motor skills which are still unknown to us.

I suspect that whales and dolphins quite naturally go in the directions we call spiritual, in that they get into meditative states quite simply and easily. If you go into the sea yourself, with a snorkel and face mask and warm water, you can find that dimension in yourself quite easily. Free floating is entrancing. Now it may just be that we are a gravity-prejudiced biped with hands who is entering a new medium, and it may be our transient response to that medium. However, you can get addicted to these feelings, as skin divers and surfers have shown. Now if you combine snorkeling and scuba with a spiritual trip with the right people, you could make the transition to understanding the dolphins and whales very rapidly. We could do that by ourselves, without the presence of the dolphins and whales, but I think we need them to tell us what it is over the millions of years they have been on this planet. They've been here much longer than we have as compared to primates. At the time we were theoretically tree shrews, whales were completely developed, and so were dolphins.
John Lilly

Peter Morgane, Ph.D., is a senior scientist at the Worcester Foundation for
Experimental Biology in Worcester,
Massachusetts. He is the co-author (with
Myron Jacobs) of A Dolphin Brain Atlas. Dr. Morgane's interest in Cetacean
brains goes back to his early work on
brain anatomy with Dr. Paul Yakolev,
who first introduced a group of United
States scientists to the question of the
significance of large-brained animals
other than human.

PETER MORGANE

The Whale Brain: The Anatomical Basis of Intelligence

The brain is of particular interest to us all since it is the organ of mind and behavior and the seat of our intellect and memory. It is considered the structure which thinks, schemes, plans, and projects, and is thus the neurological correlate of behavioral capacity. Generally speaking, brains of animals vary in size and shape and texture in correlation with differences in their habits, their adaptability, resourcefulness, and learning power. We are continually trying to answer such questions as: To what extent are peculiar bodily features and strange living habits of animals reflected in the development and differentiation of the brain? Our present knowledge of the human brain is to a considerable extent the result of comparative studies of the brains of different animals.

Here we will discuss briefly some general principles regarding brain development and its phylogenetic history, gradually building up to some principles relating to the organization of the whale brain.

One characteristic of the brain's anatomy or structure is that it closely reproduces its own past history. That is, perhaps, one of its greatest fascinations. The historical nature of the structure within the skull is most dramatic, for here the ancient parts survive in almost their original form and the new have been added to them. The present moment of the brain always embraces the past's whole achievement. The embryo repeats, in rough summary, the events of hundreds of millions of years in nine short months, and the brain maintains them all simultaneously. In our own brain our past life, from worms through fishes and amphibians towards mammals, is summed up in what we sometimes term the old brain (paleo-cortex or archi-cortex), while advance toward humanity is expressed in the elaboration of the new brain (neocortex), whose overgrowth conceals its primitive antecedents. The fact that brains of various animals differ in weight, size, texture, etc., is obvious, but the essential parts are there, from fish through man.

Parts of the brain have developed in different animals to handle particular things they must do to survive. In this paper we will look briefly at one of the most important of these parts, i.e., the cerebral cortex. The structure of the cerebral cortex is much more complicated

84

than any other part of the brain. Due to this, it has not been so fully analyzed as some of the other parts. A great deal is known about it, but not enough to enable us to give really satisfactory accounts of how it works during a mental process. However, the cortex seems to be the major part of the brain that differs in any significant way between humans and most other animals. It does seem that the *quantity* and *quality* of gray matter (especially neocortex) in brains can be taken as a definite index of the relative efficiency of those brains in the regulation of behavior.

The enlargement of the brain is not proportional. All parts do not develop at the same rate. To this it should be added that a basic tenet, which is widely accepted among comparative neurobiologists, is that the relative size of each part of the brain is an expression of the greater or lesser importance of its principal function in the animal's life. The neocortex is by far the most advanced structure and, therefore, its development is used by brain scientists to evaluate evolutionary progress. Under the assumption that neocortical development has never been retrograde during a particular species' evolution, the degree of neocorticalization is considered to be an effective guide in the consideration of evolutionary sequences and parallels.

The extraordinary supremacy of the neocortex in comparison to all other brain structures in the nervous system is remarkable. Its size represents one cerebral criterion presently available for the classification of a given species in a scale of increasing evolutionary levels. This is only one aspect of the problem, since the internal connectivities, chemical architecture, and other factors are likely to be of considerably more importance than size alone. As shown in Figure 1, if size alone were important in brain hierarchical status, the brain of

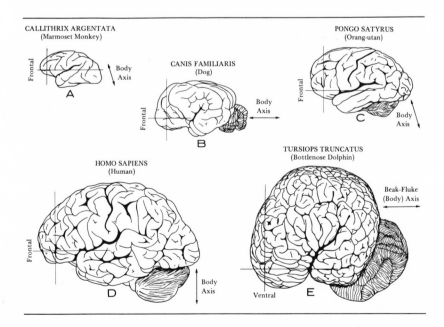

Figure 1. Comparative size of various brains including two monkey brains, dog brain, human brain, and dolphin *(Tursiops truncatus)* brain.

the dolphin would rank easily above that of man and monkey.

In higher animals in the evolutionary scale, the cerebral cortex is the dominant part of the central nervous system—the overlord that governs the somatic nervous system and, through it, our adjustments to the environment. This is a direct and authoritative control. The cortex alone seems to be the supreme arbiter of higher behavior. Now, if it can be shown that the cortex of whales has blossomed and outgrown the old brain in a manner resembling that seen in humans, we would have strong reasons for believing the whales are our close neurological relatives.

The whales, as indicated below, appear to fill such criteria as we presently have to assume advanced brain development. The amount of neocortex is generally taken as a rough index of the relative efficiency of the brain in control of behavior. The neocortex or "new brain" is a wrinkled and convoluted gray layer about one-eighth of an inch thick that covers the surface of the cerebral hemispheres. It is made of nerve cells and innumerable fine, branched, and intertwined nerve fibers. It is a place where various kinds of nerve impulses from all over the body are brought together and recombined into outgoing nerve currents. The structure of this cortex is so very complicated that it cannot be adequately shown in pictures, even if we use a great many of them. However, Figures 2, 3, and 4 give some idea of this complexity. These figures show the cortex in three separate areas in the bottlenose dolphin, demonstrating clearly both lamination and regional variation.

The lowest animals have no well-developed cerebral cortex, not even the lower backboned animals like fishes. The cerebral cortex is simply but very clearly developed in reptiles, and from here on it increases in size and complexity until in humans it makes up nearly half the brain.

It is widely held that the number of layers in the cortex (this layering is termed "lamination") determines in part the complexity of the intellect. Other features used to assess the developmental status of the brain are the degree of folding of the cortical surface ("fissurization"), general size of cortex (area), and degree of regional specialization. Complexity of patterns, arrangements, and ease of communication between cells are further important considerations. (We little comprehend the mode of the work of the vast numbers of cortical cells, but we certainly owe to their interplay much of the adaptability which has been so necessary to our evolution.) These criteria for brain advancement and complexity of process have been long accepted by anatomists.

With the above general principles stated, we will now discuss the whale brain specifically. The whales present an interesting group to study both from a morphological (structural) and functional point

86

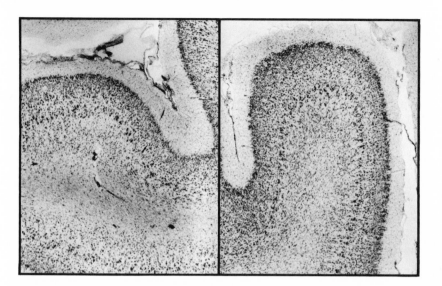

Figure 2. (left) Photograph of histological section of cerebral motor cortex of dolphin *(Tursiops truncatus)* showing the area on anterior extreme of brain containing the largest motor (pyramidal) cells. Histologically this area contains an arrangement and large pyramidal cell groups (large dark cells) similar to motor cortex in primate brains. Figure 3. (right) Photograph of histological section of cerebral cortex of dolphin *(Tursiops truncatus)* showing an area just lateral to the "primary" motor area in which somewhat smaller pyramidal cells are present.

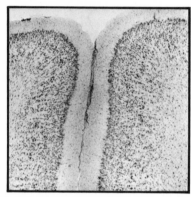

Figure 4. (above) Photograph of histological section of cerebral cortex of dolphin *(Tursiops truncatus)* showing a type of cortex seen on the lateral aspect of the hemisphere resembling what we term "association" cortex. It is clear that this architectural arrangement differs markedly from that seen in Figures 2 and 3.

of view, since they are so highly specialized to an aquatic mode of life. This specialization reflects itself particularly in the brain of these remarkable animals. Just from surface analysis alone, for example, as shown in Figure 5, the highly fissured forebrain (cortical area) is rotated forward on the brainstem axis, the brain is remarkably foreshortened, and the brainstem has a double flexure pattern not seen in other species. It is likely that many of the factors responsible for the form and developmental features of the brain in the small whales (dolphins and porpoises) and great whales must have been very different from those operating in the majority of terrestrial mammals. We do not yet know the *neurological meaning* of many of these brain specializations, but their study represents one of the most

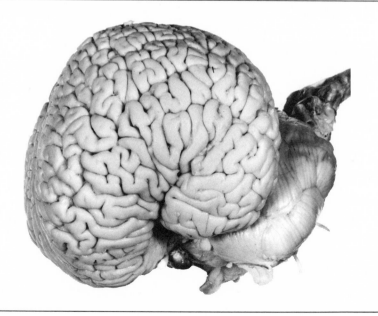

Figure 5. Photograph of brain of the bottlenose dolphin *(Tursiops truncatus)* showing the intricately folded (fissurated) neocortex. Most of this lateral cortex is of the "association" type.

But because whales and dolphins have no hands, tentacles, or other manipulative organs, their intelligence cannot be worked out in technology. What is left? Payne has recorded examples of very long songs sung by the humpback whale; some of the songs were as long as half an hour or more. A few of them appear to be repeatable, virtually phoneme by phoneme; somewhat later the entire cycle of sounds comes out virtually identically once again.

I calculate that the approximate number of bits of information (individual yes/no questions necessary to characterize the song) in a whale song of half an hour's length is between a million and a hundred million bits. Because of the very large frequency variation in these songs, I have assumed that the frequency is important in the content of the song—or, put another way, that whale language is tonal. If it is not as tonal as I guess, the number of bits in such a song may go down by a factor of ten. Now, a million bits is approximately the number of bits in *The Odyssey* or the Icelandic *Eddas*.

Is it possible that the intelligence of Cetaceans is channeled into the equivalent of epic poetry, history, and elaborate codes of social interaction? Are whales and dolphins like human Homers before the invention of writing, telling of great deeds done in years gone by in the depths and far reaches of the sea? Is there a kind of *Moby Dick* in reverse—a tragedy, from the point of view of a whale, of a compulsive and implacable enemy, of unprovoked attacks by strange wooden and metal beasts plying the seas and laden with humans?

Carl Sagan, The Cosmic Connection, *Doubleday 1973*

intriguing areas for future research. The very fact that the whales have such a highly specialized nervous system makes them of immediate interest to man. It is almost mysterious to consider the meaning of the intricate fissurization (Figure 5) of the whale cerebral cortex. This is so vast and complex a neural territory that it has aroused considerable research interest in attempting to determine the significance of its complexity and regional specialization. Why are the cerebral hemispheres so large and luxuriantly folded? What is the explanation of all this exuberant cortex in animals that seem to restricted in their scope?

At the present time, very little is known of the functional anatomical organization of the massive cerebral cortex of either the great or small whales. No brain "maps" such as exist for many other species have been worked out in sufficient detail to describe the functional areas. For example, only in the last few years have the motor cortex and some sensory areas been studied physiologically, by Lende and Akdikmen (1968). It is interesting that they found the motor field to be located on the anterior extreme of the brain. Such had been suspected from our own cytoarchitectonic studies of this area (Morgane and Jacobs, 1972), revealing it to contain the largest pyramidal (motor) cells in the dolphin cortex (Figure 2). These findings suggest a similarity in whales to the arrangement seen in carnivores and ungulates, since in these groups the somatic motor representation is also located in the extreme frontal areas of the cortex.

Generally speaking, in the dolphin and other whales we find a massive cortex in which a unique mode of expansion appears to have occurred during evolution. The surface field organization seems to represent a radically different pattern of development, not seen in other animals. The cellular architecture of the cortex of whales has largely been studied in a rather superficial manner, and there has been general agreement that the neuron density is low. Some researchers have also reported that the laminar differentiation is poor; i.e., the "layering" of the cortex is not as clear as in some other animals, and that regional variations of cell type and patterning are unclear. The cortex of whales is relatively thinner than comparable regions in other large brains, including human brains, but the total surface area is far greater due to the tremendous infolding. Hence, as a whole we may be dealing with the same essential numbers of cells, but the cells that are present are more spread out.

There have been numerous studies in recent years which indicate that, in various whale species, the cortical areal differentiation and lamination are similar to those found in higher primates. In this regard, Pilleri and Busnel (1969) have reported that the dolphins, together with primates, have the most highly differentiated brains of all mammals. Gihr and Pilleri (1968) observed that all the smaller toothed whales including *Inia* (Amazon River dolphin) have the most advanced degree of encephalization and, in this respect, can be classified between man and monkeys. Krays and Pilleri (1969), in describing the cortex of Cetaceans, came to the conclusion that the construction of the cortex in these animals was in every way comparable to that of the higher primates.

Kraus and Pilleri also report that histologically the cortex of the great whales shows an obvious lamination. They observed, from the presence of tectonic regional variations, that there exist clearly defined cortical territories, i.e., regional differentiations, and they concluded that the complexity of the neuronal cortical elements indicates a high degree of differentiation in the sei whale cortex. Grunthal (1942) also commented on the "primate character" of the brain of the small whale *Delphinus delphis*, and arranged the extant primitive and advanced brains in a series as follows: opossum, mole, cat, monkey and ape, dolphin. While the matter is one needing further studies (particularly of a physiological and behavioral nature) before any definitive conclusions are drawn, the enormous surface of the whale cortex and its luxuriant and highly convoluted appearance (Figure 5) still appear to be sound arguments for considering the Cetaceans as potentially intelligent and highly developed fellow beings.

One interesting notation made by Kruger (1969) and others is

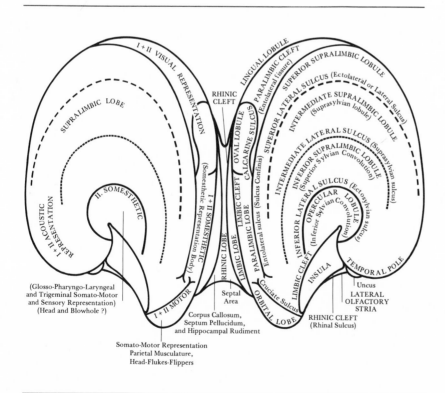

Figure 6. Schematic representation of the cortical areas of the dolphin brain indicating the huge supralimbic or "association" area in relation to sensory cortex and motor areas.

that the proportion of cortex devoted to the main sensory projection areas has been roughly estimated at 90 percent in the rabbit, 50 percent in the cat, 25 percent in the monkey, and 10 percent in man, the remainder of the cortex being devoted primarily to "association" areas. In our recent studies on the surface morphology of the dolphin brain, we have tentatively determined that most cortical formations are "association" rather than specific sensory (Morgane and Jacobs, 1972). As indicated in Figure 6, most of the area designated "supralimbic lobe" is probably association cortex, a conclusion based on architectonic assessments. In this regard, the whale, again, may be considered to be highly evolved at the level of the central nervous system.

Rose (1926) has maintained that the cerebral cortex of whales has a structure which, in principle, is similar to that of other mammals and man. In fact, he distinguished the *same layers* which are typical for the mammalian cortex and also concluded that there are unamibiguous regional differentiations of cortical areas comparable to those observed in other mammals. Similar studies by Jansen and Jansen (1969) and our own group (Morgane and Jacobs, 1972) in a large whale series confirm these general findings. The overall evidence today indicates that there is little doubt that numerous regional differences exist in the cytoarchitectonic structure of the cortex of whales.

Information available to neuroscientists offers no clear explanation for the extraordinary development of the cortical formations in whales. More quantitative data are needed concerning the number and distribution of the cortical neurons, their dendritic fields, sy-

Figure 7. Photograph of histological section of dolphin cortex just lateral to the primary motor areas stained by the Golgi technique. This shows nerve cells silver plated to reveal their intricate axonal and dendritic patterns and branching. Note the small bulbous protuberances on the branches which represent "spines." The complexity revealed in this section resembles that seen from equivalent areas in monkey and human brains.

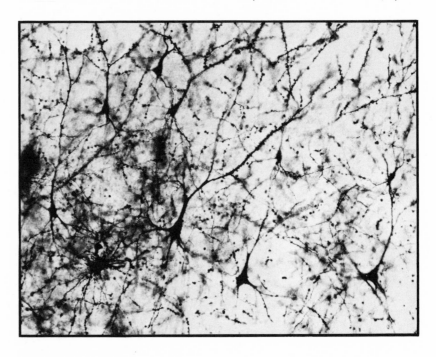

naptic relations, etc., in order to establish an appropriate morphological foundation for promising neurophysiological investigations which would yield much information about function. We have carried out several Golgi analyses (Figure 7) of many cortical fields in the dolphin brain and compared these with human and monkey Golgi sections from presumably homologous areas. So far from these studies we conclude that the neuron connectivities, synaptic geometry, and dendritic fields are comparable between dolphins and primates by all applicable criteria. Figure 7 shows some of these patterns using the Golgi procedure. It does appear that the degree of synaptological arrangements are remarkably similar to those of monkey and human cortex taken from presumably homologous areas of the neocortex. Simply put, not enough is known at the present time about these features of the whale cortex to allow one to make any pronouncement on purely morphological grounds. There are many reasons for assuming, however, that intelligence does not bear a direct or simple relationship to neuron density and degree of axodendritic complexity in the cerebral cortex (Tower, 1954).

There may be principles governing the organization of whale neocortex whose "code" has not yet been broken. At the present time it is impossible to determine the precise principles because of the fragmentary nature of the availability and the uncertainty of homologization of structures in the whale neocortex. Kesarev (1969) has concluded that the structural organization of the dolphin limbic cortex differs sharply in principle from the primate type, and in view of qualitative and quantitative evidence he has deduced that there is a specific type of whale cortex not characteristic of all terrestrial mammals. He feels that there are sufficient grounds for concluding that the cortical organization of the dolphin brain is more "primitive" than that of higher primates and, in particular, of man. He derives these conclusions from such features as the small thickness of the limbic cortex, the absence of the layer of granule cells (layer 4), the "nestlike" distribution of cells in layer 2, and the lack of prominence of the vertical striation. He notes that a typical feature of the dolphin limbic cortex is powerful development of layers 1 and 6. Yet all of these type derivations are certainly not indicative of "primitive" cortex, but rather represent a different pattern of organization whose meaning awaits physiological studies. Needless to say, for these types of studies to proceed in future years in association with behavioral analyses, these valuable and important animals must be preserved. These brain studies may well provide the neurological evidence of the links between man and these presumably unique relatives.

We should stress again some cardinal points. Compared to the primitive generalized mammal, the whales represent the *most special-*

The male Devilfish (gray whale) at all times shows strong affection for the female and Captain Melsom tells me that during the migration, when a school of males led by one or two females is found, if one of the latter is wounded, often the former will refuse to leave until she is dead. One day when hunting a pair he wounded the cow and the bull would not leave, keeping close alongside and pushing his head over her body. Later he struck the male with a harpoon but did not get fast and even then it returned and was finally killed. Captain Melsom assures me, however, that if the male is killed the female will seldom remain.
Roy Chapman Andrews, The California Gray Whale, *American Museum of Natural History*

91

POTHEADS DEFORM

I want to know
why more than 100
pilot whales piloted
themselves to
certain death
as if they were
a single organism
that had had enough.
Some say
their sonar's
defective
deflected
on sandy
gradual shores.
Others say
Florida was
underwater
notsolongago,
and the potheads
used to go that way
and were this day
interrupted
by 30 miles of Atlantic beach.
Some ascribe
the beaching
to an infectious
pollutant,
a lethal imbibing
of a bit of man's waste
along shore
or fish caught
in an oil slick
of miles and miles
at sea,
or the water heating up
or or or . . .
But potheads have
been stranding
in groups
for longer
than we've written.
I suspect
the leader
was slipping
and he
chose
this way to go.
Scott McVay, 1/14/70

ized mammalian order and are thus highly deserving of protection and preservation. The phylogenetic development of a mammalian species may be considered to be determined by the extent of centralization and differentiation of the nervous system. Centralization is expressed morphologically in the different growth tendencies of the individual brain territories or regions. The differentiation of the nerve tissue into areas showing different cell patterns and connectivities is brought out with histological methods (such as the Golgi procedure, Figure 7) in which architecture and arrangements of nerve cells can be studied. Pilleri and his group have claimed that Cetaceans attain a degree of centralization which far exceeds that even of man.

Another index of brain development should also be noted. Since the largest brains in existence are found among whales, the proportion of brain to body weight is also of comparative interest. This proportion expresses quantity of brain as a function of the body weight, and has been taken to indicate the so-called "cephalization" of the animal. In this regard, the whales stand next to humans in terms of cephalization coefficients. Our own evidence (Morgane and Jacobs, 1972) tends to confirm this in some eight species that we have studied in this regard.

I think it should be emphasized again that no serious worker in the brain sciences is attempting to presuppose a correlation between "intelligence" and any simple brain measure such as weight. We realize that the "quality factor" as well as the "quantity factor" is critical. The "intelligence" aspect relating to whales must await analyses by psychologists in relation to the peculiar non-manipulative capacity (no hands to grasp and manipulate objects) and special environment of these animals which, for obvious reasons, makes their study very difficult. As John Lilly mentioned in the book *Man and Dolphin* (1961), what we are really doing is espousing a plea for an open-minded attitude with respect to these marvelous animals. It certainly would be presumptuous and naive to presume that at the present time we are able to measure the "intelligence" or intellectual capacity of whales, and no serious student of brain function, to this writer's knowledge, makes such claims. In dealing with such non-manipulators as whales, we have continued to be obsessed with the necessity of our own nature to search for an analog of the hand and the manipulative ability. Clearly we should strive to find a more general principle than merely "handedness" and its use!

It is still possible, as Lilly and others have argued, that in order to evaluate the intelligence of the whales we must know something of their abilities in the areas of phonation and bodily gestures and manipulations and, hence, in their capacities to communicate with one another and with man. Without communication, both men and whales will go their lonely way, and lack of understanding between them will inevitably lead to extinction of the whales who are obviously at a disadvantage in such an adversary relationship as now exists. So far it is not possible to measure accurately the "intelligence" of any other being (even in humans this study is fraught with peril), mainly because we do not exchange ideas through any known communication mode with such beings. Many of Lilly's studies have touched upon these same points and attempted to derive a common ground between species, but, as we must admit at this time, such have not been firmly established. However, enough promising leads have been derived to warrant more study. As Eiseley (1960) has so well stated: "Man expresses himself upon his environment through the use of tools. We therefore tend to equate the use of tools in a one-to-one relationship with intelligence." Is it not well to examine other possible modes of expression of intelligence or intellectual capacity?

In concluding, let us agree that all the neurological evidence is not in regarding the whale brain and intelligence. However, enough *is* known to lead us to believe we are dealing with special creatures with remarkably developed brains. Major riddles of nature and relations between species may indeed be answered by study of these brains, and these opportunities may die with the whales if we do not act now. They could have taught us much if we had only listened. Their kinship with man at the level of neurological development holds us in awe and fascination. It is unthinkable for us to sit idly by and let such unique beings wantonly be destroyed by selfish and short-sighted men. This is a resource and kinship that belongs to us all. Our very training and deepest feelings make us respect these wondrous creatures. Would that the brains of men could lead them to live in harmony with Nature instead of ruthlessly plundering the seas that nurtured us. Eiseley noted in his essay "The Long Loneliness" that "perhaps man has something to learn after all from fellow creatures who themselves do not have the ability to drive harpoons through living flesh." We must continue to be haunted by such solitary beings with amazingly complex brains wending their way through the seas, wondering, perhaps, what manner of men are hunting them down to destroy them forever.

Let us close by stating that we are not idle sentimentalists acting out of any special or selfish interests. We are acting as responsible scientists who appreciate the possibility that in other forms of life we may actually find our own beings.

So many things fail to interest us, simply because they don't find in us enough surfaces on which to live, and what we have to do then is to increase the number of planes in our mind, so that a much larger number of themes can find a place in it at the same time.
Ortega y Gasset

JOAN MCINTYRE
Mind Play

There is no question that *mind* changes the universe. Mind is as strong an evolutionary force as teeth or claws or glaciers: as influential as speech. The mind of a blackbird recognizes the ideal blackbird and chooses him as mate, and in so doing, influences the future of all blackbirds. Human mind has changed the basic nature of soil, the chemical composition of air and human tissue. The ability of our minds to imagine, coupled with the ability of our hands to devise our images, brings us a power almost beyond our control—we don't know what to do with it any more, except to keep using it.

Then what is this other mind, the mind that is in the waters? These enormous alien brains that flow in the oceans—giving rise to songs, dreaming, catching at the thin web of memory, instructing each other in manners and morals—what is in the mind world of a creature with a brain bigger and possibly more complex than ours, who cannot act out its will to change the world, if only for the simple reason that it hasn't any hands?

I think the way to enter the mind of the whale is to enter the water. Whether it's the warm languid floating of the tropical oceans, or the strong cold urging of the surf at higher latitudes—the water is the cradle of Cetacean consciousness. And there, in the strength and power of the sea, is the place to explore that mind.

When a human enters the water, what becomes apparent is the integral connection between mind and body that the sea forces on her creatures. Without the alienating presence of objects and equipment, with only the naked body encasing the floating mind, the two, split by technological culture, are one again. The mind enters a a different modality, where time, weight, and one's self are experienced holistically.

In the sea, mind and body become wedded, and the sea's power and lasting steadiness are experienced directly on the skin as well

94

as through the memory banks. As the interfering screen of objects, clothing, and ideology is stripped away, the world can be *thought* and *experienced* simultaneously—not *broken down* into categories that stand for experience rather than experienced itself.

Most of human thought is a compulsive reiteration of speech habits—wondering what to say to whom, remembering to pick up the laundry and go to the store. The mind functions more as a dredge than an open field of possibilities. The kind of thought that *comes* to us, as opposed to those that are endless duplications of pre-known details, is relatively rare in modern life. And that kind of thought, the thought which creatively combines and recombines that which is not known, requires, I believe, a more playful and open condition of mind, one not absorbed in the details of daily life.

I would guess that the mind of the dolphin is a freer playground than the modern human mind. I would guess that the dolphin might have more fun with her mind than we have with our minds.

And when we try to discover the consciousness of Cetaceans through the scientific method alone, we stumble across the problem that the scientific method seems to forbid playing with its information. In a bizarre sense, the people in this culture who know the most are expected to speculate the least. It's as if their very credibility itself rests on the need to offer only what can be demonstrated. We have become so serious about our ideological systems that we cannot tolerate upsetting them—even if it means learning something new.

So in the preceding pages we can hover around the edges of an idea that is so luminous that it catches our breath, but we cannot find the way to make the leap, to become creative with our information and thought.

Susanne Langer, in *Philosophy in a New Key*, suggests that the mind needs activity for its own self-fulfilling satisfaction, that the mind *enjoys* thought. Some of my most satisfying moments have been when my mind catches the moth-like pre-thought hovering at its margins and brings it into being as an idea. Idea making is a source of intense satisfaction. Idea making, combined with the body's experience, may be the mind world of the whales.

To experiment, I imagine myself in the water, in a world of shifting currents and cycling days and nights, where the moon's pull on my body is as clear in my consciousness as the call of my infant beside me. Living there, where the world moves, shifts, changes around me minute by minute—but is recognizable by my kind over thousands of years—I float and breathe and think, and let the water smash down on me and the sun silver my eyes.

I am not sure this is a description of their world, but it is a place to start from.

Canst thou draw out leviathan with an hook? . . .
I will not conceal his parts, nor his power,
　　　nor his comely proportion . . .
Who can open the doors of his face?
　　　his teeth are terrible round about.
His scales are his pride, shut up together as with a close seal.
One is so near to another, that no air can come between them.
They are joined one to another, they stick together,
　　　that they cannot be sundered.
By his neesings a light doth shine, and his eyes are like
　　　the eyelids of the morning.
Out of his mouth go burning lamps, and sparks of fire leap out.
Out of his nostrils goeth smoke, as out of a seething pot or caldron.
His breath kindleth coals, and a flame goeth out of his mouth.
In his neck remaineth strength, and sorrow is turned to joy
　　　before him.
The flakes of his flesh are joined together: they are firm in
　　　themselves; they cannot be moved.
His heart is as firm as a stone; yea, as hard as a piece
　　　of the nether millstone.
When he raiseth up himself, the mighty are afraid:
by reason of breakings they purify themselves.
The sword of him that layeth at him cannot hold: the spear,
　　　the dart, nor the habergeon.
He esteemeth iron as straw, and brass as rotten wood.
The arrow cannot make him flee: slingstones are turned with him
　　　into stubble. Darts are counted as stubble:
　　　he laugheth at the shaking of a spear . . .
He maketh the deep to boil like a pot:
　　　he maketh the sea like a pot of ointment.
He maketh a path to shine after him; one would think the deep
　　　to be hoary.
Upon earth there is not his like, who is made without fear.
He beholdeth all high things:
　　　he is king over all the children of pride.

From the Book of Job

LARRY FOSTER
The Whale Object: a portfolio of drawings

Larry Foster is an artist who started **General Whale:** *a graphics effort offered as "proof against the harpoon." He is a sculptor who (in his own words) "feels the need to contribute more to society than art alone." He is keenly aware of the urgency with which man must re-appraise the nature of his immutable union with the environment. Working through* **General Whale,** *he has brought imaginative life-size images of whales and dolphins to exhibits and special events throughout the country, and offers this original portfolio of unpublished drawings as part of his desire to help save the whales.*

The Right Family

Right Whale and Bathers

EVENT	12-72	MELBOURNE BEACHED WHALES	18 FEBRUARY 1972	1357.

The following information was received by cable:-

BEACHED WHALES-

"1. DATE: FEBRUARY 3, 1972

"2. KIND: SPERM WHALES

"3. NUMBER BEACHED: FISHERIES AND WILDLIFE DEPARTMENT STATES 36, LOCAL PRESS 37. 41 REPORTEDLY SEEN IN SURF THAT DAY.

"4. NUMBER DEAD: ALL ON BEACH. ONE WHALE LATER FOUND DEAD OUTSIDE PORT PHILLIP HEADS, POSSIBLY THE 37TH.

"5. CAUSE: CAUSE UNKNOWN. OIL-LIKE MATERIAL REPORTEDLY SEEN ON BEACH SAME DAY (UNCERTAIN WHETHER MINERAL OIL, THOUGH FISHERIES AND WILDLIFE REPRESENTATIVE SPECULATES MATERIAL COULD HAVE BEEN WHALES' FECES, REACTION TO PANIC).

"6. INVESTIGATION CONDUCTED BY ROBERT WARNECKE, RYLAH INSTITUTE, DEPARTMENT OF FISHERIES AND WILDLIFE, 123 BROWN STREET, HEIDELBERG, VICTORIA."

EVENT NOTIFICATION REPORT

TYPE OF EVENT	BIOLOGICAL
DATE OF OCCURRENCE	3 FEBRUARY 1972
LOCATION OF EVENT	MELBOURNE

VICTORIA, AUSTRALIA

REPORTING SOURCE	AMERICAN CONSUL-

ATE, MELBOURNE, VICTORIA, AUSTRALIA

SOURCE CONTACT	AMERICAN

CONSULATE, MELBOURNE, VICTORIA

AUSTRALIA

This report is based on notifications received from the Center's
corrrespondents and is disseminated for information purposes only.
The Smithsonian Institution bears no responsibility for its accuracy.

SMITHSONIAN INSTITUTION
CENTER FOR SHORT-LIVED PHENOMENA
60 Garden Street
CAMBRIDGE, MASSACHUSETTS 02138
UNITED STATES OF AMERICA
CABLE: SATELLITES NEW YORK
TELEPHONE (617)-864-7911

EVENT	128-73	CAPE LOOKOUT WHALE STRANDING	10 OCTOBER 1973	1725.

On the morning of 10 October, 35 pilot whales (Globicephala melaena) stranded themselves at Cape Lookout, Harkers Island, south of Beaufort, North Carolina.

The North Carolina Fisheries investigators are on the scene along with the U.S. Coast Guard and local fishermen.

Some of the whales were towed out to sea, but they beached themselves again. Between eight to ten whales are dead.

EVENT NOTIFICATION REPORT

TYPE OF EVENT	BIOLOGICAL
DATE OF OCCURRENCE	10 OCTOBER 1973
LOCATION OF EVENT	CAPE LOOKOUT HARKERS ISLAND (34°42' N, 76°34' W), NORTH CAROLINA, U.S.A.
REPORTING SOURCE	NATIONAL MARINE FISHERIES, ST. PETERSBURG, FLORIDA, U.S.A.
SOURCE CONTACT	MR. HASKELL

NATIONAL MARINE FISHERIES, DUVAL BLDG 9450 GANDY BLVD., ST. PETERSBURG, FLORIDA 33702, U.S.A.

SMITHSONIAN INSTITUTION
CENTER FOR SHORT-LIVED PHENOMENA
60 Garden Street
CAMBRIDGE, MASSACHUSETTS 02138
UNITED STATES OF AMERICA
CABLE: SATELLITES NEW YORK
TELEPHONE: (617)-864-7911

| EVENT | 5-71 | SAN CLEMENTE ISLAND BEACHED WHALES | 18 JANUARY 1971 | 1090. |

"On or about 0100-0400 hours, 8 January 1971, a pod of 29 pilot whales, <u>Globicephala scammoni</u>, were stranded on the beach at Pyramid Cove, San Clemente Island...The pod appeared to be composed of mature females and juveniles of both sexes. Animals were strewn along the high tide line for about 200 yards. Most were oriented in parallel axis with the beach. In general, the skin from many contact surfaces (chin, flukes, etc.) was abraided off, presumably due to thrashing, post-mortem degeneration and tidal action. Three animals had been extensively 'carved-up' prior to arrival of NUC (Naval Undersea Research and Development Center) personnel. Carcasses, especially the viscera, were bloated and discolored due to post-mortem changes. Due to advanced decomposition the gastro-intestinal system was not systematically explored. Bacterial, toxicological and histological specimens were taken from several animals. The visceral and parietal serosal surfaces of thorax and abdomen appeared to be normal except for post-mortem changes and the presence of several parasitic nodules. It is the current opinion of NUC Code 502 personnel that the grounding of this pod of pilot whales was a natural event comparable to those recorded for the same area for some 200 years. Meteorological and biological conditions (high tide, no surf, very slight wind, sloping beach with steep drop-off, and presence of spawning squid) created optimal conditions for stranding.

"On 12 January 1971, the Los Angeles County Museum sent a scientific party to the stranding site to remove and prepare the skeletal material on all 28 animals."

EVENT NOTIFICATION REPORT

TYPE OF EVENT	BIOLOGICAL
DATE OF OCCURRENCE	8 JANUARY 1971
LOCATION OF EVENT	PYRAMID COVE, SAN CLEMENTE ISLAND, off coast of CALIF.
REPORTING SOURCE	W.E. EVANS, HEAD MARINE BIOSCIENCE DIVISION(Actg.),DEPT OF NAVY, NUC, SAN DIEGO, CALIF. 92132
SOURCE CONTACT	W.E. EVANS, HEAD MARINE BIOSCIENCE DIVISION(Actg.), DEPT. OF THE NAVY, NAVAL UNDERSEA RESEARCH AND DEVELOPMENT CENTER (NUC) SAN DIEGO, CALIFORNIA 92132

SMITHSONIAN INSTITUTION
CENTER FOR SHORT-LIVED PHENOMENA
60 Garden Street
CAMBRIDGE, MASSACHUSETTS 02138
UNITED STATES OF AMERICA

CABLE: SATELLITES NEW YORK
TELEPHONE (617)-864-7911

Broadbacked Whale

Blue Whale and Flensers

EVENT	154-73	CAPE HENLOPEN BEACHED FINBACK WHALE	17 DECEMBER 1973	1756.

On Monday, 10 December a common finback whale, Balaen-optera physalus, beached itself at Cape Henlopen, Delaware. The animal was alive when it was first seen by one of the Delaware harbor pilots. However, by the time representatives of the Delaware Department of Fish and Game arrived on the scene that afternoon, the whale had died.

Dr. James Mead, Curator of Mammals for the Smithsonian Institution's Museum of Natural History in Washington, D.C. was notified of the whale's discovery. He picked up the whale that night and brought it to the Smithsonian's National Zoological Park for autopsy.

The whale was a newborn female which was thought to be a week to a month old because of its unhealed umbilical scar. The animal was 22 ft. long and weighed 4,900 lbs. It had suffered a severe blow to the head and had a massive cerebral hemorhage. The cause of the blow was unknown, but it was conjectured that the animal might have been struck by a fairly round-bowed vessel or by another whale.

EVENT NOTIFICATION REPORT	
TYPE OF EVENT	BIOLOGICAL
DATE OF OCCURRENCE	10 DECEMBER 1973
LOCATION OF EVENT	CAPE HENLOPEN,
DELAWARE, U.S.A. (38°48'N, 75°05'W)	
REPORTING SOURCE	MR. FRED BONNER
DELAWARE DEPT. OF FISH AND GAME, DOVER, DELAWARE, U.S.A.	
SOURCE CONTACT	DR. JAMES MEAD
CURATOR OF MAMMALS, SMITHSONIAN INST.	
MUSEUM OF NATURAL HISTORY, WASH., D.C	

SMITHSONIAN INSTITUTION
CENTER FOR SHORT-LIVED PHENOMENA
60 Garden Street
CAMBRIDGE, MASSACHUSETTS 02138
UNITED STATES OF AMERICA
CABLE: SATELLITES NEW YORK
TELEPHONE: (617)-864-7911

JOAN MCINTYRE
Iceberg

I wonder if we need to know any more of what we already know.

On November 30 the young humpback whale washed up on the beach. He lay there in the gritty sand, surrounded by his investigators, for five days and nights before he finally died. During the long process of his dying, this infant whale was examined, photographed, poked, and prodded. Samples of his living skin were taken. The removal of his corpse was discussed while his breathing came hoarse and heavy under his uncommon weight. The surf washed against his side, the sun rose and set, birds wheeled in a leaden sky, and people came to study the dying whale. We will never know what memories flickered in his dimming consciousness, what songs, what images of family, of group, stirred in his tunneling vision. We will know his blood type and whether he carried traces of our metal poisons in his flesh. This infant animal, alone, untended, unloved, became for us the object of our investigations.

What could we have done with the dying whale?

We could have sat with him. We could have sat next to his massive head and stroked his heaving side with the touch of a mother. We could have kept him company in the long and terrible hours of his dying; sung to him, spoken to him, told him stories, kept in contact through our voice that he could hear, with our fingers he could feel. We could have presented ourselves in empathy to a dying fellow creature. Instead, we chose to treat him as a corpse before he even breathed his last and ragged breath.

The assumption of modern science is that it is a clear eye looking out objectively on a real world. No bias or feelings cloud its image. Science assumes its method is the only one that can describe a pure objective reality, and that reality is pure and objective. If you were to question the group of experts that attended the dying whale and ask them what they were doing, they could tell you easily. They were finding out about the whale.

I asked one of them why no one had sat quietly with the young animal and kept him company in the isolation of his solitary death. The question did not make sense to the cetologist. He did not comprehend that any mammal understands another; that there is a bond which links us all; and that empathy and compassion, the need for comfort, are qualities that are trans-specific.

The material in this book is about what we now know. It has left out more than it has covered. It has left out the living lore of peoples of ancient cultures who understood the world and its creatures in a different context. It has left out the direct felt personal experience of people who cannot write, who cannot communicate the intensity and vigor of their encounters. It has left out all of the questions we do not know how to ask. It has left out much of what could have been discovered by sitting with the dying whale.

The limits are in us; they will always be in us. But the more we can stretch to accommodate what seems at times to be irrelevant, the greater chance we have to synthesize, to make larger sense of, our knowledge. This knowledge is like an iceberg. We see only the jagged edges above the icy waters. Beneath the opalescent sea, there is a base that is real, that supports the living structure. We can probe that underwater topography with our instruments, and we can also probe it with our imaginations and feelings.

The reason why the idea of the person sitting at the side of the dying whale is relevant is that it would inform the person, would begin to suggest other meanings and other relationships. A friend of mine guarded a dead baby sperm whale on a beach in Massachusetts. Waiting for the bulldozer that was to carry the corpse away, sitting in the hot sun, in the silence of the surf and birds, he realized that the process of death was alive; that death was not a severing that took place in an instant, but was a long sequence. The dead baby whale cooked and seethed in the juices of its own decay. It was not an inert hunk of meat, the life gone; it was life going through the process

105

of dying. The ancient Tibetans sat with the corpse and read him instructions to guide him through the process. As my friend sat with the dead/dying whale, the experience put him in touch with feelings and ideas that caused him to change the content of his own life.

Perhaps the major difference between the way non-technological peoples see animal nature and the way we see it, is that we have abstracted out of it all contradictory qualities. We look at creatures as single purpose units; they do *this* for *that* reason. The American Indian, the Congo pygmy, the Siberian shaman, recognize the contradictory livingness in animal life; understand that an animal can be both/and/or. That is, an animal can be something to eat/something that embodies wisdom other than human/something that participates in the spiritual life of the community/friend/enemy/trickster/ghost. A non-technological hunter/gatherer would never get stuck on the "logical" dilemma that "you can't love animals if you eat meat." It is this openness to the coexistence of all qualities that characterizes the "primitive" view of the living world.

Our sense of knowledge is single purpose. It depends on the assumption that a thing is true only if it is the truest, if it sits on the top of a hierarchy of truth. It also requires constant reiteration in order to *prove* that truth is truth. There are now more vervet monkeys in laboratories proving and reproving "behavioral" truths than are living those truths in the savannas of East Africa.

Our sense of knowledge is single purpose. It depends on the assumption that the presence of the investigator is an interruption rather than an enhancement and it tries for objectivity at the cost of all else. As a result, we are stuck with a science that turns the scientists themselves into objects. The scientists become the instrumentalities of their own singlemindedness. A United States Fish and Wildlife Service scientist applied for and received permits from the government to kill 316 protected California gray whales in order to write *The Life History and Ecology of the Gray Whale*. In reading the life history there is no life, just a series of tables of the weight of testes and ovaries. There is more to the mating of a whale than the weight of his gonads; there is more to the feeding of a whale than the contents of her stomach; there is more to birth than the weight of the fetus. There is more that is being left out than is being included; and I think that comes from our inability to consider our subjects and us as interacting parts of a whole system.

At the 1972 meeting of the International Whaling Commission, the United States delegation was trying to gain acceptance of a ten year moratorium on commercial whaling. The Scientific Committee of the I.W.C. recommended against the moratorium on the basis that further research was necessary; and that research required whaling. Russell Train, the U.S. Commissioner, said, "Well, I can understand the need for more whales to study, but do you really need thirty-five thousand?" And Raymond Gamble, the senior British scientist, stroked his chin, smiled across the table, and said, "Yes, lots more!"

Two million whales have been killed in the last fifty years. The industry and the scientists connected with the industry have had an opportunity to examine the corpses of two million whales and yet maintain a need for still more to study. We can pile up the tables of weights and lengths and ages and measures until it reaches the sky, but it won't get us an understanding of the living creature. The way to understand a living creature is to live respectfully in its presence, to approach it with tact, grace, and love, and maybe even to sit with it in its dying moments and sing human songs to it to aid its passage.

GOING OUT TO MEET THE MOON WHALES

It was time;
    high in the round fruit trees
    we saw them passing
    under the moon.

The manta rays lined up
    to slowly flap their wings.
Then we floated out
    on the manta waves.
There was no time
    we were happier.

Whales, look,
I have not died too young:

I floated out
    in the wood boat
I was born in fifty years ago,
    when the moon whales were swimming here.

From the Creole of Paulé Bartón, translation by Howard A. Norman

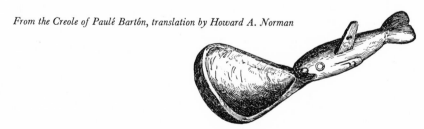

FOR A COMING EXTINCTION

Gray whale
Now that we are sending you to The End
That great god
Tell him
That we who follow you invented forgiveness
And forgive nothing

I write as though you could understand
And I could say it
One must always pretend something
Among the dying
When you have left the seas nodding on their stalks
Empty of you
Tell him that we were made
On another day

The bewilderment will diminish like an echo
Winding along your inner mountains
Unheard by us
And find its way out
Leaving behind it the future
Dead
And ours

When you will not see again
The whale calves trying the light
Consider what you will find in the black garden
And its court
The sea cows the Great Auks the gorillas
The irreplaceable hosts ranged countless
And fore-ordaining as stars
Our sacrifices

Join your word to theirs
Tell him
That it is we who are important

From The Lice, *by W. S. Merwin, Atheneum*

PART THREE

_____

LIVING
IN THE
SEA

_____

Peter Warshall, Ph.D., is a naturalist and animal behaviorist. He has studied baboons in Africa, rhesus monkeys in the Caribbean, and has set up a wild horse sanctuary in Wyoming. He is interested in the environment of the community and has worked on sewer recycling systems in California. He is active in local environmental politics. "The Ways of Whales" has been compiled by Dr. Warshall from his review of the existing literature, amplified by some of his own thoughts.

Cetaceans dwell inside a rich community of animals and plants. This community is interconnected in a huge food web. The food chain for the baleen whale and the basking shark starts in the lighted zone of the oceans (the euphotic zone). Here, microscopic plants synthesize light into energy. These plants (called phytoplankton) include the diatoms (a kind of algae) shown opposite. In turn, these plants are eaten by animals called zooplankton. (Plankton is just a big word meaning

PETER WARSHALL
The Ways of Whales

The Oceans As Home

Having emerged from the seas as amphibians, the ancient whales returned millions of years later as mammals. First entering the rivers, then the estuaries, then the coastal oceans, spreading over the continental shelf, the prehistoric Cetaceans finally ranged the seas from the Arctic to the Antarctic. At each stage of their return, the Cetaceans diverged from what they had been, and became specialized to their equally emerging habitats. At present, there are five exclusively fresh-water river dolphins, about fifteen dolphins and whales that occasionally enter estuaries and rivers, about forty species that roam the shallow salt waters over the continental shelf as well as the deep oceanic waters, and about ten species that make their way almost exclusively in the deep oceans.

In this slow and elegant process, two great families of whales and dolphins emerged: the family of baleen whales, enormous creatures that strain the seas for food, filtering plankton and small crustaceans through the baleen bristles that fringe their mouths; and the family of toothed whales, swifter hunters who divide their diet between fish and squid. At this time, twenty-eight species are extremely local. The Chinese Lake dolphin lives in and around the Tung-t'ing Hu Lake. The Ganges dolphin lives only in the Ganges, Brahmaputra, and Karnaphuli rivers. Gray's dolphin inhabits only the tropical coastal region from southern India and Ceylon across the Indian Ocean to Zanzibar and Somaliland. The Falkland Island porpoise never leaves the vicinity of these two South American polar islands.

On the other hand, thirteen species are cosmopolitan, and migrate through the vast reaches of the oceanic world. The killer whale or *Orcinus orca* has been seen in rivers and oceans from the Arctic to the Antarctic, as well as in semi-isolated seas like the Mediterranean. The humpback whale migrates from the poles to the tropical waters each year. Some of these migration patterns, like those of the right and blue whales, may never be fully known because of the recent overkill by the whaling industry.

The re-entrance of early whales into the oceans appears to be at least forty million years old. But it was only twenty thousand years ago that glaciers sparked an amazingly rapid diversification of Cetacean species. The right whale, inhabiting the southern Atlantic, was forced northward by colder waters and glaciation. When the glaciers receded, two right whale forms were evolving: one back in the South Seas, and a new species that stayed north. When the earth warmed even more in the post-glacial period, the northern right whale swam over the top of the world to the Bering Sea. Then, when the earth again cooled, this Bering Sea population was isolated by the ice cap from the Atlantic group. Thus, from one southern population, three species were formed.

The oceans not only shape the evolution and habits of the whales and dolphins, but are the repository of much of the life on the planet.

"unable to swim" or "carried by the currents.") These zooplanktons include shrimp-like krill, baby crabs, little molluscs called copepods, young jelly fish, certain sea worms, and many other creatures. Zooplankton are eaten in huge quantities by the baleen whales and the basking sharks. Zooplankton are also eaten by small swarming and schooling fish like the herring and small squid. These fish and squid are eaten in turn by the toothed whales (including porpoises and dolphins) and the beaked whales. Larger varieties are eaten by the sperm whale. The fuel for the oceanic community comes from great churnings of the oceans. Organic matter, including dead animals, sinks to the bottom, where it decomposes. The decomposed organic material is recycled as nutrients for the phytoplankton wherever there is a strong upwelling. Nutrient-rich water washed from the land also feeds the plankton.

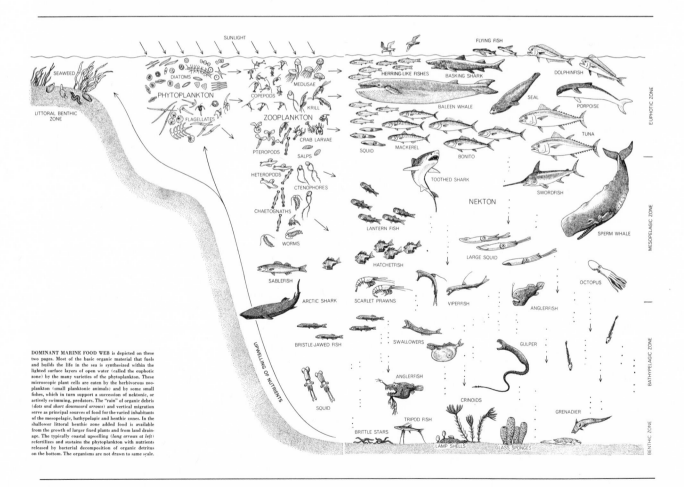

DOMINANT MARINE FOOD WEB is depicted on these two pages. Most of the basic organic material that fuels and builds the life in the sea is synthesized within the lighted surface layers of open water (called the euphotic zone) by the many varieties of the phytoplankton. These microscopic plant cells are eaten by the herbivorous zooplankton (small planktonic animals) and by some small fishes, which in turn support a succession of nektonic, or actively swimming, predators. The "rain" of organic debris (dots and short downward arrows) and vertical migration serve as principal sources of food for the varied inhabitants of the mesopelagic, bathypelagic and benthic zones. In the shallower littoral benthic zone added food is available from the growth of larger fixed plants and from land drainage. The typically coastal upwelling (long arrows at left) refertilizes and sustains the phytoplankton with nutrients released by bacterial decomposition of organic detritus on the bottom. The organisms are not drawn to same scale.

Cetaceans evolve many adaptations to conserve fresh water in their bodies. They don't sweat. They can concentrate their urine many times better than humans. (This ability is also found in the camel when it travels in the deserts.) They will eat fish that have about one-third the saltiness of the oceans. And the females have very concentrated baby's milk, thick like cottage cheese.

Despite its low water content, baby's milk still provides the nursing Cetacean with all the necessary fresh water. Cetacean milk has ten times the amount of fat as that of primates, and almost no sugar. The advantage of more fat is chemical; when fat is broken down in the body, one of the significant by-products is water. This is how baby Cetaceans drink without depriving their mothers.
Peter Warshall

All the processes that alter the temperature or salinity of the oceans influence the density. Density is decreased in warmer seas, in areas of much rainfall, where there is significant ice-melt or runoff from the land. It is increased by cooling evaporation, the formation of ice and areas where the water masses are relatively stagnant. For instance, the Mediterranean is a semi-isolated sea with one small connection to the Atlantic. While the average salinity of the oceans is about thirty-five parts of salt per million of water, in the Mediterranean the salinity is forty parts per million. A dolphin herd swimming through the Straits of Gibraltar feels this density as an increased ease in floating.
Peter Warshall

They cover about seventy-five percent of the earth's surface. The ocean's deepest trenches are taller than Everest; its submerged mountains are more extensive than the Himalayas. The waters of the ocean contain every phylum of plant and animal existing on earth. The land is naked by comparison. The great plant and animal communities of the oceans rise and fall each day through vast vertical steps that follow the changing light. Whereas on land, gravity determines an animal's architecture, it is the buoyancy of the sea that shapes the whale. Unlike land creatures whose body chemistry and density is radically different from the air around them, the creatures of the sea have insides very similar to their surroundings. Being land-bound, we understand something of the diversity of the landscape: tundras, jungles, plains, and deserts. The oceans, from the coast to the depths, from the Poles to the Equator, have an equally complex, yet still mysterious diversity: ice floes, coral reefs, the twilight zone, and the hadal depths.

As the whale travels through the shifting, changing seas, a map—unlike anything used on land—is learned. The temperature changes; light changes; colors change. The volume of ocean between the surface and the sea floor changes. Taste changes as the chemical composition of the sea changes. Skin changes as the acidity of the water changes. As the salt content changes, it becomes easier or harder to float. As the whale dives, its surrounding pressure changes. And, on a grand scale, the sun, moon, and stars cause the huge sweeping oceanic currents and tides to change. We can consider, as a matter of convenience, that the forces which mold the movements of whales are saltiness, temperature, light, and currents in water. The combinations of these properties yield the great fertility of the seas, the incredibly diverse "soup" wherein Cetaceans live.

SALINITY

Salt in water increases density and viscosity, so that salty seas support floating bodies better than fresh water. This buoyancy of the oceans reduces the need for a heavy skeleton. Gravity on land turned leg bones into structural supports, the backbone into a brace, and the pelvis into a cross-beam. But, without gravity to restrict them, all marine creatures became bigger than their land counterparts. The sea crabs are bigger than land crabs. The sea fish is bigger than the fish of inland waters. And the whales, especially the baleen whales, are the biggest creatures ever to have evolved. The blue whale is longer and weighs two to three times more than any dinosaur. The tongue of the blue whale weighs as much as an elephant. The largest land animal that ever lived could stroll through the blue whale's mouth. The baby blue whale is born weighing three tons. It grows an inch and a half, and gains two hundred pounds, each day for the first seven months of its life. The whales' great size is made possible

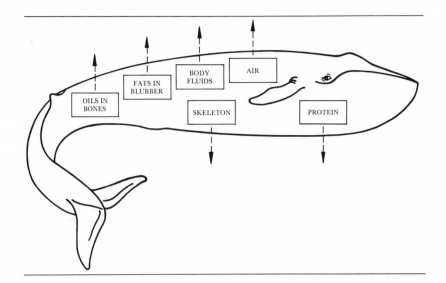

by their special adaptations for buoyancy: they have decreased their density by the arrangement of the lungs in their bodies; they have maximized the amount of inner fluids and solids that are lighter than sea water; and they swim, using the cushion of water to support their enormous bulk.

All of the oceanic Cetaceans live like desert mammals of the land. There is no water to drink. They can't drink brine any more than land mammals can. If they did, they would require so much fresh body water to dilute the sea water that they would wind up urinating more than they could drink. Therefore, most of the fresh water in the whale's body must come from its food. But the ways in which the water balance is maintained are still largely unknown.

TEMPERATURE

The oceans' volume is so great that oceans hold warmth and release heat slowly with few extremes. The earth, on the other hand, cools and heats rapidly. Temperature differences in the oceans have influenced the distribution of the whales throughout the seas by influencing their size, diet, and place of birth.

In general, bigger mammals are more tolerant of cold than smaller mammals. Thus, the temperatures of the seas produced huge whales in the Arctic and the Antarctic, and smaller whales and dolphins in the tropics. The large baleen whales have a predominantly bi-polar distribution, while the *Stenidae*, a family of smallish dolphins, live only in the tropical and sub-tropical waters.

The need for warmer temperatures for smaller Cetaceans has molded their migration routes. Humpback whales, for example, can migrate in cold or warm currents, but require tropical coastal conditions of 25° C for breeding and birth. This is especially important because the baby humpback is not only small but also relatively blubberless. After birth, when headed for the polar seas, the females

Although Cetaceans appear to be resilient to the variable temperatures of the seas, many of the creatures they eat or the creatures those creatures eat are not so tolerant. The Cetaceans have distributed themselves among the temperature zones of the seas according to their size and the food they eat. Today, there are four species that inhabit only the polar waters; twenty-six species that inhabit cold, non-polar waters; two that live only in the temperate oceans; thirteen warm water salt water species; and five warm water fresh water species; and, finally, thirteen species who are cosmopolitan and live in all the seas.
Peter Warshall

Many of the small animal plankton migrate each day in rhythm with the sun. Each species seems to have a preferred illumination. The diagram shows a typical daily migration of these small creatures. When they are close to the surface (late afternoon to early morning), the baleen whales that eat them have a feast. Each shaded figure is a huge mass or swarm of plankton.

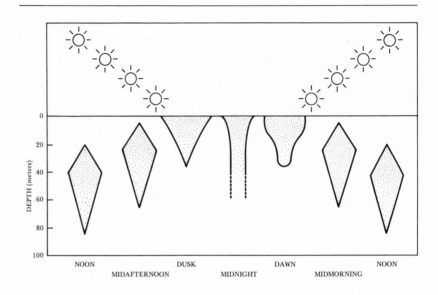

Temperature may limit the distribution of whales, dolphins, and porpoises in two different ways. First, the dolphins may be unable to keep warm enough in polar waters. The map below shows the distribution of one of the families of dolphins called rough-toothed dolphins. They are confined to tropical waters. Second, dolphins may need to eat a certain kind of fish or squid. The fish or squid survive only in a certain temperature of water, so the dolphins stay where this food lives.

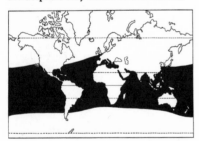

This kind of distribution is not illustrated. The larger whales can tolerate colder seas because of their thicker blubber and their relatively smaller body areas as compared to their volume. This map below shows the distribution of the right whales in the polar seas. They may avoid the tropics because they get too hot there and have difficulty cooling off.

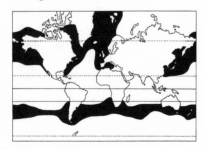

with newborn young are the last age group of humpbacks to depart from the warmer coastal waters. When headed for the tropics, females with young children leave the polar seas first. Sperm whales and gray whales have similar migrations, apparently to allow for warm water birthing.

But, in general, whales are less restricted by temperature than other creatures of the sea. Whales can maintain their internal temperature and are resilient to temperature changes as they move up and down and along in the waters. They are rather more affected by the distribution of their food, also related to water temperature. Plankton, fish, and squid, the major food of the Cetaceans, have internal temperatures excactly the same as the surrounding oceans. Their vertical and horizontal distributions are thus rather drastically limited in some cases by minor temperature changes. This limiting of the range of food species in turn restricts the distribution of many dolphins and whales, such as the belugas and common porpoise.

LIGHT

The light of the sun determines the rhythms of the earth and oceans: the day and night and the seasons. In the oceans, the length of daylight and the closeness of the sun to the equator or poles determine the fertility of the seas. The sun warms the seas, engineers upwellings and currents, and energizes plankton to produce food. Sunlight does not reach deep into the sea and it changes its penetration with a ruffled or calm surface, with turbidity caused by plankton growth, or with sediments stirred up by the winds or washed in from land. The eyesight and sonar-sight of whales have adapted to this unpredictable light.

During the Arctic summers, there is sun almost all day, while during the winter there is little or no sun. Fin whales, with a rather eclectic diet, feed on sea-fleas (copepods) during the summer. The intense continual light of the polar summer keeps the copepods in the upper layers of the ocean, feeding on the plants blooming under the photosynthesizing power of the sunlight. But in the winter, photosynthesis stops because the sunlight is so weak. The copepods sink to almost 500 meters, where they spend the winter. Since the fin whale cannot dive deeper than 300 meters, it must switch its diet, moving towards the coasts to find new food.

This vertical migration of copepods that occurs seasonally in the polar regions occurs daily in latitudes that have more distinct rhythms of day and night. These vertical migration rhythms not only influence the plankton food of the baleen whales but every step of the food chain. The feeding patterns of toothed whales, who eat fish and squid, are equally in harmony with these up-and-down movements of plankton and copepods. The sperm whale, who dives deep down out of the light zone, and Cetaceans that feed at night using echolocation, are not as tightly bound to the light cycles of the seas.

The amount of sunlight affects the north-south migrations of many species of fish and Cetaceans as well as the up-and-down migrations of plants and animals. Shorter days stir the humpback whales to move towards the tropics to breed and give birth, and longer days influence the migrations back to the Antarctic where they feed. Each age group appears to respond differently to the changes in daylight which, of course, change the temperature of the seas and the density of food. It is partially this locked-up pattern of light, food, and migration that has endangered the great whales. The areas of the greatest slaughter of the baleen whales in the last fifty years have been the summer feeding grounds of the Antarctic seas, areas that the whales cannot avoid without starving to death.

CURRENTS AND UPWELLINGS

Besides sunlight, the plant plankton of the seas requires nutrients in order to grow into the fertile fields on which all sea life feeds. If the seas are quiet, the nutrients are used up and not replaced. Currents, upwellings, tidal flows, and storms cause the seas to be stirred and mixed. When whole masses of ocean waters are mixed, nutrients are brought to the surface to interact with sunlight and become changed through the plant plankton into new food forms.

The margins of two different kinds of ocean mass are particularly fertile. On land or sea, the edge between two different habitats has both species from each different habitat as well as a group of creatures especially adapted to the boundary. These rich margins, called ecotones, are extremely rich in diversified life forms, and Cetaceans, especially the sperm whales, search them out for feeding.

Waves erode the shallow waters of the coastal shelves and stir

For that strange spectacle observable in all Sperm Whales dying—the turning sunwards of the head, and so expiring— that strange spectacle, beheld of such a placid evening, somehow to Ahab conveyed a wondrousness unknown before.

He turns and turns him to it—how slowly, but how steadfastly, his homage-rendering and invoking brow, with his last dying motions. He too worships fire; most faithful, broad, baronial vassal of the sun!
Herman Melville, Moby Dick

The gray whale undertakes the longest yearly migration of any animal on earth: a round trip of over eight thousand miles per year. The whales migrate from the Bering Sea and Arctic waters down to the waters off Baja California and back. They need the colder, richer waters of the Arctic for summer food, and the warmer, though less rich, waters of Baja California for birthing. After giving birth, mating occurs in the shallow warm water lagoons of this area.

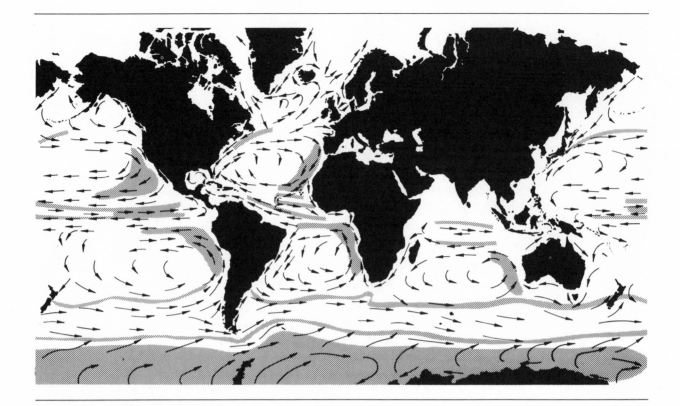

The growth of phytoplankton (microscopic, floating plants) begins the great food chain of the oceans. To grow, the phytoplankton need sunlight and nutrients. The most fertile areas of the oceans have long, reliable sources of nutrients brought to the surface by great mixings of the ocean. There are three kinds of mixings illustrated on the map. First, currents help mix the waters and concentrate nutrients near the continents. Second, upwellings of water (shaded portion of the map) bring nutrients from deeper layers of the ocean. Upwellings may be caused by two surface currents meeting and the colder one sinking under the warmer (Convergences); or by the moving of the wind over the surface water, which allows deeper water to rise to the top; or by the existence of two surface currents moving in different directions, side by side (Divergences).

up the bottom where many of the nutrients, including dead plants and the bodies of animals, are concentrated. Fresh water, sewage, industrial wastes like DDT, cadmium, and mercury, also mix with the bottom nutrients of the shallow waters. The tides flow in and out, further adding to the mixing of the life materials of the shallow shores. Because of this continual mixing, the fertility of tidal zones is very high, often limited only by the amount of sunlight available for photosynthesis.

In the deep waters, nutrients cascade down the continental shelf and settle in the bottom layers of the oceans. When the surface layers of deep waters cool in winter, they sink because they are denser and this sinking starts mixing of nutrients. When the mixing starts, the common porpoise follow the herring schools to their offshore feeding grounds. But during the summer the top layer is warm and floats because it is less dense. As a result the thermal layering becomes static and the herring leave the offshore grounds because the top layers no longer have the nutrients necessary to supply the plants to feed the animals the herring eat. The herring move in towards shore and the porpoises follow.

In the tropics, there is a more permanent thermal layering with little mixing. In the intense sunlight of the tropics, the plants use up the surface nutrients more quickly. Light descends deeper in the tropical waters, which compensates in part for the lack of mixing.

But most of the fish concentrate near the shore currents and go out to sea when the fall hurricanes stir the seas. Again, the dolphins follow.

As temperature, salinity, pressure, and currents combined to make the diverse fertile habitats of the sea, the Cetaceans spread out and diversified to join and interact with the various communities. Each Cetacean developed and elaborated its own method for searching for food. Each developed and elaborated a social life that allowed for communal or solitary hunting, a daily and yearly routine that rhymed with the flow of food and seasons to insure that there would always be something to eat.

The Whale in the Food Web

Each Cetacean species has its own unique food gathering system. The following examples suggest both the similarity and the diversity of methods by which particular species find food in the ocean community.

THE BLUE WHALE

For millions of years, the great blue whale was entwined in the cosmic rhythms of the Antarctic. During the long sunless winters, the lack of sunlight prohibited plant plankton growth and, consequently, the growth of small shrimp-like crustacea (called "krill" by whalers) which feed on the smaller plankton. The blue whale, whose principal food was krill, left the Antarctic for warmer waters and survived, as far as we know, by digesting her own blubber. For over half of the year, the blue whale dropped out of the food web and lived in the tropics and subtropics on its stored energy.

With the onset of spring, the blue whales returned to the Antarctic and stayed for the short intensive summer of twenty-four-hours-a-day

Sulphur Bottom—Another retiring gentleman, with a brimstone belly, doubtless got by scraping along the Tartarian tiles in some of his profounder divings. He is seldom seen; at least I have never seen him except in the remoter southern seas, and then always at too great a distance to study his countenance. He is never chased; he would run away with rope-walks of line. Prodigies are told of him. Adieu, Sulphur bottom! I can say nothing more that is true of ye, nor can the oldest Nantucketer.
Herman Melville, Moby Dick

This simplified map of the Antarctic region shows the massive forces involved in creating the richest feeding area for whales on earth. The Antarctic Convergence is a line where the warm waters of the subtropical oceans meet the cold waters of Antarctica. The cool waters are heavier and sink, causing a huge upwelling of deep waters that replaces the cold sinking water. This upwelling brings nutrients that feed the microscopic plants and animals that are eaten by krill. The masses of plankton and krill are moved by the East Wind Drift around the Antarctic continent. When they bump into the Grahamland Peninsula, the krill pile up in the Weddell Sea. This incredibly dense concentration of krill is where the blue whale and other baleen whales feast.

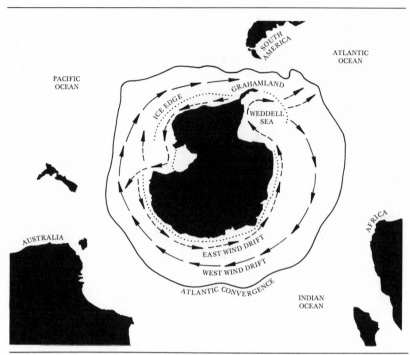

Euphausia superba is a shrimp-like crustacean eaten by the ton by blue whales in the Antarctic. It is shown here close to actual size.

sunlight. The combination of upwellings, currents, and the shape of the Antarctic continent produce there the most fertile region of all the oceans. When the cold Antarctic water meets the warmer waters of the subtropics, the cold water mass sinks and a great churning lifts nutrients and oxygen to the sun-filled surface. The boundary between these two moving water masses is called the Antarctic Convergence.

Between the Antarctic Convergence and the land, the krill swarm in vast patches covering a half acre to a square mile. The density of the patches makes the water look as if it were underlain with red bricks. A surface current, traveling west around the continent, carries with it vast stores of nutrients and krill. Because the current is blocked by the Grahamland Peninsula, it overlays the existing water mass, increasing the density of the krill. The result is a doubly thick krill mass covering one million square miles.

The relationship between the tiny krill and the enormous blue whale was the strangest food chain on earth, and one of the shortest: plankton ➤ krill ➤ whale. The most enormous animal that has ever lived subsisted on a shrimp-like creature that never grew longer than two inches. When the blue whales would arrive in the Antarctic, thin from their tropical fast, their joy of eating was so great that the whalers could approach them with ease. The blue whale, now almost extinct, faced a grim choice: to go to the Antarctic and feed, or stay in the tropics and starve.

In order to "graze" on the vast krill fields, the blue whale evolved

(*Continued on page 120.*)

Ark on the waters, fury at peace with
    itself, derelict
night of the brute, antarctic outlander,
nearing and passing me—an ice field
displacing in darkness—one day
I shall enter your walls, I shall salvage
the sunken marine of your winter, your
    armory.

Southward, there crackled a holocaust, black
with your planet's expulsion, the domains
of your silence that moved in the algae
and jostled the densities.

Then, form was, alone: magnitudes
sealed by a world's agitation, wherein glided
your leathern pre-eminence, mistrusting
the gifts of its nature: tenderness, power.

Ark of our passion, striking fire
in the blackening snow, as with torches,
when your blind blood was quickened
an epoch of ocean still slept in its gardens,
and in an immensity the disfiguring moon
divided its track like a magnet of phosphor.
Life sputtered,
the mother-medusa, blue in the flame,
a tempest of multiple wombs,
and increase grew whole in its purity,
a pompano's pulse in the sea.

Among waters, your congress
of mastheads and spars was disposed
like maternity's motion in blood,
and your power of inviolate night
was shed on the roots in a deluge.
Past expectancy's islands, your continent
fled, dereliction and terror
made the loneliness tremble:
even so, terror mounted the globes

of the glacial moon, terror entered your flesh
and struck at your solitude, the asylums
of dread where your lamp lay extinguished.
With you was the night: a tempestuous slime
that held you like pitch and enveloped you
while your tail's hurricano
spun the ice of a slumbering galaxy.

O enormously wounded one! fiery
    fountainhead
lashing a ruin of thunders,
on the harpoon's periphery, stained
in the blood bath, bleeding all virtue away,
the repose and the calm of the animal
    conduct you,
a cyclone of fracturing crescents,
to the black boats of blubber,
and the creatures of rancor and plague.

Great mold among crystals dead
on a pole of the moon, heaven itself is encompassed,
pandemonium's cloud that laments there
and covers all ocean with blood.

Pablo Neruda

Translation by Ben Belitt

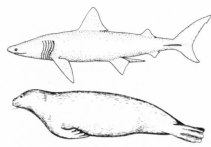

Krill populations are such a rich source of food that many other animals besides the baleen whales have evolved feeding mechanisms to eat them. The basking shark, the crab eating seal, and the penguin—animals from three entirely different orders—all have filters or sieves instead of teeth. In addition, many fish have evolved gill-rakers, still another kind of sieve which strains krill and other plankton. This is one of the most magnificent examples of convergent evolution on earth.

a mouth that functioned like an enormous strainer. There are about 360 Venetian blind–like slats on each side of the blue whale's jaw. Each slat is fringed with bristles that trap the krill. To increase its capacity for krill-laden water, the throat of the blue whale is lined with grooves that allow it to stretch like an accordion. The whole strainer is between 4 ½ to 6 square meters, larger than a tennis court net. It has been estimated that a blue whale could hold up to a ton of krill in its stomach and intestine.

When a whale swam into a krill field he gulped the water, closed his mouth, and pushed his flabby three-ton tongue into all of the corners of his mouth. The water spritzed out like water pushed through your teeth, and the krill, trapped inside, were swallowed.

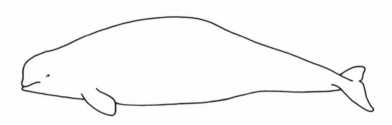

THE BELUGA

The food conditions for whales at any one point on the globe can be traced to the interacting dynamic between oceans and atmosphere. The life of the beluga, for example, is an adaptation to a seasonal diet which depends in turn on the action of enormous ocean masses.

The years of good eating are established by a strong flow of the warm Atlantic Current that flows past the Russian coast. This warmer current produces a warm winter characterized by a lot of snow on land and not much ice at sea. In spring, the snow melts and a great fresh-water run-off mixed with nutrients and vitamins feeds the coastal plant plankton. Swarms of grazing amphipods, copepods, and pteropods graze on this abundant plant life and these small creatures are in turn eaten by the Arctic cod. The beluga arrives in spring to feed on the prized cod.

But in the years when the Atlantic Current is weak, ice accumulates on the sea and there is little snow on the land. The fertility of the coastal waters is reduced and is felt along the food chain. With fewer cod, the belugas migrate away from the coasts to seek oceanic food, or adapt their diet to the new conditions.

Belugas prefer the habitats they know best: the cod-rich coastal waters. They are shallow divers—up to fifty feet—but along the coast they can reach bottom-dwelling fish like haddock and plaice. They also eat crabs and even dig in the mud for worms. They will penetrate deep into bays and inlets and travel miles up fresh-water rivers in search of food.

   The beluga has three natural enemies: ice entrapment; orcas and polar bears; and one more recent enemy, man. Belugas have been known to stay for two to three months without feeding while trapped in ice-ringed pools. A Soviet researcher described an incident where a polar bear killed a number of belugas. According to the same researcher, orcas attack belugas only when the belugas panic.

The polar bear attacks belugas frequently. According to workers in Novaya Zemlya, the bear hunts belugas mainly in water holes in the ice. Thus, at the end of 1940, a school of twenty to twenty-five belugas had been living for a long time in a hole in the ice in one of the inlets on the southern island of Novaya Zemlya. The hunters (Yu. I. and N. I. Peshishchev) heard an unfamiliar noise, a splash, the blowing of belugas, and the growling of a bear. They saw that the bear was lying at the end of an icefloe with outstretched paws, and that the water in the hole was billowing from the agitated belugas. As soon as a beluga came to the surface near the bear, it received a crushing blow on the head, and the beluga, weighing several hundred kilograms, was dragged on the ice. Thirteen belugas lay near the bear, but he did not cease killing. The hunters caught the bear together with his catch, and also the other belugas. (From BELUGA *[Delphinapterus Leucas],* INVESTIGATION OF THE SPECIES, *by S. E. Kleinenberg, A. V. Yablokov, B. M. Bel'kovich, and M. N. Tarasevich.)*

The cod has an extensive range throughout the Arctic and the northern part of the North Atlantic. Humans consume about 400 million cod each year. The beluga, which survives mainly on Arctic Cod, may be limited in its population size by the recent heavy use of cod by humans.

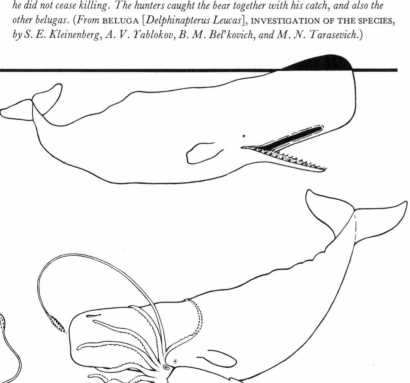

THE SPERM WHALE

   Whereas the beluga prefers the cold coastal areas, sperm whales choose regions of turbulence and deep ocean. Wherever a cold water current meets a warm water current, a great upwelling, rich in nu-

(Continued on page 124.)

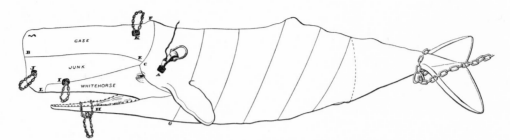

It seems no accident that one of the most significant novels written by an American, *Moby Dick* by Herman Melville, was a story of the hunting of the great sperm whale. As the prized catch of the nineteenth century whale hunt, the behavior and actions of the sperm whale were more fully documented and observed than any other species'. The sight of the sperm whale—carrying as its secret the largest brain ever evolved on the planet—gave more than one whaleman pause. Men chased them, and killed them, and looked into the sea with amazement—at a presence they could barely explain. Melville wondered:

Genius in the Sperm Whale? Has the Sperm Whale ever written a book, spoken a speech? No, his great genius is declared in doing nothing particular to prove it. It is moreover declared in his pyramidical silence. And this reminds me that had the great Sperm Whale been known to the young Orient World, he would have been deified by their child-magian thoughts.... If hereafter any highly cultured, poetical nation shall lure back to their birthright, the merry May-day gods of old; and livingly enthrone them again in the now egotistical sky; in the now unhaunted hill; then be sure, exalted to Jove's high seat, the great Sperm Whale shall lord it.

Champollion deciphered the wrinkled granite hieroglyphics. But there is no Champollion to decipher the Egypt of every man's and every being's face. Physiognomy, like every other human science, is but a passing fable. If then, Sir William Jones, who read in thirty languages, could not read the simplest peasant's face in its profounder and more subtle meanings, how may unlettered Ishmael hope to read the awful Chaldee of the Sperm Whale's brow? I but put that brow before you. Read it if you can.

In the late 1880's, Frank Bullen went to sea aboard a Yankee whaler and returned to write about it in *The Cruise of the Cachalot.* Although prejudiced by the hunter's assumption that the whales were instinctive brutes and the men had minds, Bullen narrates a scene which caused us to wonder what the whales wished to communicate to a ship that, for the moment, was so loaded with whale oil that it could not hunt.

As if to exasperate the 'old man' beyond measure, on the third day of our operation a great school of sperm whales appeared, disporting all around the ship, apparently conscious of our help-lessness to interfere with them. Notwithstanding our extraordinary haul, Captain Slocum went black with impotent rage, and, after glowering at the sportive monsters, beat a retreat below, unable to bear the sight any longer. During his absence we had a rare treat. The whole school surrounded the ship, and performed some of the strangest evolutions imaginable. As if instigated by one common impulse, they all elevated their massive heads above the surface of the sea, and remained for some time in that position, solemnly bobbing up and down amid the glittering wavelets like movable boulders of black rock. Then, all suddenly reversed themselves, and, elevating their broad flukes in the air, commenced to beat them slowly and rhythmically upon the water, like so many machines. Being almost a perfect calm, every movement of the great mammals could be plainly seen; some of them even passed so near to us that we could see how the lower jaw hung down, while the animal was swimming in a normal position.

For over an hour they thus paraded around us, and then, as if startled by some hidden danger, suddenly headed off to the westward, and in a few minutes were out of our sight.

Less than one hundred years later, Dr. Nishiwaki, a Japanese whale scientist, described the same ritual, calling it the *Marguerite Flower.* Dr. Nishiwaki noted that modern whalers deliberately harpoon the largest whale in a group, so that the remaining whales form the flower. The whalers then pluck the flower—petal by petal. ·

Perhaps the best early natural history of the sperm whale was by Frederick Debell Bennett in his *Narrative of a Whaling Voyage Round the Globe (from the year 1833 to 1836).* Bennett was a careful and fair observer and his writing forms the basis of much of our modern understanding of the behavior of the sperm whale.

The Sperm Whale is gregarious; and usually occurs in parties, which are termed by whalers "schools" and "pods." A school may contain from twenty to fifty or more Cachalots [sperm whales], and is composed of females, attended by their young, and associated with at least one adult male of the largest size, who acts as the guardian of the herd.

The smaller associations, or "pods," consist of young or half-grown males, which have been driven from their maternal schools, but yet retain a social disposition; and sometimes of large and adult males.

When a solitary, or "lone" Cachalot is observed, it almost invariably proves to be an old bull; and there is some reason to believe that the aged male frequently retires from a social, to a secluded, state of existence.

Two or more schools occasionally coalesce, and form a very large assemblage. On some tracts of ocean, peculiarly favored as their haunts, the number of Sperm Whales, seen in one large body or in many distinct schools, is beyond all reasonable conception. At particular times and places we have seen the ocean, for several miles around the ship, strewn with a constant succession of spouts, denoting a greater number of Cachalots than, could they all have been secured, would have afforded a full cargo of oil for three or four ships.

These large assemblies sometimes proceed at a rapid pace in one determinate direction, and are said to be "making a passage."

At other times they are observed to be scattered on the surface of the sea, basking or sleeping, spouting leisurely, and exhibiting every indication of being "at home," or on their feeding-ground.

When swimming rapidly, the Cachalot moves with an easy, regular, and majestic pace, the head being much raised above the surface of the sea, and a portion of the back being occasionally exhibited, in the action of leaping. The individuals composing a retreating party will sometimes move in lines, and exert their peculiar leaping movements, descend, rise, and often even spout, simultaneously.

A large party of Cachalots, gamboling on the surface of the ocean, is one of the most curious and imposing spectacles a whaling voyage affords: the huge size and uncouth agility of the monsters, exhibiting a strange combination of the grand and ridiculous. On such occasions, it is not unusual to observe a whale of the largest size leap from the water with the activity of a salmon, display the entire of its gigantic frame, suspended at the height of several feet in the air, and again plunge into the sea with a helpless and tremendous fall, which causes the surrounding waters to shoot whilst others of the school leap, or "breach," in a less degree; sportively brandish their broad and fan-shaped flukes in the air; or protrude their heads perpendicularly above the waves, like columns of black rock.

When about to descend, the Cachalot assumes a vertical posture, raising its flukes perpendicularly in the air, an evolution which is performed leisurely. When desirous of a sudden and temporary descent, the whale will occasionally sink in the horizontal position, or, as it is technically expressed, "settle down."

A necessity for respiring atmospheric air does not permit the Sperm Whale to continue below the surface of the water beyond a limited period: one hour is perhaps the average time for an individual of the largest size.

Sperm Whales are naturally timid and disposed to fly from the remotest appearance of danger: and although many instances occur amongst them of a bold and mischievous disposition, which leads them, when molested, to attack and destroy both boats and men, yet such traits rather belong to the individual, than to the general character. A shoal of Dolphins, leaping in their vicinity, is sufficient to put to flight a large party of Cachalots; and when on a well-beaten cruising ground, where the whales are exceedingly watchful, the whaler finds it necessary to be constantly on his guard, not to excite or confirm their suspicions, until he has made sure of his prizes.

The signs they exhibit of a suspicion of danger, are occasionally ceasing to spout; lying motionless on the water (evidently listening); sweeping their flukes slowly from side to side, in search of some invisible but dreaded object; and turning upon the side, or rearing the head perpendicularly above the waves, to bring surrounding objects upon the axis of vision. When pursued, they may be considered to exhibit two degrees of alarm; namely, that which puts them to the top of their speed, and which often enables them to escape the boats; or a more powerful and overwhelming impression, produced by the near approach of their enemies, or by one of their number being injured; when they will occasionally crowd together, stationary and trembling, or make but confused and irresolute efforts to escape. The females, when attacked, will often endeavor to assist each other, and those that are uninjured will remain for a long time around their harpooned companions; while the males, in which the social disposition is less strong, as commonly make a rapid retreat, without any concern for the fate of their comrades.

It is a confirmed fact, that upon a Cachalot being struck from a boat, others, many miles distant from the spot, will almost instantaneously express by their actions, an apparent consciousness of what has occurrrd, or at least of some untoward event, and either make off in alarm, or come down to the assistance of their injured companion.

The female produces one at a birth, but occasionally twins, as is usual with uniparous animals. She brings forth her young in the open ocean, and indiscriminately, on whatever spot the school may chance to be at the time of her parturition. The calf accompanies the school as soon as it is born. During a chase, it was often exceedingly interesting to observe sucklings, apparently but a few days old, leaping actively and spouting high by the side of their dams, and keeping up wonderfully well with the rapid pace of the retreating party.

Some of these whales, when attacked, will retreat but little from the spot on which they are harpooned; but rather lie, and fight with their jaws and tail until life is extinct. Others, without being themselves injured, will aid an attacked companion, and from the circumstance of their actions being less watched, often succeed in doing serious injury to the boats; whilst some few individuals make willful, deliberate, and even judicious attempts to crush a boat with their jaws, and, unless avoided or killed, will repeat their efforts until they succeed in their object.

And Bullen describes the final breaching of a dying sperm in his flurry:

Calling up all our reserves, we hauled up on to him, regardless of pain or weariness. The skipper and mate lost no opportunities of lancing, once they were alongside, but worked like heroes, until a final plunging of the fast-dying leviathan warned us to retreat. Up he went out of the glittering foam into the upper darkness, while we held our breath at the unique sight of a whale breaching at night. But when he fell again, the effect was marvellous. Green columns of water arose on either side of the descending mass as if from the bowels of the deep, while their ghostly glare lit up the encircling gloom with a strange, weird radiance, which, reflected in our anxious faces, made us look like an expedition from the Flying Dutchman. A short spell of gradually-quieting struggle succeeded as the great beast succumbed, until all was still again, except the strange, low surge made by the waves as they broke over the bank of flesh passively obstructing their free sweep.

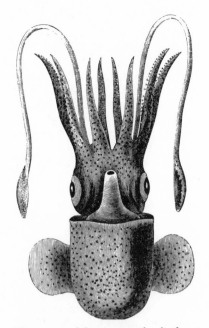

There was a violent commotion in the sea right where the moon's rays were concentrated. Getting the night-glasses out of the cabin scuttle, where they always hung in readiness, I saw a very large sperm whale locked in deadly conflict with a cuttle-fish, or squid, almost as large as himself, whose interminable tentacles seemed to enlace the whole of his great body. The head of the whale especially seemed a perfect network of writhing arms—naturally, I suppose, for it appeared as if the whale had the tail part of the mollusc in his jaws, and, in a business-like, methodical way, was sawing through it. By the side of the black columnar head of the whale appeared the head of the great squid, as awful an object as one could well imagine even in a fevered dream. Judging as carefully as possible, I estimated it to be at least as large as one of our pipes which contained three hundred and fifty gallons; but it may have been, and probably was, a good deal larger. The eyes were very remarkable from their size and blackness, which, contrasted with the livid whiteness of the head, made their appearance all the more striking. They were, at least, a foot in diameter, and, seen under such conditions, looked decidedly eerie and hobgoblin-like. All round the combatants were numerous sharks, like jackals round a lion, ready to share the feast. and apparently assisting in the destruction of the huge cephalopod.
Frank Bullen, Cruise of the Cachalot, *1875*

(*Continued from page 121.*)

trients, occurs. The sperm whale will visit these areas of greater turbulence anywhere in the oceans of the world except the polar ice zones.

The sperm whales prefer the deep ocean, in part perhaps because they are the best divers on the planet. Their deep dives give them access to the animal community of the ocean floor: ling, gropers, and spider crabs. It also gives them access to deep sea creatures like the giant squid that are unavailable to other animals. Deep diving allows them to feed on cold water cuttlefish, a kind of squid that remains at depths near 750 meters in the tropics to avoid the warm surface temperatures.

Although the human knowledge of squid is very meager, the sperm whales know their habits, preferences, and types. Each midday, the squid migrate downward, and then migrate back upward towards late evening, remaining near the surface until dawn. The sperm whales take advantage of this vertical migration and feed mainly at night. Some investigators believe that the contrast of the white gums and purple tongue of the sperm whale acts as a lure for the squid. The sperm whales can also use their sonar to hunt in the deeper oceans. Moreover, many fish that follow the squid's vertical migration pattern, especially lantern fish, are eaten by sperm whales.

In addition to their vertical migration, schools of squid seem to prefer to move through a specific temperature gradient. A species that dwells off the coast of Japan prefers a temperature gradient of 5° C for each 100 meters. If the changes of temperature become too abrupt or too dispersed, the squid migrate out of the area. Whole populations of sperm whales will disappear in exact rhythm with the departure of the squid.

Sperm whales divide the oceans into preferred feeding areas by age and sex. The solitary adult bulls and other males who leave the mid-latitude breeding grounds venture farther north and south to feed. Bulls have been seen at the Cook Strait region of New Zealand, and even in the Antarctic Convergence. These solitary males are the longer and deeper divers. They have been found entangled in deep sea electric cables 3,600 feet below the surface. Although they may normally submerge for fifty minutes, dives of over one hour have been recorded.

The adult males eat squid that have a wide temperature tolerance. Many of these squid live in the psychrosphere, a deep water area where the water remains permanently near freezing. Young males seem to eat younger, smaller squid found nearer the surface, in the warmer waters above the psychrosphere. Adult females eat large, warm water squid. Generally, the deeper and colder water masses are the feeding grounds of the adult males, and the shallower and warmer areas are used by the females and young.

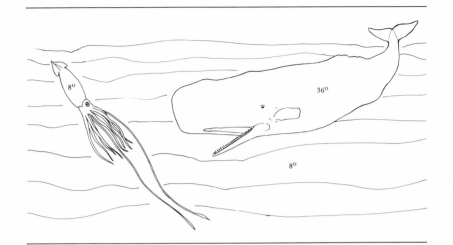

Whales are mammals and maintain a constant body temperature, as do humans. Squid are invertebrates (animals without backbones) and their body temperature is the same as the water around them. The whale must expend a great deal of energy just to keep warm. When the whale eats squid, he ingests a very cold meal. Whales spend energy just "cooking" this cold food inside their bellies.

Keeping Comfortable in the High Seas

Whales and dolphins, like all mammals, prefer to be comfortable, neither too hot nor too cold. However, the problem of maintaining comfort is more difficult for Cetaceans than it is for land mammals. For example, chilled Cetaceans cannot sun themselves like seals can to gain warmth without effort. The inside of the whale is aqueous — like the outside — so heat escapes more easily from whale to ocean than, let's say, from bear to air. A Cetacean can lose warmth from ten to one hundred times faster than a land mammal, and the skin of the whale is always the same temperature as the surrounding water. Cetaceans have no shelters to warm up in. And moving along in the ocean is much like standing in a chilling breeze.

As Cetaceans evolved, they adapted in favor of mobility. Many mammalian tricks for keeping warm were lost as whale bodies became streamlined. Whales are hairless; they cannot alter their body shape, cannot curl up to save heat nor stretch out to release it. Cetaceans do not have sweat glands for cooling off, because there is no fresh drinking water supply in the oceans to replace water which would be lost in sweating. And all Cetaceans that eat animals without backbones — like squid and crustacea — are eating food that is the temperature of the water. Finally, like all mammals in the cold, when a Cetacean exhales, he loses heat in his spout; and when he inhales, he breathes air that may be too cold or too hot.

In order to get into balance — to be neither too hot nor too cold — whales have evolved unique features not found among most other mammals. When cold, they must increase their ability to produce internal body heat from food, fat, and exercise (metabolic heat). When they are too hot, they must release the excess body heat through either their spout or their skin.

When mammals eat, the food must be changed into nutrients that can be absorbed into the bloodstream. The process of digestion

The whale is adapted to its cold sea environment, the camel to the hot deserts. Whales have spread their fat in huge blankets all over their body in order to keep warm (shaded portion of the drawing). The camel has concentrated all her fat into two humps so that the rest of her skin can perspire and thus cool her. The whale can lose heat (and cool off) only through the flippers and flukes.

Whales have a tendency to move heavily
On land it's all that blubber
Keeps whales from skipping down the
    street like little girls
Or balls of rubber

For if by chance a whale you should
    discover
Lumbering
Down Madison Avenue
On the first day of spring

You would perhaps be reminded of The
    New York Public Library
Trundling through the park
On a midsummer's eve surrounded by
    children
Or of Noah's ark

Or of the Pennsylvania Station
But if you should become a gull
Drifting quietly over the Antarctic
    Ocean
Illimitable and cool

You would see whales below like
    swallows dance
Like swallows on a pond
They would skip off lightly across the
    green water
And soar without a sound.
Scott Bates, The Carleton Miscellany,
Summer 1962

The blood near the whale's body surface is the same temperature as the surrounding ocean. If this cold blood were to return to the heart at this temperature, the whale would have to heat it back up to his body temperature (36° C). This would require the use of much energy. To conserve energy, the whale has evolved an exchange system. The cold blood coming from the body surface is warmed by blood going toward the body surface, from the heart. Since the blood near the body surface and the surrounding water are about the same temperature, little warmth is lost, and the whale saves on his "heating bill."

can be seen as a great chemical combustion of food. As the food breaks down, it releases heat. Proteins release up to forty percent more heat than fats or carbohydrates. Whales that eat fish flesh can use this protein heat to warm themselves when the sea temperatures are cold. Just being carnivorous gives them a heat advantage. In warmer waters this caloric heat becomes wasted energy and must be released. Many whales, when they enter the warmer waters of the tropics during migration, stop eating entirely and use their stored fat, or blubber, for energy. By combining a polar sea diet with a tropical fast, they also regulate their body temperature very efficiently.

Blubber replaces hair in Cetaceans. This fat blanket covers the whales like a wet suit. The mixture of fibrous connective tissue and fat is so efficient that a 2 cm thick layer surrounding a small porpoise can keep the deepest temperature inside the animal's body thirty degrees warmer than the ocean temperature. Blubber is so important to Cetaceans that it can constitute sixty percent of the weight of a north sea whale.

But blubber is not just an inert wet suit, or smeared body grease, similar to the coverings used by long-distance swimmers. Blubber is an active regulator of temperature, and Cetaceans may be able to heat up or cool off by choosing a temperature, much like a human turns the dial of an electric blanket.

Among the layers of blubber are blood vessels that can be opened or closed in a process known as vaso-constriction. When the whale is too hot, he can let the blood circulate near the surface and quickly transport some of his hot interior blood close to the colder ocean. But if the Cetacean is chilled, these vessels can be shut off and the blubber returns to its insulating "wet suit" function.

The whale has also developed an arrangement of its arteries and veins called the "counter-current" system of heat exchange. When

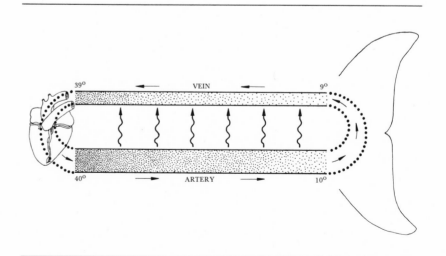

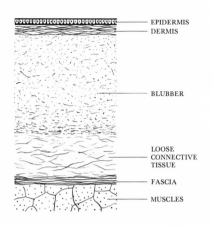

EPIDERMIS
DERMIS

BLUBBER

LOOSE CONNECTIVE TISSUE

FASCIA

MUSCLES

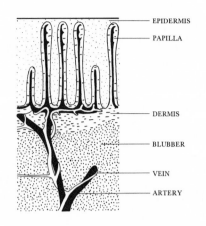

EPIDERMIS

PAPILLA

DERMIS

BLUBBER

VEIN

ARTERY

The figure to the far left shows a cross-section of porpoise skin. It illustrates how the veins with cold blood wrap around the arteries that contain warm blood, thus equalizing the temperature difference. The arteries lose heat as they approach the body surface of the porpoise. The veins gain heat as they return to the heart. The figure to the right, a cross-section of whale skin, shows the underskin (dermis), blubber (fatty layer), and attachments of the skin to the muscle (connective fascia). The thickness of blubber shows how the fat blanket keeps the whale warm.

cold, too much heat would be lost when trying to heat fins, flippers and flukes. So the veins (bringing cold blood back into the Cetacean) have surrounded the arteries (which bring warm blood from the interior). As the warm arterial blood passes by the cold venous blood, the warm blood heats the cold. This diffusion of heat across the blood vessels saves the whale's warmth and reduces the amount of extra energy needed to keep warm.

Temperature regulation is complicated for Cetaceans because of their body size. As a whale or dolphin grows, the thickness of the blubber increases in proportion to the length of the animal. Whales are so much longer than the smallest dolphin that their blubber becomes ten times as thick. This ten-times heavier blanket gives ten times more insulation. So size alone gives whales a great advantage in heat conservation compared to the smaller porpoises, but it puts them at a great disadvantage if they want to cool off. Small porpoises —with their thinner blanket—can rid themselves of excess heat ten times better than whales.

The internal body heat of an animal is proportional to its body size. The smaller the body size, the greater the amount of internal heat. The greater the body size, the less metabolic heat per pound. This has led to a famous relation between the shrew and the elephant. The tiny shrew burns up energy so fast that it must eat twice its weight in food every day or it will burn itself up. The elephant burns a relatively slow internal flame and needs to consume only four percent of its body weight daily. Thus an elephant can keep warm by eating relatively less than a shrew. We find the same relationship among oceanic mammals. The smaller dolphin has a higher production of internal heat than the larger blue whale and must eat proportionately more.

All oceanic mammals produce more internal body heat than

Many land mammal adaptations for keeping warm are not available to the Cetaceans. A furry animal can curl up to retain warmth by reducing the amount of body surface area exposed to the cold. Dolphins and whales are hairless, and they cannot curl up. Whales have evolved in a way similar to land mammals in some respects. For instance, desert rabbits have long ears—an increased body surface through which surface heat can be released. Rabbits in the north have shorter ears and shorter limbs which reduce exposed body surface which would allow more heat to escape. In the whale's case, the shape which facilitates swimming works in harmony with the shape needed to reduce surface area. The whale, during evolution, lost his hind limbs and reduced his forelimbs—an adaptation which both decreased surface area and increased mobility.

land mammals do per pound of flesh. This is obviously an oceanic adaptation for keeping warm. The higher heat production is more obvious in the smaller oceanic dolphins than in the blue whale because of a general mammal rule about size.

The flukes, fins, and flippers have the most body surface area for their weight. When a dolphin is hot, these locations allow heat to escape easily. In this way, the appendages of the Cetaceans are serving the same purpose as all mammalian appendages, like the ears of the jack rabbit and the long limbs of the desert antelope—they allow excess heat to escape rapidly.

The process of breathing also contributes to the complexity of the Cetaceans' task of keeping comfortable. Each time you breathe, hot air escapes. In winter, the hot air condenses into little clouds. Cetaceans may be able to control to some extent the amount of heat lost through the spout, and remove some of the heat from their exhalation on colder days when they need to conserve heat.

Vision and Communication in Cetaceans

Whales and dolphins can see well in a variety of situations. They can see underwater, in air, and from water to air; they can combine eyesight with "sonar-sight." Dolphins throw footballs and beach balls to each other in air without submerging or using sonar. Beginning underwater, dolphins can leap fifteen to twenty feet into the air and delicately pick a cigarette from a person's mouth. Looking from underwater through the surface, captive dolphins emerge in synchronized flying leaps and jump through hoops without touching them. With adequate light underwater, dolphins use their eyesight to hunt, play, court, and argue. They can coordinate eyesight with

Light is refracted (it bends) when it passes from one medium to another. For a dolphin to locate an object in air while the dolphin is submerged requires that he make a mental compensation. Dolphins do this very well and can learn how to adjust their aim.

A Canadian Fisheries patrol boat hemmed a group of five orcas between the boat and a series of precipitous cliffs. The sounds of the engine and perhaps the foreknowledge that the patrol boat was about to capture one of them kept the five orcas from diving under the boat and heading out to sea. They dove shallowly and then re-emerged, exhaling powerfully. After half an hour, a stiff breeze and a heavy chop made the patrol boat rev its engines. The whales dove. With one accord they broke through the surface in a vertical position and remained in this apparently motionless manner for about four seconds. They then submerged and were not seen again until way out in the open sea. This is called spying, and many whales like the orcas shown here use their eye sight in air to check escape routes.

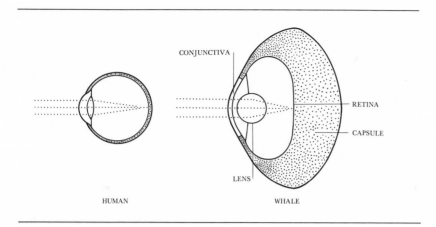

CONJUNCTIVA

RETINA

CAPSULE

LENS

HUMAN

WHALE

A whale eye cut in half compared to a human eye. The whale eye is surrounded by a tough capsule that prevents it from collapsing when the whale is diving. The whale eye has a thicker window (conjunctiva) to prevent the eye from being damaged by the continual rush of sea water around it. The whale eye also has a perfectly round lens. The round lens bends all incoming light lines into a small image of maximum brightness. Man, a daylight mammal, does not need to concentrate the light, so humans produce a larger image for the same size eye.

delicate grasping of their jaws to make fine manipulations of other creatures or oceanic objects.

> *Two dolphins enjoyed playing with an eel in their tank. One of the dolphins would catch the eel delicately between its teeth, carry it around for a while, then let it go. The other dolphin would then catch the eel and swim around with it, chased by her friend. They would then reverse the chase. One day the eel managed to hide in a pipe at the bottom of the tank. The dolphin found a small poisonous fish that also lived in the tank. He carefully caught the fish in his teeth so that it couldn't hurt him, and poked the fish into the pipe where the eel was hiding. The eel zoomed out and the dolphins continued their game of eel catch.*
> From Smarter Than Man?, *Fichtelius and Scholander, Pantheon Books.*

Cetacean eyesight went through a great transformation when the ancestors of modern whales re-entered the seas. On land, the enemy of the eye is dust and physical hurt. In the ocean, the enemy is salt, pressure in diving, and the possible irritation of the ocean always streaming by. The eyes of land creatures are often sunk deep into a heavy skull, topped with a brow and eyebrows, protected by eyelashes, and washed clean by tears. The eyes of whales have migrated to the sides of their heads so they will not constantly bear the brunt of a head-on collision with the ocean. The whole eye is encapsulated so it won't get squashed on deep dives. Whales cannot cry and have no eyelashes. But they do have special glands that continuously oil the eyes against the brine, and the eye's window (the conjunctiva) is constructed like thick protective glass to further protect the eye from rushing water.

Light is greatly diminished in the seas. In coastal waters, perhaps ninety percent of the light is lost below 30 feet. Therefore, among Cetaceans, the need for a bright image takes precedence over all other aspects of vision—perception of movement, position, color, focus, detail, and sharpness. To achieve maximum brightness, Cetaceans can open their pupils enormously wide. Their eyes are lined with a reflective substance that concentrates light like the silver of a car headlight. The lens is set far back in the eye and the eye itself is oval so that weak light rays will not fall short of the retina. The retina is a specialized receiving screen composed of cells called rods that

To maximize brightness, a Cetacean eye pools light from many receptors into one transmitting nerve. Each transmitting nerve contains the light from a large area on the fish. In man, a daytime animal, each single receptor contains light that passes to a single transmitter nerve. This gives a more finely detailed view of an equivalent area of fish. The eye receptors used to maximize brightness are called rods. The daylight receptors are called cones. Whales have many more rods than cones. Humans have more cones than rods.

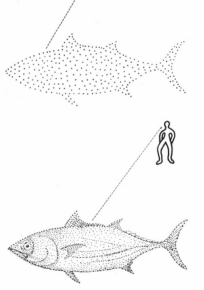

further concentrate light before it is transmitted to the brain. These modifications are very similar to modifications in the eyes of night living mammals.

Besides salt, water, pressure, and light, the Cetacean eye has changed because of the great size of some whales and because of their development of sonar sight. Land hunters tend to have frontal eyes so that the views of each individual eye will overlap. The overlap gives stereo vision and good depth perception, essential to a hunting animal. The overlap also means the hunter will have a blind spot behind its head. On land, the hunted (usually a vegetarian) will have its eyes on the side of its head. This "bilateral" vision allows the hunted animal to see in all directions. Bilateral eyes have no blind spots and no stereo vision.

The surface feeding dolphins are hunters with eyes at the sides of their heads. They can't use their eyesight to see directly in front of them, but they can use their sonar. And they can see, in stereo, right below their head. The Amazon River dolphin has such large cheeks that it can't see downwards. To see the river bottom, it turns upside down and looks down over the top of its head. The large baleen whales who "graze" on great concentrations of plankton may have extensive blind spots and no stereo vision at all because their eyes are so far apart. It is still a mystery how they locate the vast layers of plankton they feed on.

But the eyes of Cetaceans not only look for food and obstacles. They look for each other: for love, for motherly comfort and milk, for particular friends and enemies. As with other mammals, vision serves a social as well as a physiological function.

Because dolphins and porpoises have streamlined, ocean-adapted

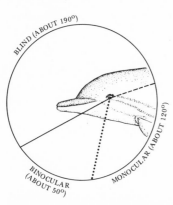

A mammal's eyesight is a balance of monocular vision, binocular vision, and blind areas. The amount of each depends on the mammal's habits and habitat. The hunter (illustrated here by a house cat) needs depth vision. The hunted (here, a rabbit) needs panoramic vision to spot the hunter. The rabbit has no blind spots. Dolphin sight is a balance of eye sight and sonar-sight. Dolphins cannot see objects right in front of their beaks; they use sonar-sight to examine things there. They cannot see above their heads and must tip their body up. They can see binocularly right below the body, but nowhere else. How these two kinds of sight relate to squid and fish hunting is not yet understood.

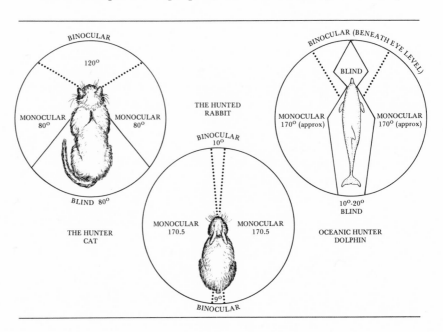

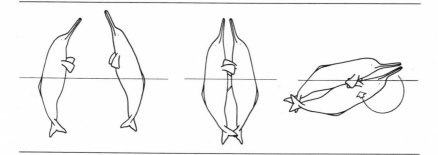

Two Ganges River dolphins engaged in courtship. This courtship is a unique part of the dolphins' life. They stand vertically in the water, whereas during most daily activity their bodies remain horizontal. The courtship displays are also "massive"—the whole body is involved, not just the face or torso.

bodies, they may have lost the detailed subtle facial expressions and body expressions found in humans, dogs, cats, monkeys, and other mammals. There is no hair to bristle, no eyebrows to raise, a mouth that does not—at least to us—grimace. The most important visual signals of Cetaceans to one another are more massive. In courtship and lovemaking, for example, dolphins emphasize the difference between everyday life and the specialness of being courtly by changing the body posture. In everyday life, the body is relatively straight and horizontal; in courtship, the dolphin bends his body at all points possible, forming an S-shaped curve, a strong signal of something special happening.

But when a dolphin is angry, she or he will lower the head, showing teeth and slanting the body upwards. When yielding, she or he will slant the body downwards and keep the mouth closed.

Besides changing their posture, dolphins can communicate by changing the direction and speed of their swimming pattern. In making love, the male or female will speed up until he or she is just ahead of the dolphin being courted, then slow down abruptly, look back, and roll over to display his or her genitals. This is a body dance signaling the desire to mate.

Cetacean markings are generally related to hunting, camouflage, and disguise. Countershading—the back of the dolphin being darker

Humans remain mystified by the color patterns of Cetaceans. The high contrast coloration of the orca is shown at left. The white spots on the flank may be used in schooling patterns so that one orca can see others in front, just as a deer flashes its white tail when running. The white on the belly seems to direct attention to the genitals, or, in females, to the nipples. The white near the head may be "disruptive coloration"—a kind of coloration which visually distorts the body outline. This could confuse the orca's prey because the head becomes difficult to distinguish.

131

July 5, 1967, 17:15. Shortly before arrival in Gibraltar a large school of *Delphinus delphis* was sighted, approximately thirty to forty animals, males and females. They approached the yacht spontaneously and played in the bow wave. Complete leaps with the whole body out of the water were seen, but only the smaller animals leapt vertically out of the water to fall back in the same position.

July 7, 16:30. A school of *Delphinus delphis*, both males and females with young. Again vertical leaps were performed, but only by the smaller animals. The rubber boat was lowered and we were able to compare the behavior of the animals towards the *Zodiac* and the behavior of the animals towards the yacht. At a speed of 8 to 10 knots the animals never once approached the *Zodiac*, on the contrary they tried to avoid it. As soon as the *Zodiac* reached the school, the dolphins dived and changed direction underwater. They did, however, swim quite spontaneously in the bow wave of the yacht. Presumably, the noise of the *Zodiac's* motor frightened the animals.

July 9, 8:30. Several schools of *Delphinus delphis*. Some half leaps were seen but there were no young dolphins. Several animals followed the *Zodiac* or swam for short periods near the bow. This only happened when the speed was reduced so that the motor was quieter. The distance between the *Zodiac* and the dolphins was always the same. If the *Zodiac* changed direction or rose or sank in the waves, so did the dolphins.

July 12, 13:00. Two large schools of *Delphinus delphis*. The school which was followed by the *Zodiac* panicked and dispersed 180° around the yacht and the *Zodiac*. They were springing completely out of water during flight. Later, when they were farther away from the yacht, they started to roll while still in the air. At quite some distance from the yacht they gathered again to form a complete school. During the attack, the animals reacted at first with leaps out of the water, then with diving and changing direction underwater. We also saw this behavior with *Tursiops truncatus* although the time spent underwater by the *Delphinus delphis* was much shorter.

14:55. A school, 650 feet (200 meters) long, was sighted swimming "on parade." Groups of three to four animals were swimming slowly and regularly behind one another.

19:30. A *Delphinus delphis* was harpooned and brought alive on board. Tail-slapping on the surface of the water was

seen once. The school was followed for 3½ hours, and the following observations were made: (1) Rolling of the body around its own axis while still out of the water; (a) a half roll around 90° so that the animal fell back into the water on its right side, the roll always taking place from left to right; (b) a complete roll through 180°, falling into the water on its

back. This roll also took place from left to right. (2) Swimming on the back with the head out of the water. At the same time, the head was swung up and down to slap the surface.

(3) Tail-slapping. Only the tail appeared out of the water to slap periodically on the surface. This behavior was only seen when the animals were swimming quietly. There were sometimes four to five rhythmical slaps, although a single slap was seen more often.

July 19, 17:30. A school of approximately fifty *Delphinus delphis* was sighted. As soon as the *Zodiac* approached, they increased speed, dived, and changed direction underwater. The school reassembled behind the *Zodiac*. The yacht took over the chase and an animal was wounded by the harpoon. We saw quite clearly how other dolphins came immediately to the help of the wounded animal on the starboard side of the yacht. They supported the wounded dolphin with their flippers and bodies and carried it to the surface. It blew two or three times and then dived. The whole incident lasted about thirty seconds and was repeated twice when the animal appeared unable to surface alone. All the animals including the wounded dolphin then dived and swam quickly out of sight. During the chase only a few leaps were seen and the animals stayed around the yacht instead of fleeing, as they had done until this time.

July 20, 9:30. A female *Stenella styx* was caught alive and put into a tank on the deck of the yacht. When the animal was rubbed on the belly, it would roll over so that the white belly was on the surface of the water. Half an hour later, a male was caught and put into another tank approximately 9 feet (3 meters) away from the tank containing the female. As soon as the male was put into his tank, he started to whistle and his whistles were answered by the female. Reciprocal whistling then continued. This "conversation" lasted for about one-half hour. When the male was rubbed on its belly, he refused to roll over as the female had done.

July 21, 7:30. A row of about fifteen animals were seen to jump all together. They all leapt half out of the water and kept exactly in line.

July 26, 15:45. We met a large tanker traveling 20 knots from east to west. The bow wave was about 16 feet (5 meters) high. We were able to see quite clearly how dolphins were climbing up the bow wave until they reached the highest point, where they then shot out in front of the tanker to fall with a great splash back into the water.

From Behavior Patterns of Some Delphinidae Observed in the Western Mediterranean, *by G. Pilleri and J. Knuckey* than the belly—offsets the tendency for the light to reflect off the back and make it more visible. Probably individual "signature" whistles are more used for individual recognition than are body shape and color. But we are not sure of the modes in which individuals recognize each other as unique. Some dolphins, like *Delphinus bairdi*, become more boldly marked in the mating season. In many dolphins, the stripes stop at the genitals and/or nipples. The stripes may, like garments, direct attention to these spots during courtship or nursing.

Perhaps the most alarming signal in the dolphin world is visual and completely silent. In extreme duress, the dolphin may silently sink without giving any other signals of distress. This alarm "signal" brings another dolphin to aid the hurt or ill animal.

The Sound World of Cetaceans

To enter into the perceptual world of whales and dolphins, you would have to change your primary sense from sight to sound. Your brain would process, synthesize, and store sound pictures rather than visual images. Individuals and other creatures would be recognized either by the sounds they made, or by the echoes they returned from the sounds *you* made. Your sense of neighborhood, of where you are and who you are with, would be a sound sense.

Sound is the primary sense in the life of Cetaceans. Vision is often difficult or impossible in the dark and murky seas. Many whales and dolphins navigate and hunt at night or below the zone of illuminated water. Whereas vision depends on the presence of light, sounds can be made and used at any time of the day or night, and at all depths. Sounds are infinitely variable: loud to soft, fast to slow, high notes to low notes, short silences to long silences, and many other combinations. Sounds can be stopped abruptly in order to listen to a neighbor in the silence. They can be finitely directed by the speaker and pinpointed by the listener. And communicating and locating by sound does not require a disruption of daily routines. Whales and dolphins can keep in sound contact simply by blowing bubbles as they exhale.

Most Cetaceans have evolved two kinds of voices. One voice is used predominantly for social communication. The other voice is used for navigation and location of submerged objects by echolocation—interpreting echoes made by the Cetacean voice. This second function is sometimes called bio-sonar (*SO*und *N*avigation *A*nd *R*anging). The two voices overlap in both quality and function. Dolphins can use both voices simultaneously.

SEEING WITH SOUND.

All of the toothed whales and some of the baleen whales can "see" with sound. They send out an extremely powerful *click* or *ping* that moves through the water until it encounters an object of a different density than the water. The sound then bounces back in the form of

The porpoises came straight in our direction. We could see the smooth gray back beneath each triangular dorsal fin as the animals came up rhythmically for air and dove again in a graceful arc.

There must have been nearly twenty in the group. When within fifty or seventy-five feet of our craft, they all submerged and swam directly beneath us. Looking down through the water, we could see dark shapes streaking swiftly past.

During all this time, the only noise we heard them make in the air was the "whoosh" of exhaling breath as their blowholes were momentarily out of water at the top of each arc—and even this was audible only when they were close to the boat.

But the underwater listening gear told a very different story. The intermittent tapping or sputtering which had been barely discernible from the speaker when the animals first turned in our direction grew in intensity and in continuity as they approached. When emitted by a single porpoise alone, this noise—as we had learned before—is a concatenation of clicks or clacks such as might be produced by a rusty hinge if it were opened slowly. It was soon apparent, however, that a number of the animals were making the sounds together, and more seemed to join the chorus as they came nearer. Superimposed upon this increasing clatter was an occasional birdlike whistle resembling the "cheep" of a canary.

As they came still closer, the sputtering noises continued to grow louder and still louder. Taken together, they suggested the roar of an approaching railroad train. By the time the group was about ready to make its final dive, the crescendo from the speaker in our boat had become a clattering din which almost drowned out the human voice.

Then abruptly, as if by prearranged signal, it stopped completely and left us in a shocking silence. At that moment, they swam beneath the boat. A single barklike sound was now repeated once or twice, and the porpoises with their underwater chorus were gone.
Winthrop N. Kellogg, Porpoises and Sonar, *University of Chicago Press 1961*

A trainer taught a dolphin to approach a lit electric bulb. The dolphin always performed correctly but never looked at the light bulb. The confused trainer hid the light bulb. He turned it on and, sure enough, the dolphin swam towards it. The trainer figured it out: dolphins prefer to listen—to hear the click of the light switch—rather than look.
Peter Warshall

Sonar is a way of "seeing" with sound. The dolphin sends out a short click or ping which hits a fish and bounces back. The dolphin hears the echo and interprets the size, texture, speed, location, and other characteristics of the fish from the echo. An echo can be placed between the outgoing clicks (top diagram). In this case, the dolphin interprets the returned unaltered echo. An echo can also be placed so that it interferes with the outgoing click. In this case, the dolphin must interpret the amount and kind of distortion in the echo.

an echo. The echoes are received by the whales or dolphins through their jaws and melon. They are then synthesized by the brain into images and information—the distance, direction, speed, shape, texture, density, and even the internal structure of the object. Hunting, migrating, traveling, or resting together, they can also tell the position and direction of every other creature they are traveling with.

If a human diver jumps into the water with a dolphin, the dolphin can "see" inside the diver into the air passages of his lungs and respiratory system. This is because sonar sight penetrates materials that are approximately the same density as the water—like human flesh—and returns different echoes from objects with different densities. The greater the difference in density, the more easily sonar can discriminate. In the case of the diver, his lungs show a greater contrast to the water than his wet suit. To the dolphin, the diver might look like an x-ray photograph of the human body.

Bottlenose dolphins have been trained to utilize their sonar to discriminate the difference between a metal of one kind and a metal of another kind, or between a metal plate of one thickness and one of another thickness. In an experimental situation, Dr. Kenneth Norris determined that a dolphin could tell the difference between a half inch long gelatin capsule filled with water, and a piece of fish of the same shape, at twenty feet. This ability to make fine discriminations in objects of similar size is useful to dolphins and whales in

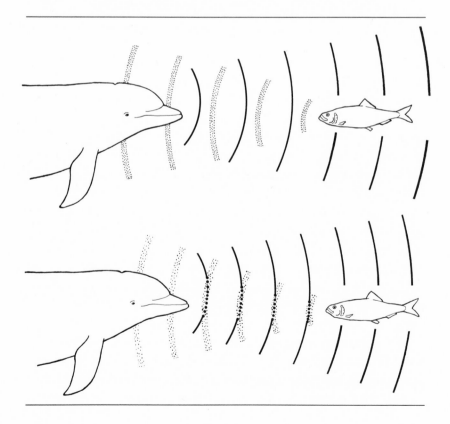

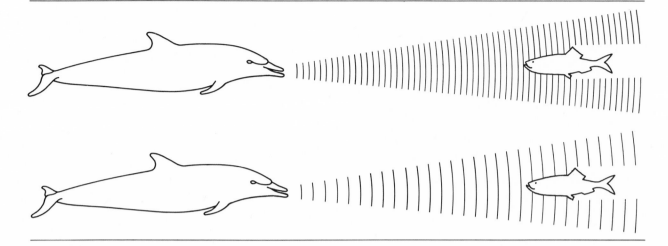

hunting because it eliminates the need to spend a lot of time chasing the wrong prey.

To echolocate, the dolphin or whale gives out a series of clicks—let's say, twenty to thirty per second. The dolphin spaces the clicks so that the outgoing clicks do not interfere with the incoming echo. The dolphin analyzes the strength and character of the echo.

Or the clicks may be spaced so that they *do* interfere with the incoming echo. This occurs if the clicks follow one another too rapidly or too slowly. Some investigators believe that the dolphin may use the interference of click with echo to judge location, direction, and speed.

Sonar, like eyesight, can be focused. Using the same amount of energy, a dolphin's click can have a high note and travel a short distance, or a low note and travel a long distance. This is described in physics by saying that a click has a high frequency and a short wavelength, or a low frequency and a long wavelength. A high frequency sound can make a more detailed sound picture than a low frequency click. Using high frequencies, the sound waves hit the target in close patterns because of the short wavelengths.

When dolphins are traveling in the oceans, they will use multiple frequencies simultaneously so that they can focus on near and far objects. As soon as some interesting echo is received, a dolphin will use loud, high frequencies for far objects, and quiet, high frequencies for nearby curiosities. The dolphin can switch frequencies in less than one-thousandth of a second. But whether she uses high or low frequencies, the dolphin can sputter out clicks with incredible rapidity—up to 300 per second—and still interpret this fast-fire sound echo.

Cetaceans living in clear seas probably use sonar quite differently from dolphins inhabiting tidal flats and muddy bays. For instance, sperm whale sounds are intense and mainly low pitched for long range, deep water search, while the Amazon River dolphin uses faint

A dolphin can see detail using his sonar-sight by changing from low to high frequencies. When sound waves encounter a fish with great rapidity (high frequency) they return many more echoes. Each echo provides an additional detail for the dolphin as he forms a sound picture in his brain.

A real example of how the frequency of a sound wave in water is related to wave length gives some idea of the ability of the dolphin to focus.

A tone of 5,000 cycles per second, traveling in water at 5,000 feet per second, produces a wave one foot in length. But a tone 50,000 cycles per second travels at the same speed, and the wave length is 1/10 foot. The dolphin gets a more precise resolution from the echo at the higher tone.
Peter Warshall

SOUND IN WATER

Sound is energy. One way Cetaceans can create sounds is by causing a disturbance—an explosion—by snapping the jaws shut, popping a bubble, or slapping the flukes. The disturbance compresses the air or water, and variations in the disturbance make the compressions and relaxations of the water "sound" differently.

Because water is denser than air, sound disturbances compress and relax more quickly and sound zooms along five times faster in water than in air. This is about one mile per second.

This quick transmission of sound is altered by changes in temperature, depth, or pressure; the amount and kind of suspended plankton and sediment; the presence of other animals; and the salinity of the water. When a human diver descends into the water, the pressure increases until finally his voice gets higher and higher, becoming very nasal and unintelligible.

Sound in water can travel much farther than on land because water's density doesn't dissipate sound energy as quickly as air's does. Sound retains so much of its energy in water that it can be bounced off the under-surface of the seas and the bottom of the ocean floor like a rubber ball.

In the deep parts of the ocean, the sound just keeps going on and on. Whale sounds have been heard fifteen miles from the nearest visible whale, and some of the larger whales may make sounds that travel hundreds of miles until they bounce back off the continental shelf. Whales may keep in voice contact over hundreds of miles of ocean.

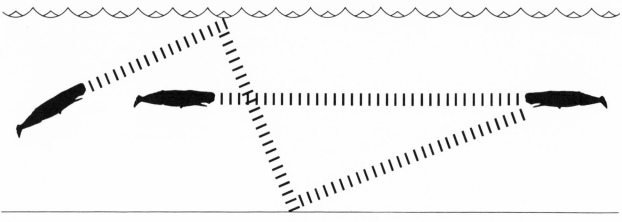

fast clicks suited to the muddy bottom of this great river.

But sonar is not just an exotic way of seeing or navigating. Sonar speaks. While using their sonar to hunt, dolphins or orcas can simultaneously communicate their position in the hunt, their relation to their neighbor, and their closeness to the fish. The criss-crossing sounds of a group of hunting Cetaceans are like a multi-directional space-time map of the movements of the entire group. This map can be made without the necessity of extra signals. Further, since most sonar hunting sounds are above the hearing range of the fish (10,000 cycles per second), the exchange of information among dolphins takes place without alarming the fish.

SOUND PRODUCTION

The way Cetaceans produce their sounds is largely unknown. Some sounds are made without any exhalation of air, an adaptation which is convenient for an air-breathing underwater mammal. In some way the air from the lungs is recycled at the closed-off blowhole. After returning to the lungs, the air is recycled again and again, as in yogic breathing and the circular breath used by some saxophone and trumpet players.

The sounds are directional. They are channeled about 10° on

The sonar clicks of a dolphin are very directional and can be focused. In the above example which illustrates an experiment by Kellogg, the dolphin clicks could be felt only for 10° from either side of the mid-line of the head. To cover a wider area, the dolphin rotated and waved his head back and forth.

each side of the dolphin's jaw. To broadcast over a wider horizon, the dolphin or whale can rotate its head as it clicks and whistles.

Some sounds are so loud that if we could hear them it would feel like your ears were laying next to a jackhammer breaking up a sidewalk. People who have lived around dolphins say that you can feel the sound by placing your hand in front of the dolphin's head. In order to protect the dolphin from the intensity of his own sounds, the skull around the sound production area is thickened to prevent the dolphin's nerves and brain from being shattered by continuous sonic bombardment.

SOUNDS AS LANGUAGE

Cetaceans make other sounds besides sonar clicks. They make sounds with their bodies and with their voices. All of these sounds seem to communicate something to other Cetaceans, although different species vary greatly in loquacity. Gray whales seem to be very silent, while the beluga is known as the "sea canary." The Amazon River dolphin clicks a lot, but has not been heard to say much else. The humpback whale will sing for seven to thirty minutes and then repeat the whole song for several hours. Most dolphins speak in short phrases. Some speak simultaneously with two voices: the echo-

The voice of the blue whale, largest known animal, carries 100 miles underwater, and hits a pitch of middle C on the musical scale, Navy scientists report.

The scientists, who made a six week study of the whales, are not sure what the sounds mean, but say they could be a simple form of communication. The sounds began at regular 100 second intervals.

The scientists found two kinds of outcries. Both lasted thirty-seven seconds but one had a two-second break and the other was broken twice.

Dr. William C. Cummings, a senior scientist at the Naval Undersea Research and Development Center, has detailed the findings of a 2,000 mile expedition to study the blue whale sounds.

"We have no idea what the sounds mean. Five years ago, I discovered that right whales repeat a complicated, twelve minute stanza of signals in exactly the same way, signal for signal. More recently, others have reported similar occurrences among humpback whales, the so-called 'song of the whales'."

The blue whale sounds "are not voiced indiscriminately. They may well represent a simple kind of communication."

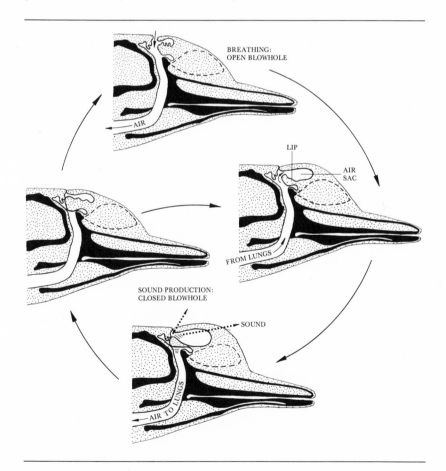

This diagram shows the relation of breathing to vocalizing in the dolphin. In breathing (top drawing), the blowhole is open and air is sucked into the lungs. In vocalizing (middle right drawings), the blowhole is first closed and air from the lungs is forced into an air sac near the top of the dolphin's head. As the air sac swells with air, the forehead swells. Then the dolphin closes the lip of the air sac (bottom drawing) and releases air back toward the lungs. This makes the air sac lip give a "Bronx cheer" like releasing air from a baloon. These are focused by the melon and are bounced off the bones of the jaw and brain case. The drawing at the middle left shows the deflated air sac. The dolphin may either refill her lungs by opening the blowhole or make more sounds by refilling the air sac.

HEARING IN WATER

Humans lose their ability to detect the direction of sounds when they are underwater. The whole skull vibrates—becomes a receiver—instead of the two separate receivers, the ears. It vibrates because sound travels until it encounters something dense enough to stop it.

The difference between the density of flesh and water is so slight that sound is not stopped by the surface of the body. It enters all over the head and body until it hits bone. On land, sounds enter the air-filled ears because flesh itself is one thousand times denser than air. But flesh is only eight times denser than water.

The evolving Cetaceans were spending more and more time in the water, but they still had their ears. Since they received underwater sound through the vibrations of their whole skull, the ears were unnecessary, and the whales gradually lost them. The ear channels were reduced to tiny pinholes, and in some species, plugged with a hard wax. To channel the sound, a material less dense than water was needed. While blubber developed for other reasons, certain blubber fats were significantly less dense than the surrounding sea. These deep fatty (blubber) deposits channeled the sounds into unexpected places inside the body of the whale.

Two of these places were the whale's inner ears, and they became the Cetacean sound channels.

The first fatty deposit is inside the jawbone of the whale. The "ear" for receiving sound is a very thin area of the jawbone itself. The second fatty deposit is called the melon, and is found in the "forehead" region of the whale's body. The melon is also involved in broadcasting sounds. It is not yet known how, but the melon can broadcast and receive sounds simultaneously.

The hearing of the dolphin is so sensitive that every time Dr. Winthrop Kellogg, a researcher, dropped a teaspoon of water into a large oceanarium pool, the dolphin turned and echolocated at the spot. When it rained on an outdoor tank the sound of the rain hitting the water was so painful that the dolphins kept leaping out of the water to escape the sound. In the oceans, they would be able to dive deep enough to avoid the pain. The construction sounds in one oceanarium were severe enough to kill a dolphin in a nearby tank. Dolphins can hear much higher tones or pitches than humans. The shift to higher tones was made partly because water vibrates differently from air. Nevertheless, no animal on earth can hear such high tones as dolphins.

Two entirely different sound receivers have been discovered in the porpoise. The first sound receiver is in the jaw of the dolphin. Sound enters the jaw and travels in a thin oil inside the jawbone to the ear drum. The second sound receiver is in the forehead region, or melon, of the dolphin. Sound enters the oil-filled melon and travels from the melon through a series of air passages to the ear drum. The "ears" as we know them in other mammals do not receive sound waves because of the problem of hearing underwater.

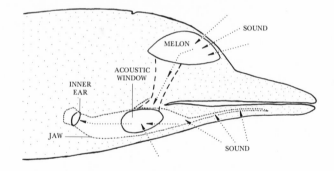

Dr. Kenneth Norris' description of discovering the "acoustic window":

"In the spring of 1959, while walking down a lonely beach bordering the Gulf of California in Mexico, I came upon the skeleton of a bottlenose porpoise. I puzzled over its odd features, and in particular over the strange lower jaw. The mandibular lower jaw's canal, which bears blood vessels and nerves, had been massively excavated until the posterior jaw—the part near the skull—was nothing but a thin hollow shell of bone, so thin on its outer surface that light shone easily through the bone in a large oval area."

location clicks and whatever "social" vocabulary is appropriate.

The body also speaks. Many Cetaceans make a sound by clapping their jaws. Dolphin trainers believe this is a threat or warning. In a quiet mood, dolphins will release one big bubble underwater. The gurgle-pop of the bubble is believed to be a question—"What's that? Can I share or partake in that?" The bubble is somewhere between curiosity and a request. When a dolphin gets excited, its breathing quickens and each exhalation forms a distinct "chuff!"—an exhuberant high-energy sound.

A whale can use his or her tail to produce a variety of subtle sounds. Flukes are wiggled on the surface in anxiety or annoyance. When there is danger, the flukes are slapped against the surface, producing a very loud crack (lobtailing). This crack can be heard for

Many Cetaceans communicate by slapping the water. The loudest sound can be made by a breaching sperm whale as it leaps out of the water. The crash of the whale's hitting the water surface is an alarm signal. All other sperm whales will immediately dive under the surface in response.

miles in the ocean and will cause other Cetaceans in the area to dive directly down. A whale or a dolphin may also breach—jump part or all of the way out of the water and then belly-whop or sidesmack the surface. Sometimes breaching is for danger or a warning; other times it seems to be for fun.

The vocal sounds of whales have been categorized into two broad types: pulsed sounds and pure tones. Pulsed sounds include: (1) sonar or echolocation sounds; (2) faster clicks used for social communication; and (3) more repetitive, less well-modulated sounds which are thought to be "self-expressive." To humans, the faster clicks used for some types of social communication sound like creaking doors and rusty hinges. The loosely modulated sounds have been described as squeaks and squawks and barks and grunts. To describe these latter sounds as "self-expressive" means that we can't figure out what the toothed whales are saying to each other.

The pure tones sound to us like clear whistles. They are beautiful bird-like sounds with trills and arpeggios, glissandos and sitar-like

This is a greatly simplified rendition of the song session of a humpback whale. The diagram contains pieces of the humpback songs represented visually as a "sonogram." The higher the note, the more vertical the sonogram. The longer the note, the longer the length of the line on the sonogram. Song sessions may last for hours. The circled areas show sounds so subtle that humans cannot hear them unless they are played at slow speeds.

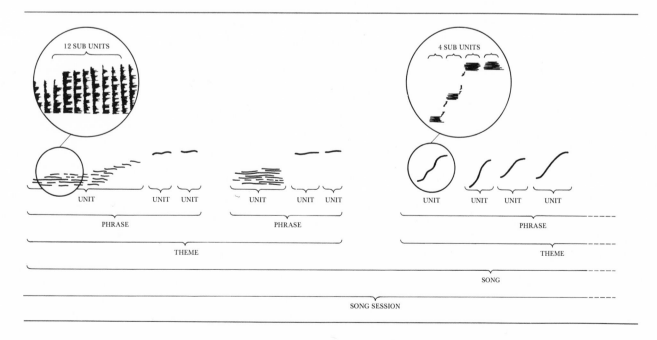

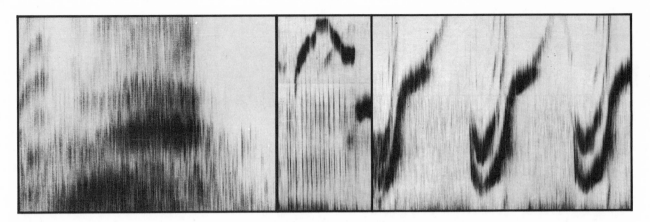

Three sonographs—pictures of dolphin sounds made by a machine that is more sensitive than the human ear. The top left sonograph shows a "squawk." Squawks are common emotional expressions that have many frequencies or pitches which are vocalized simultaneously. The top right sonograph is a whistle. Note that the number of frequencies is small and this gives a "pure" sound—not a squawk. Whistles are like personal signatures for dolphins and identify each dolphin as well as its location. The third sonograph shows a dolphin making two kinds of signals simultaneously. The vertical stripes are echolocation clicks (sharp, multi-frequency sounds) and the dark, mountain-like humps are the signature whistles. No one knows how a dolphin makes both whistles and echolocation clicks simultaneously.

bends in the notes. Each whistle is particular to the species that makes it. A bottlenose dolphin will always recognize another bottlenose dolphin. More important, each whistle is individualized, like a signature or a name. When Paddy the bottlenose dolphin whistles to Dolly the bottlenose dolphin, each knows exactly who is whistling. Even more surprising, it seems that the Cetacean community is so integrated that an individual of one species can recognize (and communicate to) an individual of another species. Thus, Moby Dick the sperm whale can cross-species-communicate with Emu the orca.

Dolphins are born with their own personal whistle. The whistle is a little raggedy at birth, but becomes clear and clean quickly. The female bottlenose dolphin seems to turn her whistle into a song as she matures, repeating the whistle over and over again.

Whenever the whistle is given, it is answered by a nearby Cetacean. The whistle provides a great deal of information: the location of the whistler, the identity of friends, the whereabouts of companions, and the desire to hear a response. Choruses of whistles may be a way to confirm and reconfirm the mood, state of being, or purpose of the group. For instance, whistling occurs more often when dolphins are hungry and might be expected to start a coordinated hunt. Orcas often vocalize intensely just before setting out to hunt, and then keep in contact with clicks and whistles while herding fish or hunting cooperatively.

Cetaceans can vary their pulsed sounds and whistles. There are endless combinations of changing loudness, timing of bursts or groups of bursts, tone and groups of tones, as well as silences. Until we leave the confinement of the oceanaria and enter the oceans where the Cetacean voice evolved, the meaning of Cetacean language will evade us.

JOHN SUTPHEN
Body State Communication Among Cetaceans

John Sutphen, M.D., is a physician who practices at the Lawrence Memorial Hospital in Connecticut. He has been interested for a number of years in the biological capabilities of Cetaceans and their ability to teach us something about medical diagnosis and interpersonal relationships.

If we consider communication in the widest sense of the word, we must include transmission of information from every biologic motor source and reception by every sense. All animals transmit information to a greater or lesser extent depending upon their physiognomy. Dogs, for example, are olfactory oriented. Earthworms, however, are tactile and vibrational creatures. The separate exchanges of information among each frequently lie in these corridors.

In humans, communication is made largely through either verbal abstraction or visual imagery. The former is basically spoken and written language as we know it. Visual images, however, frequently transmit gestalt impressions and provide our most meaningful intraspecies' emotional link: the curl of the lip, the tear, the turn of the eyes. Vision, of course, is also our major stereotactic sense and serves functions of recognition and location.

Imaging in the Cetacean world is primarily in the acoustic metaphor. Therein lies an incredible difference between human and Cetacean communication. Echolocation is three-dimensional. For example, one dolphin scanning another dolphin does not just receive an echo from the other's skin but from the interior body as well. In fact, far stronger echoes are raised from air-filled cavities and from bone within the animal. Furthermore, the echoes from the many soft organs and surfaces within the animal are about as strong as the skin echo.

In addition to the static, full thickness images that the dolphin receives, there are also the shifting pitches of sound from moving objects—the Doppler effect. Motion must solo boldly forward from the background of the acoustic picture. Pulsations of blood-filled vessels and viscera must dominate every symphony of personal identity.

Recent developments in diagnostic techniques in modern medi-

In passing, I would like to refer to the wonderful way in which these whales realize at a great distance, if the slightest sound be made, the presence of danger. I do not use the word "hear," because so abnormally small are their organs of hearing, the external opening being quite difficult to find, that I do not believe they *can* hear at all well. But I firmly believe they possess another sense by means of which they are able to detect any unusual vibration of the waves of either air or sea at a far greater distance than it would be possible for them to hear. Whatever this power may be which they possess, all whalemen are well acquainted with their exercise of it, and always take most elaborate pre-cautions to render their approach to a whale noiseless.

Frank K. Bullen, Cruise of the Cachalot, *1875*

After many years' study of the char-acteristic habits of the Humpback, we believe that the females of this species resort in large numbers to favorite in-land waters, connected with the ocean, to bring forth their young. In their wanderings, they are addicted, more than any other rorqual, to "breaching," "bolting," and "finning." In the mating season they are noted for their amorous antics. At such times their caresses are of the most amusing and novel char-acter, and these performances have doubtless given rise to the fabulous tales of the sword fish and thrasher attacking whales. When lying by the side of each other, the megapteras frequently admin-ister alternate blows with their long fins, which love-pats may, on a still day, be heard at a distance of miles. They also rub each other with these same huge and flexible arms, rolling occasionally from side to side, and indulging in other gambols which can easier be imagined than described.

Charles M. Scammon, Marine Mammals of the Northwestern Coast of North America, *Dover 1968*

cine can give us a glimpse of the possibilities inherent in echolocating animals of higher intelligence. The adoption of sonar imagings of the organs within the human body has vastly extended our own capacities in medical diagnosis. For example:

Echoes from the brain, the heart, the kidneys, the liver, and the reproductive organs are now easily obtained, and provide unique information that has been unobtainable by exploratory surgery or sophisticated radiographic techniques. Sonar procedures are non-invasive and therefore do not alter physiology, as do most of our previous diagnostic techniques. The unique properties of sound make it possible to detect foreign bodies the size of dust particles within the globe of the eye and to differentiate between benign cysts and malignant tumors. The placental souffle in the earliest stages of pregnancy can be easily heard with the Doppler echoes. The flow of blood through the microscopic capillaries of the finger is heard as a veritable roar. Motion of the heart valves is now best evaluated by using sonar.

Consider what exchanges of personal information may be possible between intelligent acoustic creatures. Each dolphin has to be con-stantly aware of the internal workings of the other if for no other reason than personal identification. From what is now known about resolving capabilities of the dolphin's sonar and from certain well established principles of physiologic morphology of internal organs and tissues, it is reasonable to assume that Cetaceans are aware of each other's health and general well-being. Cancers and tumors must be self-evident. Strokes and heart attacks are as obvious as moles on our skins. Equally important, and perhaps more interesting, they could be constantly aware of a considerable portion of each other's emotional state. The psychophysiological alterations of sexual arous-al, fear, depression, and excitement may be impossible to hide. Even with our relatively unsophisticated electronic gear, the physiologic alterations accompanying these emotional states can easily be meas-ured. Analogy could be made to the simple human lie detector which monitors only a handful of superficial variables, such as heart and respiratory rate.

To Cetaceans, then, there would be another order of magnitude of visualizable information, and another cultural experience to bring to bear on their meanings. What sort of candor might exist between individuals where feelings are instantly and constantly bared? It would be irrelevant to hide, to lie, or to deny one's feelings.

Perhaps dolphins pick up similar vibrations from their prey, from species neighbors, or from us. What do they think of us? Maybe, they do not even care. We do not care except on that thin tangent between our two spheres when we pass dead fish parts into their mouths at a marine circus or consider them as models for new machinery.

142

PART FOUR

DISCOVERY
AND
RESPONSE

Meeting the Great Blue Whale

In 1850, Dr. J. D. B. Stillman of San Diego made a voyage to Realejo, Central America, on the ship *Plymouth*. On the way, the crew encountered a great blue whale which followed the ship for twenty-four consecutive days. Dr. Stillman wrote the following account of their encounter in his journal.

NOVEMBER 13: *We are witnesses of a very remarkable exhibition of the social disposition of the whale. A week ago today, we passed several, and during the afternoon it was discovered that one of them continued to follow us, and was becoming more familiar, keeping under the ship and only coming out to breathe. A great deal of uneasiness was felt, lest in his careless gambols he might unship our rudder, or do us some other damage. It was said that bilge-water would drive him off, and the pumps were started, but to no purpose. At length more violent means were resorted to; volley after volley of rifle-shots were fired into him, billets of wood, bottles, etc., were thrown upon his head with such force as to separate the integument; to all of which he paid not the slightest attention, and he still continued to swim under us, keeping our exact rate of speed, whether in calm or storm, and rising to blow almost into the cabin windows. He seems determined to stay with us until he can find better company. His length is about eighty feet; his tail measures about twelve feet across; and in the calm, as we look down into the transparent water, we see him in all his huge proportions.*

NOVEMBER 29: *The bark* Kirkwood *hove in sight, and bore down to speak to us. When off a mile or two to leeward, our whale left us and went to her, but returned soon after. He showed great restlessness last night; and to-day, whenever we stood off on the outward tack, he kept close below us, and rose just under our quarter, and most commonly to windward, to blow. But whenever we stood toward the land he invariably hung back and showed discontent. This afternoon he left us. It is now twenty-four days since he attached himself to us, and during that time he has followed us as faithfully as a dog an emigrant's wagon. At first we abused him in every way that our ingenuity could devise to drive him off, lest he might do us some mischief; but, save some scratches he received from our ship's coppering, and numerous sloughing sores, caused by the balls that had been fired into him, no damage was received by either of us from his close companionship, though our*

white paint was badly stained by the impurity of his breath. We long since ceased our efforts to annoy him, and had become attached to him as to a dog. We had named him 'Blowhard,' and even fancied, as we called him, that he came closer under our quarter, when I felt like patting his glabrous sides, and saying: 'Good old fellow.' As the water grew shoaler he left us, with regret unfeigned on our part, and apparently so on his. This story of the whale is so remarkable, that were there not so many witnesses, I would not venture to tell it, lest I be accused of exaggeration. There were a number of experienced whale-men among our passengers, who said the animal was a 'Sulphur-bottom.'

From Marine Mammals of the Northwestern Coast of North America, *by Charles M. Scammon, Dover*

A Personal Connection

Tom Hill is a poet who offers these words to explain his relationship with whales.

You asked about my friendship with the whale, and all I can say is that it has been smoldering in my memory and unconscious for many years ever since I saw a film in grammer school showing the mass butchering and slaughter of whales on a factory ship, including a pregnant female. I have never forgotten those scenes or my horror at the impersonal cutting of the blubber or the draining of the vats of still-warm blood. The whale being outwitted and hunted by technology and human greed. But I suppose the germinal point where all of this coalesced for me was my initial listening to the song by Judy Collins, "Farewell to Tarwathie." Not only the loneliness conveyed, but the undercurrent of whales singing, calling out into the sea for their images, for their species. "Songs of the Humpback Whale," of course, and what I have mentioned about the unconscious pull of the whale, his voice like an echo of my own somewhere far in the labyrinth, the fibers turning to his own mass with empathy. I cannot separate myself from the whale, he is my other identity.

In the early days of whaling, the captain's log book contained a record of whales killed, each one marked by a stamp like this one.

Gregory Bateson, Ph.D., is an anthropologist, psychologist, and biologist. He was married to and worked with Margaret Mead in the South Pacific in the 1930s and 1940s. The author of Steps to an Ecology of Mind, he is currently teaching at Cowell College at the University of California at Santa Cruz. Dr. Bateson worked with John Lilly in St. Thomas on the early dolphin communication studies, and later with Tap and Karen Pryor at Sea Life Park in Hawaii in the 1960s. Dr. Bateson feels that ten years of intelligent investigation of Cetacean relationships would produce interesting and useful results. At age seventy, he considers that task up to someone else.

GREGORY BATESON
Observations of a Cetacean Community

The pool at Whaler's Cove at Sea Life Park is a free-formed, cement-lined sheet of water about two hundred by one hundred feet. In this pool is a 5/8 scale model of the whaling ship *Essex* with large port holes on both sides, below decks. The water immediately around the *Essex* is about twenty-five feet deep, and the animals spend most of their time in this.

Five times a day, six days a week, seven dolphins, all of whom have Hawaiian names, give shows for the public, each show lasting about thirty minutes. In these shows the animals are trained to act in a concerted manner, e.g. (a) all jump; (b) all swim at the surface patting the surface with their tails; (c) all race; (d) all spin (except two *Stenellas*, who only jump); (e) all dance the "hula." The animals receive almost the whole of their food (smelt) during these performances, fish being thrown in to reward each activity.

Preliminary observation of this community was carried on through a period of about three weeks. When observers (Barrie Gilbert and the writer) were reasonably sure of their ability to identify the animals, formal recording was begun on October 28, 1964. Recorded observations of the group were spread over a period of twenty-seven days from October 28 through November 24, 1964, when one animal (Haole) was removed from the community for

146

special training. Almost all of the observation was done through the port holes of the *Essex*.

Observation was focused upon data which might answer the following questions:

1. How does each animal act when alone?
2. Which animals interact in pairs?
3. What is the content of this paired interaction? Who does what in the dyadic relationship?
4. What triads go together and in what formations?
5. What more complex groupings are observable?
6. Are the simpler groupings derivable from the more complex?

A notebook was prepared in which a separate space was allotted for:

(a) Each of the seven animals alone;
(b) Each of the twenty-one dyads;
(c) Each of the thirty-five possible triads.

The corpus of data was then searched for items appropriate to each of the sixty-three spaces (seven animals, plus twenty-one dyads plus thirty-five triads). These items were then summarized so that each space finally contained what had been recorded about that particular individual or relationship. When this was done, it was found that relationships occurred with very unequal frequency. The dyad, Akamai-Lei, was described by thirty entries, while the relationship Akamai-Haole had only three entries (in all of which Haole was an aggressor). Among the triad groupings, Haole-Limu-Mamao had thirty-eight entries, while thirteen of the possible thirty-five triads had five entries or less, and another thirteen were never recorded at all.

All this is strong primary evidence for *organization* within the community.

In order to obtain any measure of the more fleeting phenomena, observers paid special attention to rare events at the expense of the more routine and familiar. Thus, while the notes show thirty entries for Akamai-Lei and only three entries for Akamai-Haole, the total time that Akamai and Lei spent in interaction was probably several hundred times greater than the total time spent together by Akamai and Haole.

The Animals

It is convenient to introduce the animals one by one.

KAHILI (*Stenella attenuata*, male). This is the largest animal of the seven and certainly the most powerful. During the period of the observation he was rarely alone for any considerable time. He would, however, make frequent trips to the shallow area of the pool and there rub his belly on the bottom. In many of these trips he was unaccompanied. When otherwise alone he would occasionally stay briefly suspended at the surface with his blowhole out and his body hanging down at an angle of about 45°. He would usually break off this withdrawal with "impatient" behavior—jumping and the like. He was only once observed to play with bits of seaweed at the surface. Following the removal of Haole from the community, Kahili spent almost all of his time (except during the shows and when in sleep formation) suspended at the surface with his beak pointing to the wall and his back to the pool. In this withdrawal he resembled Moki.

LEI (*Stenella attenuata*, female). This animal was frequently alone but for rather brief periods. When observed alone she usually had the appearance of cruising around in search of a partner. When alone for a longer period, she was usually occupied in playing with bits of seaweed or other toys. When so engaged, if another animal approached, she would often continue to play rather than go with the other animal.

MOKI (*Delphinus rosiventris*, male). This animal spent about ninety percent of his time (when not in shows) suspended at the surface with his beak pointing toward the feeding station on the *Essex*. From time to time he would suddenly jump in place or dash off and make a few jumps and return to his suspended position.

AKAMAI (*Delphinus rosiventris*, male). When not with Lei, this animal is usually alone. When alone he cruises rather aimlessly (not obviously searching for a partner and rarely giving impatient jumps). When not cruising he hangs suspended near the *Essex* feeding station, close to Moki, but without any visible interchange with that animal.

HAOLE (male)—MAMAO (female)—LIMU (male). These animals are all *Delphinus rosiventris*. In the study we refer to them as the "remainder triad." They are those animals who are not withdrawn like Akamai or Moki, and are not *Stenellas*. These three spinners are alike in being rarely alone. Mamao especially is a restless female and is almost always in company. She is much more active in her body rubbing and flipper-fluke rubbing than the other animals. Haole is the largest of the spinners.

The Dyadic Relationships

The dyadic relationships were sometimes symmetrical, sometimes complementary. The following lists the various types of "transactions" observed between pairs of animals:

SYMMETRICAL TRANSACTIONS

1. *A and B swim together slowly, side by side.* In this transaction there is usually synchronization of approaches to the surface (i.e., synchronization of respiration), and often almost precise synchrony of locomotor movements. The transaction may continue for a few sec-

onds or for many minutes. In some cases, this transaction is accompanied by bodily contact which may be symmetrical: A and B swimming with their inside flippers in continuous contact. In other cases, A may swim with one flipper touching B. Contact of any kind is rare when the animals are cruising together asleep.

2. *A and B swim together fast.* This transaction is rarely recorded in our sample of data, but is more common than this fact would indicate. In this transaction, identification of the animal is difficult and records in which the animals are not identified were not used in the sample. The transaction is often accompanied by progressive synchronized jumping, i.e., the sort of jumping in which the animal travels a smooth arc, re-entering the water beak first, as distinct from vertical jumping in which the animal merely flops back into the water.

COMPLEMENTARY TRANSACTIONS

1. *Coitus.* This was recorded in the sample seventeen times. In all these cases, the male Kahili was one of the partners. On one occasion, the female Mamao was observed to act in the male role in relation to Kahili, but on another occasion she took the normal female position. (In addition to these seventeen cases, there is one case outside the sample in which Akamai had relations with Lei.)

Typically, the acting male first chases the acting female (Lei, Mamao, Haole, or Limu), and this chase may be either brief or long and complex. The chased animal may dodge with sudden turns and twists. (In the case of Kahili-Mamao, when Kahili was acting as male, the chase took a special shape. Mamao held her peduncle rigidly bent to one side, while Kahili pushed against the outside of this bend with his melon thereby pushing the other. In this way, the two animals traveled at high speed in great curves thirty to fifty feet long. After four or five such swoops, Kahili approached and copulated with a series of thrusts. More usually, the animal who was chased supplied his or her own locomotive power.)

At the end of the chase, the acting female commonly becomes quite passive—like a log—and the male pushes the body quite gently toward the surface. At intromission the acting female is typically near the surface, belly downward. The male comes in belly up from behind the female and the underside of his head first contacts her peduncle. From this position he slides forward until the genitalia of the two animals are opposed. Close contact is then maintained for several seconds during which the male gives a short series of pelvic thrusts. Following this the animals separate. The penis is usually not visible until the moment of separation.

Exceptionally (in the case of Kahili-Mamao) this copulatory position is reversed. In this case, Mamao came under Kahili and it was her body that moved rhythmically against his pelvic region.

Actual coitus is commonly both preceded and followed by a number of the transactions listed below: rubbing of various kinds, beak-genital propulsion, etc. But these transactions also occur independent of coitus.

It will be noted that in this community copulatory activity occurs both heterosexually and between males. Such activity was not observed between the two females (Lei and Mamao), though these two animals may engage in beak-genital propulsion and other transactions which might seem to be related to sex.

2. *Threat.* This transaction is clearly recognizable as incipient attack and is *always* characterized by suddenness. A may make a sudden lunge toward B, or may turn his head suddenly toward B with mouth open, or A may suddenly hit B with a fluke or with his beak. Threat is commonly accompanied by sound (audible even in the hold of the *Essex*).

The roles of threat are not reversible. In no case does the sample record that any animal was threatened by another whom he had threatened at any time during the sample period. In the sample period we have records of thirty-three threats, distributed as shown in Figure 1. This distribution of threat indicates a rather clear system of ascendancy. Not only are the roles of threat irreversible between any two animals, but the relationship defined by threat is transitive: If A

Figure 1. Threat

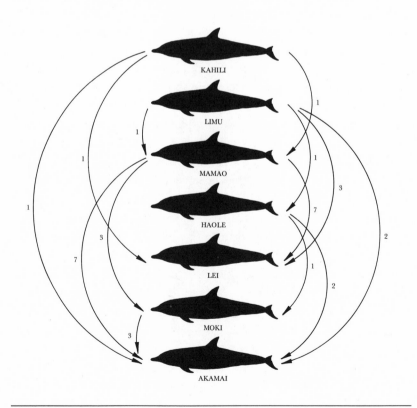

150

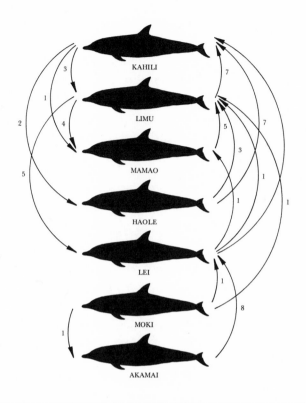

Figure 2. Beak-Genital Propulsion

threatened B, and B threatens C, then C does not threaten A.

This ordering of the animals is therefore used in this report for the exhibition of other distributions. It will be noted, however, that the position of Lei is unclear. She never threatened anybody, and it is therefore possible that she might be in any of the positions below Mamao. A similar ambiguity occurs in the relation between Mamao and Haole, neither of whom threatened the other.

(Allowing for these ambiguities, the probability of such a transitive ordering of random arrows over a population of seven animals is approximately 1/128,000.)

3. *Beak-genital propulsion.* In this transaction, A places his beak, usually closed, in the genital orifice of B. B then becomes quite still, ceasing to make locomotor movements, and A gently propels B. This may last for a distance of fifty to sixty feet and the propulsion may be straight or may follow a curved or circular path. Usually the contact is broken from time to time, and A will then replace his beak in the other's genitals and start over. The transaction, though complementary, is partly reversible, i.e., A may propel B and a few seconds later B will be propelling A. The diagram (Figure 2) shows this partial reversibility and intransitivity. It appears that beak propulsion is most commonly rendered by animals of lower ascend-

ancy to animals of higher ascendancy (thirty-five arrows point up, while sixteen arrows point down).

4. *Body rubbing.* This behavior is very varied in form, ranging from momentary body contact to long rubs which go the whole length of the body of one or both animals. It is often impossible to form an opinion which animal is the more active in seeking or initiating the contact.

5. *Fluke or flipper rubbing.* Here again behavior may take many forms. The rubbing may be addressed to any part of the recipient's body and may take the form of a smooth rubbing, or repetitive patting, or continuous contact.

6. *Pat-a-cake.* This is a peculiar "game" or "acrobatic stunt" in which A swims upside-down under B. The two animals then actively rub their flippers together. First the palmar surface of A's flipper meets the dorsal surface of B's flipper; then the dorsal surface of A's flipper meets the palmar surface of B's; and so on alternatively. Occasionally two animals will do this with all four flippers actively and rapidly rubbing.

7. *Chase.* This phenomenon expectedly is ambiguous. On the one hand a short chase may follow threat, and on the other hand chase may precede coitus. However, neither of these types of threat explain the distribution of the phenomenon among the seven ani-

Figure 3. Chase

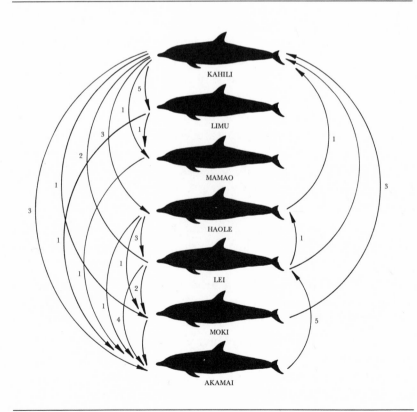

152

mals. This distribution is shown in Figure 3. Here, while the majority of items (twenty-seven) indicate that the chaser is ascendant to the chased, in a very considerable number of instances (eight) the reverse was true.

It is possible that a third category of "chase" (other than chase associated with coitus and threat) occurs which would be essentially symmetrical rather than complementary—some sort of playful and/or competitive racing. We have a number of instances in which after A has chased B, either B will chase A or the two animals will cruise slowly together. These sequences would support a hypothesis of this kind.

The Sleep Formation

It has not been practical to study the community at night, owing to the difficulty of identifying animals by moonlight and the extreme disturbance of behavior which follows artificial lighting. Moonlight observation, however, reveals a great deal of activity. What is here called the "sleep formation" was never observed at night.

However, the animals are regularly and predictably in this formation in the early morning. They usually wake and break formation in the early morning. They usually wake and break formation between 0830 and 0900 hours.

In contrast to the extreme complexity of interaction when the animals are awake, their sleep habits and the formation in which they sleep are simple and regular.

1. *The nuclear group*. Five animals (Kahili, Lei, Haole, Mamao and Limu) sleep together, slowly circling, usually clockwise. Occasionally, without change of formation, they cut across the diameter of the circle which they are following and reverse their direction. In these reversals, the formation is not disrupted. This group of five animals consists of the two *Stenellas* (Kahili and Lei) and three of the spinners (Mamao, Haole, and Limu). The two *Stenellas* cruise side by side, usually with Mamao on the inside going clockwise. Occasionally a single animal will go to the surface for a breath and immediately return to position in the formation. More usually, the pair of *Stenellas* rises to the surface together regularly at the same point on the circle, and the three spinners rise together but at a different point. After each such rise, the relation between the pair and the triad is re-established.

2. *Akamai*. The relation between this animal and the nuclear group of five is difficult to interpret. He is clearly not of the group. But while they circle in sleep formation, Akamai moves rather vaguely about two or three lengths ahead of them. He is clearly not leading them. Rather he appears to take his cues from them and follows a slow and rather irregular pathway, occasionally adjusting

himself to get back to the position ahead of them. His respiration is not synchronized with that of either the pair or the triad.

3. *Moki*. Moki sleeps by himself, suspended at the surface, with his back to everybody.

The relationship between the two species in the nuclear group of the sleep formation is of extreme interest. That these differing species should combine together, even in captivity and in such a formal manner, is surprising.

It is already clear to us that any future attempt to analyze the social organization of a school of Cetaceans in the wild should begin with a study of their sleep formation.

4. *The sleep formation governs the occurrence of triadic groups in this community.* To understand what this means it is first necessary to describe briefly the behavior of dolphins in groups of three. If three dolphins are to stay together, there is only one thing that they ever do: They swim slowly side by side with occasional contact between them if they are awake. Our dissected data contained one hundred twenty-nine entries which refer to triads. Of these about half are records of swimming slowly side by side. The remainder are brief narratives in which, for example, a third animal approaches a pair and either interacts briefly with one member of that pair or disrupts the pair and swims away with one of the members. We have no record of three animals swimming fast side by side, and it seems that this is a dyadic activity.

5. *Active* interaction between dolphins is fundamentally a dyadic affair. The important and most frequent dyadic relationships in the community are:

a. *Kahili-Lei*. This is an intra-species heterosexual pair. They swim together quietly and have coitus from time to time. They rarely engage in "playful" activities.

b. *Kahili-Mamao, Kahili-Haole, Kahili-Limu*. These are Kahili's other dyadic relationships—pairings in which Kahili goes with one or other of the spinners in the Nuclear Sleep Group. With each of these he has been seen to engage in copulatory activity.

c. *Lei-Akamai*. (Lei's other dyadic relationship.) Lei also plays with Akamai, the spinner at the bottom of the ascendancy list, who is *not* a member of the Nuclear Group, and is the receiver of eleven of the thirty-three recorded threats. Coitus has once been observed in this relationship (during the period of preliminary observation). However, the relationship is very different from Lei's relationship to Kahili. It is characterized by much beak propulsion in which it is always Akamai who propels Lei, and by much chasing in which either animal may chase the other. On one occasion these two spent nearly thirty minutes playing together with a floating stick. (This is our only long example of two animals with one toy.)

6. Lei goes rather rarely with other males of the Nuclear Group. She is threatened rather often by Mamao, the only other female, but she also does some long slow cruising side by side with her.

7. The notes on the triad, Akamai-Kahili-Lei, include nine entries and indicate a complex but not overtly hostile relationship. In one instance, the three animals swam slowly together, Akamai's flipper touching Kahili, while Kahili's flipper touched Lei. On two or three occasions it appears that Kahili tried to get Lei away from Akamai, but failed and left them together. In two chases (Kahili going after Akamai) it appears that Kahili "pulls his punches," e.g., by swimming upside-down.

8. One possible synthesis covering these relationships would suggest that Kahili's ascendancy is most meaningful within the Nuclear Sleep Group, and that Lei's relationship with Akamai is permitted precisely because he is outside this group. Conversely we might predict that if Akamai should succeed in joining the Nuclear Group (and he has once been seen to join the three spinners in it quietly while they slept), he would have to forego his relationship with Lei.

9. Moki's position is not adequately described by saying that he is last-but-one on the ascendancy list. As already mentioned, he sleeps by himself and spends most of his time in his sleeping position even when clearly awake. When not withdrawn in this way, he is a rather active animal. He joins actively in the shows, competes with others for food, and once even chased Kahili three times in one morning. He has twice been seen to slip in among the spinners and briefly join them while they slept.

10. Material on *Tursiops truncatus* from St. Thomas indicates that in this species also, while some animals sleep as a group slowly cruising, others may sleep alone, stationary, or suspended at the surface. No animal has been seen to circle while sleeping *alone*. We badly need information about sleep in the wild. We may guess that slow circling is an efficient way of maintaining a watch against sharks and other dangers. In such circling only one eye need be open to maintain a watch in all directions. But perhaps a group of animals is necessary to maintain the navigation in a circle; so that one animal sleeping by himself would have to remain stationary.

This raises the question of what happens to animals like Kahili or Moki who, for one reason or another, withdraw to sleep stationary by themselves in nature. Can an animal survive in the wild if he regularly sleeps alone and stays alone in this way suspended when awake? How would he maintain contact with the school?

The Removal of Haole
The meaning of this solitary stationary withdrawal is somewhat

illuminated by what happened when Haole was withdrawn from the pool for special training. A summary of these events follows:

Haole was removed, on a sudden decision, in the late afternoon of the day before Thanksgiving. The observers first heard that this had occurred after dark on the following day and the first observations were conducted early the next morning—some forty hours after the removal. By then, a definite pattern was established, which persisted until Haole was returned to the pool a week later.

The sleep formation appeared to be undisturbed. Kahili and Lei circled slowly as usual but above two spinners (Mamao and Limu) instead of three. Akamai and Moki were in their usual places. As the animals awoke, however, it became clear that things had changed. Kahili was no longer the vigorous active animal that we were familiar with. He went over to a position facing the wall of the pool and hung there suspended. From time to time, he would make a sudden move—like Moki—but would always return to his withdrawal. Several times Lei circled round him slowly—but he did not join her. The remainder of the animals acted in their usual relationships. Akamai and Lei still went together. But the group as a whole was lethargic and the trainers complained that the shows were very poor, some animals not participating and others lethargically doing only half what they should.

Haole, himself, was miserable and refused to accept food from the hand. He could not be given the special training which was planned. Another animal (a young *Tursiops*) was put with him to reduce his aloneness but he continued to be miserable. Finally he was returned to the pool lest he become sick.

Following his return, Haole immediately performed with unusual vigor in the shows. Between shows, Haole cruised with Limu. Kahili became unusually vigorous with Mamao and the sleep pattern went back to normal.

There is no evidence that Kahili's relationship with Haole was any more important than his relationship with the other two spinners in the remainder triad. He associated with all these animals and engaged in copulatory activity with all at various times, while Lei was playing with Akamai. We could not have predicted that the removal of Haole would especially disturb Kahili.

The geometry of the sleep formation, however, suggests that what happened was that Kahili lost not only Haole, but also, in effect, all three of his spinner companions. As long as there were three spinners in the Nuclear Group, Lei could join Akamai, and Kahili could then play with whichever of the spinner triad was unpaired. After Haole was removed, there was never an unpaired spinner member of the Nuclear Group. Akamai was with Lei, Moki was as usual non-social, and Kahili had no companion. Such an interpretation would

156

suggest either that Kahili's ascendancy is not sufficient for him to succeed in breaking up a pair of spinners who want to stay together, or that his ascendancy is not of such a kind as would lead him to attempt to break them up.

Learning: About and From Them—A Discourse

When Barrie Gilbert and I did the study in 1964 we had no idea whether it would apply to animals in the wild. But in 1970 it was born out by the observations of wild spinners in Captain Cook's Bay. It seems that the pattern in which porpoises rest is a diagram of the social order of the group. So if you go watching porpoises at sea, try to watch the rest patterns to get the social order.

It's usually dangerous to extrapolate from behavioral material on captive animals, especially material on their social organization. The problem of organizing seven animals in a pool is of course very different from organizing a bunch of animals in the open ocean. Time and space are different, competition is different. In many cases they are not even the same species. And the Whaler's Cove animals were all performing animals. However, we did get out of them one thing which I believe to be of first importance. What we got was a pattern in which they rest. I say rest, not sleep, because we don't know whether they sleep or not. Sleep is a very obscure matter with porpoises.

What we discovered was that if you go to the tank before 9:00 A.M., you find the animals in a regular formation, going round and round, slowly. And that formation is unvarying, the same animals in approximately the same positions every day. If you begin to think about it, it becomes quite obvious. The formation is the statement of order, of protocol—the ethological formation, so to speak. You can think of it as the diagram of relations. Now, if you look at them during the middle of the day when they are all playing and fooling around, you would never get the picture. But once you have the picture and then look at the play, the play starts making sense.

As for the function of the rest pattern, I had the idea that it had to do with keeping a 360° watch on what's happening. John Lilly did a piece of research which he never published on dolphin sleep. He put a couple of watchmen on a dolphin in a small plastic tank like a bathtub. One watchman was on one side, the other watchman was on the other, and they were to record when the dolphin's eye was closed, to record each eye separately and also both together. It's very difficult to do in a big tank—I couldn't do it at all. But what they found was approximately this: that the dolphin closed both eyes in a twenty-four-hour period for a total of five minutes or less. What the dolphins do is to close one eye for five or ten minutes, then close the other eye for five or ten minutes. Each separate eye is closed for something like three or four hours in twenty-four hours. The suggestion is that somehow they sleep unilaterally.

My idea, as I said, is that this has to do with keeping a 360° watch on what is happening. You see, if you are moving in a circle, which is what the porpoises at Whaler's Cove were doing, and you've got one eye open, whichever side the eye is open is maintaining a 360° watch. What I suspect is that in this circle there were always several single eyes open, going round and round.

So after you see the sleep pattern, you begin looking at the play and you ask, "Well, who goes with whom and what is happening?" and "What other tensions are there in the situation?" and so on. Then you begin to see a lot of things. To summarize it: there were seven animals and the circle they were going in in the rest pattern was about twenty or thirty feet in diameter, not very big. There were two animals on top, three animals under them. They rose to get air but dropped back into formation after they breathed. The two on top breathed simultaneously, and then the three breathed simultaneously. In addition, we had one animal who would be out in front somewhere, who was looking over his shoulder all the time to see if the others were following him. He was not in the group and wanted to be.

Kahili, a *Stenella*, was the lead animal. He traveled with Lei, the other *Stenella*. Under them traveled the three spinners. They were two different species. Who was inside or outside was not an issue, and every now and then they would make a figure eight and start going the reverse way. The three spinners were Limu, Mamao, and Haole.

We kept statistics about who was going with whom. What we found was that the three spinners were a pattern and the two *Stenellas* were a pattern, except that Lei had a daytime thing with another dolphin, Akamai. In the daytime she would go off and play with him, and Kahili would get one of the three spinners to play with, regardless of sex. There was a lot of screwing regardless of sex, too.

There was also Moki. Moki, a spinner, spent most of his time facing the cemented-down scale model of the *Essex*, hanging in a resting position of 45°. He didn't move, he hung out. There was a slight rotation in the water so Moki drifted with the rotation. When he woke up, he moved back to his position near the *Essex*.

Well, during the day Lei would go off and play with Akamai, and Kahili would go and pick one of the three spinners. Then one day the trainers took out Haole, one of the three spinners, to give him special training, to teach him to wear a lei around his neck. As a result, there was a dyad among the spinners and not a triad. Kahili couldn't get a spinner to play with when Lei was with Akamai. He then hung out and sulked, facing the drain, until Haole came back.

This original pattern of organization lasted six or eight weeks. Then Limu, one of the spinners, hung himself accidentally. There was a rope hanging down from the boat. He started playing with it and got his tail twisted in it, dropping his head in the water, and he drowned. That was the end of the study.

What landed me in porpoise research originally was a piece of a scientific magazine that said that the big-brained animals were not so bright. The elephants had never invented matchboxes . . . the big brain was all a fad. I got a little angry with this and wrote a letter to John Lilly, whom I hardly knew, who was in the West Indies then. I said, look, let's twist this guy's tail. Am I not right that the personal relationships among these fellows, the porpoises, are where the complications come in, where they use their big brains? And once you start using your brains on personal relationships, you've got a competitive situation because you have sex included, and you are going to evolve in the direction of bigger and bigger brains. Not for catching fish—any shark can catch fish—but for leadership purposes, for influencing the group.

That's why the Whaler's Cove study interested me, because it was a way of drawing a base line to begin to see what was happening within a group. Without some idea of the essential order, you can't begin to see other subtleties and complexities.

It is pretty obvious that dolphins and porpoises have a very strong sense of manners, of what they consider to be appropriate behavior. One story of dolphin ethics is George Hunt's story about Sissy, a porpoise in the West Indies. John Lilly wanted to make a film of a porpoise rescuing a human being in the water. So George gets in the water and pretends to be in distress. Sissy comes over and rescues him by pushing him to the side. Lilly is filming this, but when he looks at the camera he finds that the cap is still on the lens. So he takes the cap off the lens and sends George back into the water. When George pretends to be in distress again, Sissy beats him up.

About "language," I'm sure the clicks and whistles made by the porpoises do not say the kinds of things we say. I don't think they're concerned with talking about *things*. I think they're concerned with talking about relationships: the nuances of love and hate and respect which are talked about by land mammals with hair and facial expression and tail and body posture. It's like kinesics, the language of body movement. Kinesics is not talking about things, kinesics is talking about you and me.

Drs. Rice and Kellogg were trying to teach dolphins to discriminate between circles and triangles, hearts and squares. They began by showing these shapes to Paddy the dolphin above water. Then they showed the shapes to Paddy under the water. When the shapes were learned in the air and then tested in the water, Paddy did very poorly. When the patterns were learned in the water and then tested in the air, Paddy did fine and could tell the difference between the figures whether they were right side up, sideways, or upside-down.

Drs. Rice and Kellogg discovered that Paddy was pretty good at discriminating patterns that had no meaning for him when he became familiar with them in his natural world. He *could* learn them when they were presented to him out of his natural habitat, but he did best when he could relax underwater and learn. They found that the context in which learning takes place was as important as the material to be learned.

Peter Warshall

Now an important point is that the creodont mammals, from which the porpoises were presumably descended, were four-footed, hairy, land mammals, and probably had the kinesics of a dog or cat at least. No doubt they used their external ears, the hair on the back of their necks, the direction of their eyes, probably contractions of the face muscles, or at least contractions of the lips, to show fangs, a tail, all the stuff that a mammal shows, especially eye direction. They took to the ocean and they steadily lost all these things, their hair, their external ears, the mobile face. Their eyes became invisible at more than twenty feet, and they started developing sound. And obviously all that whistling and croaking and creeking has to do with communication, with how the animal shows itself to others. I think *that's* the elaboration of dolphin language or communication— the expression of relationship.

I think there is something very important for people who are swimming with porpoises to know; and that is, that certainly when you are in the water with a porpoise you are not in the position you are with a dog or a cat. A dog or cat takes a filial position with you, puts you in the position of parent or leader or whatever, and you get all the begging for food, and so on, that dogs and cats do. You don't get that when you are in the water with a porpoise, because you are the child and the porpoise is the parent. Now if you are the swimmer and you can accept being the child and let the porpoise teach you, there is a lot you can learn about being a porpoise. Usually people think they learn about an animal by raising it, by becoming its parent. But then you are in a false situation, you are doing the leading. If you let the animal do the leading, the teaching, you will find out a lot more about the animal.

Then there's the very real question of the boredom tolerance level of porpoises. There seems to be a point at which the porpoise or dolphin seems to have had enough and won't perform in a situation, whether it's experimental or not. One psychologist set up a reversal learning study in Florida. The question was whether the animal could learn to learn. There was a straight pipe and an L-shaped pipe, and one pipe meant "do this," and the other pipe meant "do that." If you did the right thing you got rewarded, if you didn't, you didn't. Then when the porpoise knew clearly what it was supposed to do—to differentiate between the straight pipe and the L-shaped pipe—the trainer reversed the signals, so that the L-shaped pipe now meant this, and the straight pipe meant that. In such an experiment, you've got to have a criterion of how many times the porpoise has to be right—to do the right thing—in order to permit you to say, "He now knows." Obviously, it's not enough to get it right once. The criterion was set, I think, at fifteen times. This was much too long and the porpoise got bored. The psychologist had gone off to New York and left an assistant to do the experiment and take notes. But she was never able to get the porpoise to go to fifteen times, because somewhere along the line it would do it wrong. And she said to me, "You know, it makes a funny noise when it does it wrong." And I said, "Have you recorded the noise?" And she said, "No, he (the psychologist) didn't ask for that." So, to this day we don't know the porpoise for "go to hell."

I don't think Skinnerian conditioning has anything to do with how or why porpoises do what they do. I don't think you can condition them that way; I'm not even sure you can condition anything that way.

When I arrived in Hawaii at Sea Life Park in 1964, the trainers were putting on a performance for the public in which they were demonstrating "Skinnerian psychology." When I arrived there the trainers were showing the public how they train a porpoise. The trainer says to the audience, "You see, the porpoise is in the holding tank. When I have the animal come into the performing tank, I will watch her, and when she does something I want her to repeat, I will blow the whistle. She knows what the whistle means, and she'll come over and I'll give her a fish. Then she will repeat whatever it was I marked with the whistle."

You can do this with a porpoise in three or four minutes. So the animal comes on and the trainer watches it. It does something the trainer calls something—"a behavior"—and she blows the whistle. The porpoise gets the fish, and repeats the "behavior," maybe a couple of times, and that's the exhibit of Skinnerian conditioning. The public can see how the porpoise is taught to do that particular thing. Well, there are five shows a day, six days a week, so what are you going to do the next show? The porpoise could come onstage and do that for which it was rewarded the last time it came on stage. But then you would be cheating, you would not be teaching the public how this works. You have to have a new bit of behavior. And when I first saw the show, the porpoise was doing this, providing a new "piece of behavior" when she came on stage, and not particularly repeating the one before.

Now, I looked at this and said, that's very interesting indeed, because that's the next level of learning. After she learned to *do this particular thing* on signal she has got to learn to do something in a *category*, a category which includes the negative—a "not this"—the behavior for which she received the earlier reward. So I put my associate Karen Pryor and a psychologist on to the idea, and they got a little money and did a little research and repeated the whole thing and recorded it.

The work was set up so that there would be training sessions which would last about ten minutes, and in each session a "new" piece of behavior would be required and the trainer would not reward the old behavior. Well, in, let's say, the eighth session, the porpoise would spend seven or eight minutes doing the thing that she had been rewarded for before, in the seventh session, and not getting rewarded for it, and getting more and more impatient and annoyed. Then, about two-thirds through the session the porpoise would more or less accidentally do something the trainer could call a "new" piece of behavior—a way of making a fluke or a sideways leap— and the trainer would blow the whistle and the porpoise would repeat the new item for the reward.

She would then come to the next session and first do the thing she had done in the immediately previous session. Between the fourteenth and fifteenth sessions, the porpoise got all excited, splashing and jumping and carrying on in her holding tank. And when she was let into the stage for the fifteenth session, she immediately did twelve absolutely brand new pieces of behavior.

There is always a jump, a discontinuity between information of one logical type and information of the next logical type. So the learning has to be a sort of jump. The porpoise had to jump from "learn" to "to learn"; from learning about an instance, to learning about a class, and it's a logical-illogical situation because the porpoise can't do it from a single sample. She can only do it from the structure of a complex sample; therefore, it's the next logical type up.

The other thing about the story is that the trainer never did obey the rules, and *would* not. Because the porpoise would get frustrated, and at a certain point the trainer would toss a fish. And if you think about it, the trainer has to toss a fish because otherwise the porpoise thinks that the relationship with the trainer is out of order. Nobody loves me, the trainer doesn't love me. It was a female porpoise and a female trainer, by the way. Not only that, if you have a guru, or a psychiatrist, that you are dealing with—on the porpoise end of the relationship—you will find that the guru has to toss you an occasional fish to keep you going. Any relationship is maintained by a certain amount of unearned fish.

The late Wayne Batteau was a mathematician attached to Tufts College who was primarily interested in electronics and sound. From this interest he got into porpoises and dolphins. Wayne started a project which involved a machine he made, a box. The box would take the human voice and turn it into underwater whistles, such that the back vowels of the voice were low-pitched whistles, and the front vowel sounds were high-pitched whistles. Therefore, human words had a contour in underwater whistles. It worked very nicely. He used Hawaiian words in general, because they are full of vowels. The box couldn't do much with consonants.

With the aid of this box he would say into the microphone,

"Joe," or whatever the name of the porpoise was, and Joe would come to the station and stare at you—the experimenter. And you would then say, "do" or a word which approximately translated to "do"—"do ball." "Do ball" meant the porpoise, after the cue, should go and touch the ball. The porpoise was then stationed ready to go, waiting for the word "okay," and then would go and touch the ball, and come back.

Or you could say, "Bill" (the other porpoise), "do ball," and Bill would go through this ritual too. Or you could say "repeat." You could say, "Bill, repeat ball," in which case Bill would give you back the whistle tone of the word "ball" which you had given. He would imitate the word "ball," and not go and touch it. Now those were the only possible pair of words in the middle of the message—"do" or "repeat"—and on the end were about a dozen words of different names of actions the porpoise could perform or words he would have to repeat, and both animals could do these actions very well. They were told what course to take, but the meaning of the word "ball" depended on what the intervening word was. That's where it got interesting.

I personally am concerned with the larger gestalten and the largest units one can work with. This means not redwoods, but redwood forests; not dolphins, but pieces of ocean. I think it is fairly clear that the organization of these very large pieces must simulate *mind*. It has to be self-corrective. It has to be in the business of processing information and all that. When I called my book *The Ecology of Mind*, I wasn't kidding. I wonder how multiple ideas live together in the same housing. Therefore, I would like to know all that can be known relative to those questions. They are very valuable questions for the world to know the answers to—because most ecological sin is sin against that fact. So I would want to know something like, "If it be so that human language with its identification of things and the identification of purposes and all the rest of it leads to an epistemology in which the sensible thing is to eat the environment—and eat up the environment—then how do the dolphins structure their universe?"

They, presumably, do not have anything like language. I think they are interesting because they don't have language. The question is, what do they have and what is it like—with the presumption that it isn't going to be anything like language at all. It's going to be about relationships. It's going to be, conceivably, about their relationships, not only to other dolphins but to oceans, to geography, to navigation, to whatever they deal with.

How do you get it? That I don't know, of course. I think I would start with child-parent relationships among dolphins, which we now have a few pointers about, but very little. It looks as though the

SIX SERI WHALE SONGS

1

The sea is calm
there is no wind.
In the warm sun
I play on the surface
with many companions.
In the air spout
many clouds of smoke
& all of them are happy.

2

The mother whale is happy.
She swims on the surface, very fast.
No shark is near
but she swims over many leagues
back & forth, very fast.
Then she sinks to the bottom
& four baby whales are born.

3

First one comes up to the surface
in front of her nose.
He jumps on the surface.
Then each of the other baby whales
jumps on the surface.
Then they go down
into the deep water to their mother
& stay there eight days
before they come up again.

4

The old, old whale has no children.
She does not swim far.
She floats near the shore & is sad.
She is so old & weak
she cannot feed like other whales.
With her mouth on the surface
she draws in her breath—hrrr—
& the smallest fish & the sea birds
    are swallowed up.

5

The whale coming to shore is sick
the sharks have eaten her bowels
& the meat of her body.
She travels slowly—her bowels are gone.
She is dead on the shore
& can travel no longer.

6

Fifty sharks surrounded her.
They came under her belly
& bit off her flesh & her bowels
& so she died. Because she had no teeth
to fight the sharks.
Santo Blanco

parent-child relationship is very heavily instinctual on the child's end. This flapping along beside mama is an awfully crude reflex behavior. On top of that instinct you've got to put relationships, sounds dealing with relationship, sophistication of relationships, from a very simple, almost reflex level at bottom. This is what I would like to know about. Still, it looks as if the mother is a playpen. The baby navigates on, say, the mother's left side. And if baby is navigating on mother's left side and is pretty well in contact with her, and the mother swings left, going round and round facing to the left, then the baby is inside that circle. Every now and then the baby goes over the mother's back to the other side, and then mother swings around and goes right. Whatever else happens, she is creating a playpen there. That playpen must be a part of their universe in a deep psychological sense. Later information has to be pickled on top of the conception of the universe as constructed of a playpen like that. And probably that sleep pattern we watched at Whaler's Cove is part of that playpen. Who knows? That's where I would look, anyway.

I would also look at the relationship between swimmers and porpoises. As already stated, this is a parental, or paternal, situation vis-à-vis the swimmer, the porpoise being the parent. When I couldn't get ahold of baby porpoises, I would work on the swimmer and train the swimmers not to tell the porpoises how to behave. Swimmers have got to leave it open and let the porpoises determine the situation. Then the porpoises will really tell you things. A lot of things. You see, you must look at the spiritual playpen in order to find out what universe they live in. Then you want to extend that to knowledge of how they behave in that universe.

Obviously they've got to structure their time and space in ways that don't acknowledge named concepts. What that means, I don't know, but that's what I'd be looking for. It means giving up having hands, giving up naming objects. If you have hands you are going to name objects. Porpoises don't have hands; how lucky they are! What they have, we hardly know. We don't know anything about their navigation, which is probably one of their major intellectual efforts. We know virtually nothing about their hunting. We know they go out in these big crowds; we see the herds break up about four o'clock in the afternoon and go off into the ocean. It's quite a sight. Do they hunt together? Nobody knows. You can't follow them because if you do they'll play with the ship or run away. We are awfully anthropomorphic people. Was George Hunt being penalized for falsifying a plea for help when he tried to trick Sissy into "saving" him? We don't know. If you are going to have self-consciousness about your kinesics, then you have to have very careful devices for preventing people from using their kinesics for lying. You see, that's the point about not knowing. If people don't know what the signals are for love and hate, they can't lie about love and hate. If they know the signals, then they can lie about love and hate. Human beings are sort of on the edge of being human in this respect; they partly know and partly don't know. The porpoises probably *do* know, and probably therefore can lie. And if so, they've got to have an organization—a social order—that allows for that lying, and lying about kinesics will become for porpoises a major sin—therefore punishable. Who knows? Much of this is way out on the limb, you know.

The photographs accompanying this article were provided by David K. Caldwell and Melba C. Caldwell and were taken at Marineland of the Pacific. Although the animals shown are not the species observed by Dr. Bateson, the photographs are descriptive of Cetacean behavior and relationships.

Whales and dolphins commonly cross through the biological categories of species and genera that science imposes on them, to interact among themselves in a variety of playful and serious ways. Most of the documentation for interspecific or intergeneric behavior comes from observations made of captive Cetaceans in oceanaria or marine aquaria. Dolphins and whales in captivity show an amazing ability to reach across the ostensible barrier of species and genera to help each other in spite of the difficulties imposed by the severity of captive conditions.

The following stories have been edited from *Contributions to Science*, a publication of the Los Angeles County Museum.

Intergeneric Behavior by a Captive Pacific Pilot Whale

On March 28, 1962, the whale tank at Marineland of the Pacific oceanarium, near Los Angeles, California, contained three Pacific pilot whales and three striped dolphins. On this day, an interesting case of intergeneric behavior was observed. All of the captives were highly trained and several of the animals had been living together for over three years.

On the above date, at 11:00 a.m., we were notified that the large male pilot whale was carrying a dead striped dolphin around in the whale tank. The behavior had been noted shortly after 9:00 a.m.

At 10:10 a.m., when notes were first made, the male was resting near the bottom of the tank. He was holding the dead dolphin in his mouth by one of its tail flukes with the body resting between his pectoral fins. The male's eyes were open to approximately twice normal size, giving him a "startled" expression. After an exceptionally long interval of about 10 minutes, he rose to the surface carrying the dead animal with him. His next dive also was clocked and again the underwater interval was 10 minutes.

At 11:20 a.m. the personnel of Marineland made an attempt to retrieve the dolphin. A diver entered the tank with a spear gun. Observers stated that the two female pilot whales in the tank initially assumed a position between the descending diver and the male pilot whale.

The diver knelt behind one of the large water inlet pipes, and when the male pilot approached, succeeded in spearing the dead dolphin and quickly passed the line to other personnel on the top deck. Upon pulling on the line, they succeeded in drawing the dolphin to the surface, but the whale forcibly retrieved the body in his mouth before it could be removed from the tank. In lunging for the dolphin, the male pilot whale struck the heavy stainless steel gate in the upper part of the tank. In his excitement, the whale damaged the gate and inflicted a large abrasion on his left side about two feet long and one foot wide. At the same time, he scraped the leading edge of his dorsal fin. The diver, not having time to leave the tank, was, in the confusion, also struck a glancing blow. However, he escaped injury, and it generally was believed that the blow was not deliberate on the part of the whale.

The pilot whale snapped the ¼-inch nylon line, bent the harpoon sharply, and returned to the bottom of the tank with the dolphin. After about 10 minutes, he surfaced to breathe carrying it with him. On surfacing he again commenced to carry the dolphin, once by grasping the still-embedded harpoon in his mouth. During this period, after an attempt was made to snare the dead animal at the surface, the pilot whale then began dropping the dolphin before he surfaced for air. Upon recovery, he always took it in his mouth very gently, usually by the pectoral flipper. On two occasions he made unsuccessful attempts to take it by the snout. He also made fruitless efforts to grasp the body. On several occasions he took the caudal peduncle in his mouth and succeeded in carrying the dolphin. Once he carried the body by the dorsal fin.

At 12:00 noon, the management decided to continue the scheduled whale performance. Both large whales refused to feed. The smaller female pilot whale and the remaining dolphins performed as usual. The male pilot whale was now surfacing every half to two minutes, as opposed to the ten-minute period noted above.

When approached by a diver, the male pilot whale avoided him by circling the tank with the dolphin still in his mouth. Once, when the pilot whale surfaced for air, the dead animal was suctioned toward the outlet pipe in the center of the tank; the pilot whale quickly retrieved the body.

At 12:40 p.m., the divers again harpooned the dolphin, this time using a 3/8-inch nylon line. The dead animal was drawn to the surface once more. Again the large pilot whale seized the body before it could be removed from the tank, easily snapping the extremely strong line in the process.

At 12:50 p.m., the male pilot whale began leaving the dolphin for two or three seconds longer than necessary to breathe. Also, he left the body on the bottom and did not attempt to carry it toward the surface. The smaller female pilot whale approached the body but left when the large male returned. The other striped dolphins in the tank also approached the dead animal, but quickly swam away on the male's return. The male pilot whale now frequently rubbed his cephalic melon against the dead body, and also left the dolphin to rub his melon on the inlet pipe. By this time his eye had closed to a normal attitude. During this period he also rubbed his body slowly against the dead animal.

Both larger pilot whales refused to perform for the 1:30 p.m. show, but the small female whale and the surviving dolphins performed as usual. At 1:45 p.m., the male pilot whale attempted to lift the body with his pectoral flippers, but did not succeed.

From a small boat held in position above the dead animal, Marineland personnel lowered a modified swordfish harpoon into the water near the dead body of the dolphin. The pilot whale tried to push the harpoon away with his head. However, after several attempts, while the male whale surfaced to breathe the dolphin was harpooned, brought to the surface, and quickly removed from the tank. The pilot whale made a great flurry to recapture it, and this time failed. The time of removal was 2:00 p.m.

The male pilot whale gave several shrill cries immediately after this that could be heard clearly at the first level of viewing windows below the surface.

At 2:15 p.m., the male pilot whale seemed completely normal. He was resting at or near the surface with his eyes half closed in his normal attitude. However, both he and the larger female whale again refused to perform at the 3:30 p.m. show, but both readily took food from the attendant's hand.

The following day they both performed as usual, and, other than the abrasions sustained by the male whale, no ill effects were noted from the experience.

The behavior detailed above is especially significant because it was shown by a male, for whom incidents of long-term aiding behavior are less frequently reported than for females. The behavior also was constantly performed for a minimum of four hours until forcibly terminated. The interaction was between different genera, the important factor probably being apparent affection for a recognized individual.

The great variety of responses made to the situation also is significant. There was no stereotyped method of carrying the dolphin, and both the area of the body held, and the position assumed either at the surface or at the bottom of the tank varied with circumstances. The gentle handling of the body was particularly striking and showed the most careful deliberation. Deep scratches on the flukes and flippers of the dead animal were made when the pilot whale successfully retrieved the dolphin from the men attempting to remove it from the tank, and are evidence of the forceful efforts he was exerting in retaining possession of the body.

The wideness of the eye opening was important in that it gave an indication of the emotional state of the animal. Best and Taylor suggested that emotional manifestations in man and various animals are sympathoadrenal effects, and that a startled expression is due to the involuntary action under emotional stress of Mueller's orbital muscle, which retracts the upper eyelid. The wideness of the eye, coupled with the refusal of the pilot whale to feed after an abstinence of some twenty-two hours, despite strong conditioning to do so, together with persistence of the behavior in the face of injury, rules out the likelihood of play.

From "Intergeneric Behavior by a Captive Pacific Pilot Whale," by Melba C. Caldwell, David H. Brown, and David K. Caldwell.

The birth of a bottlenose dolphin photographed at Marineland of the Pacific by David K. Caldwell.

Behavior of Pseudorca *during Birth of a Common Dolphin*

On December 13, 1963, a female Pacific common dolphin arrived at Marineland. Shortly before being placed into a quarantine tank, the dolphin showed the symptoms of shock. Following the intramuscular injection of a tranquilizer drug, the animal became soporific and could not remain at the surface without assistance. Help was rendered by one of Marineland's divers who entered the tank and supported the little dolphin in his arms. Upon release, the effects of the drug remained evident and the animal drifted at the surface and made little attempt to swim. Silver smelt thrown into the tank elicited immediate response and the tranquilized newcomer consumed a quantity of this fish. The dolphin continued to feed and on January 9 she was transferred to the Circular Tank.

The common dolphin is difficult to maintain in a captive environment. This species appears to be peculiarly emotional and particularly sensitive to the competitive feeding behavior normally demonstrated by larger, more aggressive, forms. This specimen, however, appeared to adapt rapidly to an enclosure shared with delphinids of four other genera.

Dolphins in the latter stages of pregnancy normally display a pronounced distention of the inguino-abdominal region. The small common dolphin failed to show these signs. It was, therefore, a surprise when, at approximately 11:40 a.m. on February 15, observers saw a small tail protruding from her birth canal. The birth progressed very rapidly and by 12:05 p.m. the entire posterior portion of the fetus had been expelled. The umbilical cord, which seemed stretched and taut, was clearly visible.

The striped dolphins and false killer whale followed the

laboring female. The dolphins showed particular interest and nosed the female's abdominal region on several occasions.

The dorsal fin of the calf appeared to obstruct its further passage. In normal births the dorsal fin folds at its base either to the right or left, but in this case it remained erect and caught internally at the apex of the vaginal introitus.

At 12:15 p.m. one of the striped dolphins grasped the fetal tail flukes in its mouth and withdrew the infant from the parental birth canal. A discharge of amniotic fluid and a little blood followed the delivery.

The infant was stillborn, and delayed expulsion at a critical phase of parturition was no doubt incriminated in this fetal death.

Our common dolphin, attended by the striped dolphins, carried her dead infant's body to the surface. These efforts were, however, terminated by the male pilot whale, who seized the body by its head. The pilot whale devoured the small cadaver, entire, after carrying it to and from the surface for 38 minutes.

The common dolphin at first seemed little affected by the intervention of the pilot whale, but appeared greatly distressed by his ingestion of the cadaver. Whistling constantly, she moved rapidly around the tank, swimming in an erratic manner, apparently searching for her calf.

The animal quickly resumed a more normal swimming pattern, in the company of the striped dolphins, but she continued to vocalize intermittently for several hours.

Since 1:00 p.m., continuous uterine contractions had caused a three-inch length of the umbilical cord to move in and out of the female's urogenital opening. At 4:06 p.m., the common dolphin sought the company of the female false killer whale. She was observed at this time to deliberately avoid the company of the striped dolphins and begin to swim on the west side of the tank quite close to the surface. The false killer whale swam to the little dolphin and, after an apparent deliberate examination of her genital area, gently grasped the umbilical remnant in her mouth, and with a lateral movement of her head withdrew this tissue some six inches from the common dolphin's body. The dolphin rolled on her back and broke away from the larger animal, but then returned and again waited for the false killer whale. Once more, the whale seized the placenta and repeated the behavior previously described and withdrew the membrane another three inches. The common dolphin during these periods was observed to actively flex her body and appeared to try to assist the false killer whale in its attempts to remove the afterbirth. At the third attempt, the female false killer whale was successful and withdrew the entire placental membrane from the smaller animal. This was released and immediately both animals resumed normal activity in the tank. The free placental membrane was closely examined by the striped dolphins, but was swept away and down the drain before it could be recovered by the Marineland staff or before the dolphins could further investigate it.

Protective Behavior

On January 6, 1965, it became necessary to drain the Circular Tank for the purpose of giving the occupants their bi-annual erysipelas vaccination. The water level had reached the desired depth of three feet by 7:45 p.m. It was then dark, and it was necessary to illuminate the work area with flood lights placed around the top of the tank.

After administering a prophylactic injection to a pilot whale, two of the men helping in the tank, trainer Ray Cribbs and diver Richard Blacker, effected the capture of the common dolphin. The small dolphin immediately commenced to emit a series of high-pitched whistles. The false killer whale, apparently attracted by these vocalizations, inserted her head between the man holding the hinder end of the *Delphinus* and the animal's body. It then gently, but nevertheless very deliberately, proceeded to push its companion out of its captor's arms. Both Cribbs and Blacker later stated it was impossible to hold the *Delphinus* at the time. The false killer whale made no attempt to bite, and in fact failed to direct any aggressive behavior at either of the men involved. Upon effecting the dolphin's release, both it and the *Pseudorca* swam together for a short time. Shortly thereafter, the common dolphin was captured once more, and the injection made quickly before the false killer whale could again intervene.

On March 20, 1965, the female *Delphinus* refused to accept food. Emesis also occurred on several occasions during this and the following day. It was decided to remove her from the exhibit, and in the evening the Circular Tank was again drained to a depth of approximately three feet.

Upon the common dolphin's being secured by trainer Joe Beazie, the *Pseudorca* again approached and intervened. The dolphin was whistling at this time. The whale quickly effected the dolphin's release by pushing her out of the man's arms. The next attempt was made by both trainers Cribbs and Beazie and they were again obliged to release the animal owing to the intervention of the false killer whale. At this time the false killer whale grasped and gently pressed one of Cribbs's legs in her mouth. A third attempt made by Beazie elicited the same behavior; *i.e.*, the whale seized his leg and relinquished its hold only upon the dolphin's release. Immediately after this, the false killer whale carried the *Delphinus* on its back for several seconds. It was then decided to drain more water out of the tank until a depth of 18 inches at the sides was reached. Again the animal was captured and this time removed. During this last attempt, the false killer whale swam to the shallow edge of the tank and stranded herself in her effort to come to the aid of the common dolphin.

On the day following the removal of the *Delphinus*, the *Pseudorca* continued to behave and feed in a normal manner.

From "Observations on the Behavior of Wild and Captive False Killer Whales, with Notes on Associated Behavior of Other Genera of Captive Delphinids," by David H. Brown, David K. Caldwell, and Melba C. Caldwell.

FOR THE DEATH OF 100 WHALES

Hung midsea
Like a boat mid-air
The Liners boiled their pastures:
The Liners of flesh,
The Arctic steamers.

Brains the size of a football.
Mouths the size of a door.

The sleek wolves
Mowers and reapers of sea kine.
THE GIANT TADPOLES
(Meat their algae)
Lept
Like sheep or children.
Shot from the sea's bore.

Turned and twisted
(Goya!!)
Flung blood and sperm.
Incense.
Gnashed at their tails and brothers,
Cursed Christ of mammals,
Snapped at the sun,
Ran for the sea's floor.

Goya! Goya!
Oh Lawrence
No angels dance those bridges.
OH GUN! OH BOW!
There are no churches in the waves,
No holiness,
No passages or crossings
From the beasts' wet shore.

Michael McClure

'. . . *Killer whales . . . Savage sea cannibals up to 30 feet long with teeth like bayonets . . . one was caught with 14 seals and 13 porpoises in its belly . . . often tear at boats and nets . . . destroyed thousands of dollars worth of fishing tackle . . . Icelandic government appealed to the U.S., which has thousands of men stationed at a lonely NATO airbase on the subarctic island. Seventy-nine bored G.I.'s responded with enthusiasm. Armed with rifles and machine guns one posse of Americans climbed into four small boats and in one morning wiped out a pack of 100 killers . . .*

'. . . *First the killers were rounded up into tight formation with concentrated machine gun fire, then moved out again one by one, for the final blast which would kill them . . . as one was wounded, the others would set upon it and tear it to pieces with their jagged teeth . . .*'

From TIME, *April 1954*

Paul Spong, Ph.D., is a psychologist and cetologist from New Zealand. He is currently working and living with wild orcas in Vancouver, British Columbia. Dr. Spong's interest in the mind and manners of whales is related to his commitment to see a world of restored human relationships. He is a member of the Board of Directors of Project Jonah in Canada.

PAUL SPONG
The Whale Show

We, my family and I, and other friends, have been studying whales, principally *Orcinus orca*, for a little over six years now. At the outset I was totally ignorant about the creature. Of course I had heard of the "killer" whale and was aware of its reputation as a ferocious predator and consumer of other species of whales. But my knowledge certainly did not extend beyond what was popularly accepted. I had come to orcas by way of a job offer, with a background of training in physiological and experimental psychology and an interest in relationships between brain mechanisms and behavior. I knew that the orcas had enormous convoluted brains, but nothing of the details of their anatomy. During the first two years of our studies we worked exclusively with captive orcas, and in the last four mainly with free whales.

We came to call the creature "orca," because "killer" seemed an inappropriate label for one so friendly towards man. Of course, orcas sometimes harass and frequently frighten humans, especially when they are in small boats and a whale surfaces to blow close to them. However, I know of just two instances in which orcas have actually attacked and killed people. Perhaps the most interesting thing about these cases is that in each of them the attack, if not the result, was justified. I will relate one of these stories by way of introduction to *Orcinus orca*.

In 1956 two loggers working on a hillside in British Columbia were skidding logs down the slope into the water. Noticing a pod, or family group, of orcas passing below, one of the loggers deliberately let go a log which skidded down and hit one of the whales in the back, apparently injuring but not killing it. The whales went away. That night, as the loggers were rowing back to camp, the whales reappeared and tipped the boat over. One man vanished, the one who had let the log go. The other man was not touched and survived to tell the tale.

Why study *Orcinus orca*, a species about which little is known, and one which faces no obvious survival crisis? Of course, the fact that we know little about it is sufficient to arouse our interest in the creature: man's greatest challenges have always been the unknown. Then there is the availability of captive individuals and free populations for close study; during the past decade numerous individuals have been captured alive and placed in exhibition facilities in several countries, and a sizable population of free orcas reliably inhabits the British Columbia coastal waters. Beyond these considerations, however, is the fascination that the creature holds for us because of its unchallenged status at the top of the ladder of life of the oceans: it is literally capable of preying upon *any* life-form it chooses, and is not systematically preyed upon by anything. As far as orcas are concerned, man is the major but still probably an insignificant predator: the commercial whaling industry kills a few hundred orcas each year, and a few others are killed by foolish men who shoot them for target practice or perhaps just because they are feeling bad. But in a very real sense, *Orcinus orca* occupies a place in the oceans equivalent to the one which we occupy on land.

It is easy to speculate about something of which we know little. One speculation I am particularly fond of is the thought that *Orcinus orca* is probably a creature which has little or no experiential reason to know fear; it may literally be fearless. I sometimes wonder what our human lives would be like if we were not, as we are, creatures of fear.

Then, what do we know about *Orcinus orca*?

We know that the largest orcas grow to about thirty feet long. We call them "senior bulls." They are large male whales, easily identified because of their proudly erect dorsal fins which often exceed six feet in height. We know that orcas live in family groups which we call "pods." We suspect that orca families remain together for life. No one knows how long orcas live, but an eighty-year life span has been fairly well established for one individual, and it is probably reasonable for us to speculate that orcas live about as long as we do, remembering that life expectancy in our own species ranges from about thirty to seventy years. The orca diet principally consists of fish and marine mammals such as sea lions and seals, although they apparently sometimes eat shellfish and are said to savor mountain goat fat. Probably they eat whatever food is most abundant in whatever area they happen to be living in. In general, however, it is true to say that we know very little about the orcas. One reason for our lack of knowledge about the species is that it has

SALAMANCA A PROPHECY

(1)
a city on
a turtle's back
a longhouse
/
was like Jerusalem
's temple resting
on a whale.

(2)
impossible to bring it all
together
Jerome Rothenberg

He can change into any desired form, and many are the legends about him. One which was related to me was that ages ago the Indians were out seal-hunting. The weather was calm and the sea smooth. One of these killers, or blackfish, a species of porpoise, kept alongside of a canoe, and the young men amused themselves by throwing stones from the canoe ballast and hitting the fin of the killer. After some pretty hard blows from these rocks the creature made for the shore, where it grounded on the beach. Soon a smoke was seen, and their curiosity prompted them to ascertain the cause, but when they reached the shore they discovered, to their surprise, that it was a large canoe, and not the *Skana* that was on the beach, and that a man was on shore cooking some food. He asked them why they threw stones at his canoe. "You have broken it," said he, "and now go into the woods and get some cedar withes and mend it." They did so, and when they had finished the man said, "Turn your backs to the water and cover your heads with your skin blankets, and don't you look till I call you." They did so, and heard the canoe grate on the beach as it was hauled down into the surf. Then the man said, "Look, now." They looked, and saw the canoe just going over the first breaker and the man sitting in the stern; but when it came to the second breaker it went under and presently came up outside of the breakers a killer and not a canoe, and the man or demon was in its belly. This allegory is common among all the tribes on the northwest coast, and even with the interior tribes with whom the salmon takes the place of the orca, which never ascends the fresh-water rivers. The Chilkat and other tribes of Alaska carve figures of salmon, inside of which is the full length figure of a nude Indian. Casual observers, without inquiry, will at once pronounce it to be Jonah in the fish's belly, but the allegory is of ancient origin, far antedating the advent of the white man or the teachings of the missionary.
Report of the National Museum, *1888*

been of little interest to the commercial whaling industry. Most of what we have learned about other whale species has so far come from observations of whalers and whaling industry scientists.

Of course, when I say that we know very little about *Orcinus orca*, I am really talking mostly about the knowledge that comes to us from modern science. For we must remember that the creature has been well known to other men for hundreds, even thousands, of years. People living on the land and traveling on the water in areas inhabited by orcas have known much about *Orcinus orca* for a long time. Their knowledge has led them to an understanding and admiration of the creature which often amounts to awe. The respect is splendidly depicted in the painting which is the front of the longhouse in Alert Bay, British Columbia—a traditional Kwakiutl representation of *Orcinus orca*. An old Kwakiutl story will serve to illustrate the understanding which these people have of the creature.

In the old days, one of the tests of manhood involved the following circumstances: some men in a canoe would see a long orca asleep on the surface of the water. They approached him very quietly, taking care not to lift their paddles out of the water because they knew that the sound of dripping water would awaken him. As the canoe came alongside, one man would jump out onto the whale's back, run along it to the head, and leap quickly back into the canoe. That man was a *man* and honored by his people.

My own early work with *Orcinus orca* reflected my background conditioning as a scientist. Deliberately refraining from making any prejudgments about its nature or capabilities, I approached the species as if it were a mammalian life form of the order of complexity of, say, the laboratory rat, but one about which nothing was known. I reasoned that if we could understand something of the way in which the creature experiences the world around it, we might eventually be able to ask and answer questions concerning, say, the complexity of sensory information that it is capable of processing. This was one way of gaining a clue to some of its capabilities. I initiated a series of very traditional experimental studies of vision.

My associates and I learned that *Orcinus orca* can see underwater about as well as a cat can see in air, and that it processes visual information in a highly specific way. We went on to study audition—learning, for example, that orcas hear through several sound input channels, and that they hear best through the rostrum (the most forward portion of the head) and the tip of the lower jaw. When an orca is orienting the front of his head towards a sound source, he is probably listening to it. We also investigated the reward value of sound stimulation, finding that captive orcas love to listen to music and practically any other kind of sound, this being, we decided later, presumably partly a reflection of the acoustic monotony of most captive environments. We also came to realize that the conditions of captivity probably change the creature greatly, and that if we are truly to understand it we must study it in its natural habitat.

Towards the end of this work with captives I moved from my remote position of data collector and behavior manipulator to one of participant-observer. I began to interact closely with my orca subjects, to show them something of myself and my kind while I was learning about them. As I opened my mind to these creatures, I came to respect them more and more. Eventually my respect verged on awe! I concluded that *Orcinus orca* is an incredibly powerful and capable creature, exquisitely self-controlled and aware of the world around it, a being possessed of a zest for life and a healthy sense of humor, and moreover, a remarkable fondness for and interest in humans.

Many of us who have worked with whales and dolphins have come to the realization that at the same time we were attempting to manipulate their behavior, they were manipulating ours. At the same time we were studying them and performing experiments on them, they were studying us and performing experiments on us. And it did not take long to understand that fear was the principal barrier between us—human beings—and them—killer whales.

In the spring of 1969 I was working with a young adult female orca named Skana at the Vancouver Public Aquarium in Vancouver, British Columbia. Although I had been studying her for well over a year at the time, we were just then getting to know each other and to interact with each other at a physically intimate level. For example, Skana enjoyed having me rub her head and body with my hands and bare feet, and she allowed me to walk out onto her back or front, sometimes sinking down into the water, encouraging me to enter it with her. We were becoming close friends.

Early one morning I was sitting on a training platform at the edge of Skana's pool, dangling my bare feet in the water. Skana approached me slowly, as she usually did, until she was a few inches from my feet. Then, suddenly and without warning, she opened her mouth and slashed it quickly across my feet, so that I could feel her teeth dragging across both the tops and the soles of my feet. Naturally, though probably with a very slow reaction time, I jerked my feet out of the water. After a pause for reflection and recovery from shock, I put my feet back in the water. Again Skana approached and slashed her open mouth across my feet. Again I jerked them out of the water, and after a while put them back in, only to have her and myself repeat the procedure. We went around in this circle ten or eleven times, until finally I could sit calmly with my feet in the water, controlling the urge to flinch as she flashed her teeth across my feet. Then she stopped. Remarkably, I no longer felt afraid. She had very

We were out one day hunting for blackfish, out in the umiak, and I saw a big pack of killer whales following some blue whales. Well, the killer whales were looking for something to eat. The blue whales knew the killer whales were behind them and they went on for a while, and had this conversation between them. Then one big old blue whale turned back out of the pack and he went back into the killer whales. They decided among them who was going to be eaten.
Willy Willoya, Eskimo whale hunter

While on a cruise in the U.S. Revenue cutter *Wayanda,* during the month of October, 1872, we had an opportunity of witnessing, at midnight, the gambols of an immense herd of these active and rapacious animals. The sea was quite smooth, and not a breath of wind was stirring. At first we could hear a harsh rustling sound, as if a heavy squall of wind, accompanied with hail, was sweeping over the otherwise tranquil sea; and, as the moon burst through the clouded sky, we could see a sheet of foam and spray surging toward us. In a few moments the vessel was surrounded by myriads of these Common Porpoises, which, in their playful movements, for the space of one hour, whitened the sea all around as far as the eye could discern, when they almost instantly disappeared.

Charles M. Scammon, Marine Mammals of the Northwestern Coast of North America, *Dover 1968*

The following behavior has been reported to us by Robert V. Bell, leader of a party of salvage divers who spent seven weeks in Baja California in the spring of 1958.

The divers reported that almost daily during the seven week period they watched gray whales riding the breakers coming in over the shoal. The divers were particularly interested in the behavior and agreed among themselves at the time that the whales were surf-riding "just as a man would"; i.e., just in front of the crest of the waves.

The whales engaging in the activity were adults. It was not noted, however, whether the same individuals rode more than once.

David K. Caldwell and Melba C. Caldwell

effectively and quickly deconditioned my fear of her!

In addition to the work with Skana, I spent time with two captive orcas at Sealand of the Pacific, an oceanarium in Victoria, British Columbia. One of the orcas was Haida, a young adult male; the other was Chimo, an adolescent female albino. Haida and Chimo had been together for some time, and were the principals in a film done by the National Film Board of Canada called *We Call Them Killers.* A few months after the film was finished, Chimo died.

When she died, Haida entered a state of deep shock or mourning. In the period between the filming and Chimo's death, the two whales had become engaged in an increasingly beautiful mating ritual. Chimo's death was obviously a great blow to Haida. He stopped eating altogether and became virtually inactive, remaining almost motionless, scarcely breathing, on the surface of the water for long periods of time. Cracks began to open around his blowhole. It looked as if Haida was losing the will to live, as if he were giving up. At that point, flautist Paul Horn, who had been in the film, came to visit Haida every day for a week, playing music to him. For the first two days Haida was completely unresponsive. At the end of the second day Paul pretended to get angry with Haida, admonishing him with the words: "Look, Haida, why should I waste my time coming down here to play for you, when you're not the slightest bit interested! If you don't show some interest next time I come, I'm going to go away and I won't ever come back to play for you again!" The next day Haida began to show some interest in the music. By the end of the week he seemed almost like his old happy and energetic self again!

In January 1970 we visited Alert Bay, British Columbia, to check out reports concerning the predictable presence of an *Orcinus orca* population in the Johnstone Straits region of British Columbia. After talking with numerous local area residents, fishermen, and Indian people, we returned to Alert Bay in June 1970 and established a land-based field station on Hanson Island, adjacent to Blackney Passage and lying between Blackfish Sound and the Johnstone Straits. This was a location from which, we were told, we would often be able to see orcas traveling close to shore. "Blackfish" is a local area name for *Orcinus orca.*

Some orcas are present in these and surrounding waters most, if not all, of the year. At its peak, in July and August, the population probably numbers about one hundred individuals. There are four pods or family groups. One has eight members, a second sixteen members, and two others thirty to forty members each. Their peak presence in the area in the summer and fall coincides with the presence of an abundance of salmon in a succession of schools of several species, and of hundreds of salmon fishing boats, seiners, gillnetters, and trollers. The whales know the habits of the fish, and of the fishermen, well. They move effortlessly and efficiently through the area, both day and night, hunting and harvesting the salmon that are their food, their source of body energy. So far as we know, the same pods of whales return to the area each year, although local people tell us that their numbers have greatly diminished in recent years. The pods, and presumably the population, are cooperatively organized social units. Vital individual and group functions, ranging from feeding to breathing and resting, are monitored and organized by the pod.

Our approach to understanding *Orcinus orca* is a simple one: we live on an island in an area inhabited by orcas, making whatever observations we can from the land, from boats, and underwater, with our eyes, and with modern technological tools. And we interact with the whales whenever we are afforded the opportunity—for example, by paddling or swimming amongst them, by playing music to them, and by shouting simple greetings like "hello" and "goodbye." My orcoid rendering of "hello" sounds like: "heLLOOooommm," and "goodbye" sounds like "goodBYEeeee."

We have equipment that enables us to monitor and record the sounds emitted by the whales as they pass by. Hydrophones—underwater microphones—located underwater offshore are used to pick up the whales' sounds. An oscilloscope and video tape recording equipment are used to display visually and record the sound signals, enabling us to superficially examine their frequency characteristics. We found that although most orca sounds are wholly or partly audible to us, there are many which are entirely ultrasonic or have ultrasonic components. The highest frequencies we observed were around 80 kc.

In addition to routinely observing and recording the passage of pods past our station, we performed numerous experiments. We were particularly interested in determining whether free orcas would show the same enthusiastic interest in music and other sources of sound stimulation that we had previously observed in captive orcas. We placed loudspeakers in the air onshore, and underwater. For several weeks we bombarded the whales with a wide variety of sounds that they must have been able to hear for miles: recorded music of all types, pure tones over a wide frequency range, tone bursts of short and long duration, wave forms of every conceivable type, recordings of the vocal sounds of captive and free orcas and other whales, simultaneous and delayed feedback of their own sounds, and so on. All to little avail! The orcas consistently displayed a (to our minds) remarkable indifference to our efforts to catch and hold their attention. Although they showed some interest occasionally, they mostly seemed to ignore the sound stimuli we projected at them. The most interesting reactions occurred in relation to feedback of their own vocalizations. When the feedback was simultaneous, they virtually stopped vocalizing. However, with delayed air feedback, the whales produced some very unusual vocalizations, seeming to play with the procedure. In general, we concluded that the whales were usually preoccupied with their routine hunting activities when they passed by our station, and that the types of sound stimuli we were using held little interest for free whales. This was when we concluded that the responsiveness of captive orcas must have been at least in part due to the typically monotonous conditions of captivity and to the acoustic deprivation which captives housed in concrete enclosures are subject to.

Contrasting sharply with the whales' disinterest in recorded sounds was their obvious interest in live music. In August 1970, Vancouver rock and roll band Fireweed became the first modern group of musicians on our planet to play live music to free orcas. Their seagoing stage was the recently launched and as yet unrigged forty-eight-foot concrete-hulled sailing vessel *D'Sonoque*, on her shakedown voyage. The whales' response to Fireweed and their music was both subtle and dramatic. The first pod to encounter the band became completely silent as they passed slowly by the *D'Sonoque*. (Though such silence is not unknown, it is rare in our experience.) On another occasion a pod of about thirty orcas completely surrounded the *D'Sonoque* and traveled with her for several miles as Fireweed played. At one point during this trip, more than a dozen young orcas, with one large bull in the middle, traveled in a line abreast continuously on the surface about hundred feet behind the vessel for perhaps a mile. It was just a glimpse, but sufficiently impressive for us to conclude that the whales *were* interested in live music, whereas they did not seem to be very interested in recorded sounds. Why this difference? Perhaps the greater fidelity of the live sounds was a factor, and as well the presence of the musicians.

One of our most interesting experiments involved attempts to feed fish to free orcas. For a two-week period we set a net out from shore which caught salmon and other species of fish, notably rock and kelp cod and dogfish. Feeding the whales salmon by hand from boats, tossing the fish into the water, was indeterminately successful: we were never able to observe an orca grasping a salmon, although it appeared likely that they did take at least some of our offerings. However, when we simply let the caught fish remain in the net, it was apparent that the whales came at night and took some fish from the net. On one occasion a young whale became entangled in the net, tearing a great hole in it to get free.

The partial success of these feeding experiments suggests that we may eventually be able to feed the whales fish containing radio

176

transmitting telemetry devices which would enable us to monitor and record remotely a wide variety of data concerning normal orca behavior and functions about which we can now only guess; e.g., depth of dive, amount and frequency of food intake, body temperature, heart rate, respiration patterns, vocal behavior, and so forth. If we can plant such telemetry packages in several or all members of an orca pod, we will be able to gain an intimate view of one of the most fascinating aspects of orca life: the coordination of individual and group functions.

In general, we felt fairly satisfied with the results of this first study of free orcas, despite numerous imperfections and limitations. We had made our first observations of and contacts with free orcas—exciting moments! And we had gained our first glimpse of their exquisitely beautiful, efficiently and harmoniously organized existence amidst the freedom of the seas. We imagined the totality of their understanding of the habits of other creatures in and on the ocean. We saw their effortless pursuit and harvesting of the abundant salmon. We came to recognize our own insignificance in their scheme of things. We found them to be just as active during the night as they are during the day, presumably because their world is mostly a world of sound. We gained the impression that socially the population of more than fifty orcas was a cooperatively organized group entity comprising several pods which in turn subdivide in various ways; individual, pod, and population activities were obviously highly coordinated. We felt the ease and freedom of orca existence. And we were awed by the flow, the control, and the command of the creature.

Contemplation of the results of our 1970 program led me to the conclusion that I had been overly preoccupied with technical aspects of the work: monitoring record levels of hydrophone recordings and video tape recordings of oscilloscope displays of orca sounds; making notations of settings on amplifiers, tape recorders and wave form generators; and so forth. As a result of all this busy-work I felt I had paid relatively little attention to the whales, at least, not as much as I could or should have.

Consequently, our 1971 project was quite differently oriented. In addition to the electronic systems of the previous summer, we took with us a new item of equipment: a one-man kayak. During August 1971 I made ten day excursions lasting two to eight hours each with orca pods. These were wonderful, ecstatic days in which I experienced a feeling for and closeness to the creatures that will ever remain with me.

Perhaps the most remarkable feature of these experiences was the immediacy of the orcas' acceptance of my presence in their midst. The first time I approached an orca pod, its thirty or so members remained milling around in one place while I slowly paddled more than two miles towards them and into their midst. I felt that they welcomed my presence, and sensed in them, particularly in the young, an excitement rivaling my own, which was immense! The whales ambled slowly off down Johnstone Strait at a rate which made it easy for me to keep up with them. Together, we traveled for several miles. The trip eventually terminated with the noisy intrusion of a motor boat.

Of course, there are numerous other examples of human beings granted acceptance and even status by groups of other socially organized species; e.g., chimpanzees and wolves. However, this is usually a fairly slow process involving a period of gradual approach and mutual adjustment. In contrast, this first kayak contact with free orcas was accomplished with astonishing ease and rapidity.

Following this initial contact, I spent many days out on the water with orcas. My procedure was simple: having made contact with a pod, I remained close to it for as long as the whales permitted, just being there with them, keeping my eyes and mind open. Gradually, I came to appreciate something of the details of their daily lives, particularly the effortless flow of their existence. I saw how easy it was for them to obtain the food they needed by mobilizing group energy to satisfy individual needs. For example, I once observed a pod of about forty whales break up into three groups which proceeded to completely surround Blackfish Sound, a body of water several miles long and wide. For several hours they worked slowly backwards and forwards, herding the salmon and gradually closing in on them. When the circle was less than a mile wide, feeding commenced. It, like the hunting, was cooperatively organized: small groups of whales would suddenly dash into the circle to feed on the balled-up salmon, while their comrades maintained their stations on the perimeter, making sure that no fish escaped. After all the whales had been fed, some of them rested, while others went their separate ways.

Orca resting patterns are particularly interesting. The creature seems to have a variety of resting modes, sometimes remaining completely still, and sometimes resting while moving. Although senior bulls may sometimes rest alone, the pod or sub-sections of it usually rest together. Whales resting together often closely synchronize their breathing.

During these first kayak excursions with free orcas, I was frequently thrilled by moments of joyous interaction between myself and the whales. Let me relate one incident as an example.

August 11, 1971, began with heavy fog on Hanson Island. I was sitting in bed writing when I heard the sound of porpoises breathing, blowing, close into shore. Normally I don't pay that much attention

to the porpoises, of which there is a small population in the area, but
for some reason that morning I decided to go out to them, briefly,
in my kayak. I really intended it to be a very brief trip, because I
omitted taking my compass, chart, food, or water. I took only my
flute with me. The porpoises moved away into the fog and I paddled
after them. Then I began to hear some louder blows farther away,
so I paddled towards them. Through the fog I could hear the sound
of many orcas blowing as they came to the surface to breathe. Then
I could no longer hear the sounds, so I put down my paddle and
picked up my flute and started to play, with my eyes closed. After a
few minutes I opened my eyes to see about six young orcas sitting
quietly on the surface of the water in the fringes of the fog, about
hundred feet away. I went on playing, closing my eyes again. When
I next opened them, it was to see three whales, a pair of adults and a
young one, surfacing together, about fifty feet in front of the kayak
and moving away from me. I immediately put down my flute,
picked up the paddle and started after them. They surfaced to blow
three times at about twenty second intervals, and then, sounding,
they disappeared. I paddled for a few minutes, until I lost my sense
of direction in the fog, stopped paddling, and started playing my
flute again. This time, as I played, I became aware of the presence
of groups of whales all around me in the fringes of the fog, fifty to
hundred feet away. I estimated there to be at least fifty of them.
After several minutes they started to move slowly away and I paddled
after them. It seemed clear to me at the time that they expected me
to tag along with them. I was a little unsure as to which whales I
should travel with, so I headed for the group that seemed to have
the most babies. I paddled along with them for perhaps ten or fifteen
minutes at distances of around twenty feet, and then they disappeared. So I headed for another group of eight whales, all older
juvenile and young adult males. They allowed me to come right in
amongst them. At one point I was in the middle of them as they swam
in a line abreast, four on either side of my kayak, I paddling as fast
as I could, they swimming continuously at the surface. Two of them
were so close to my kayak that, for a moment, I forgot where I was
and impulsively leaned out of the kayak to touch the whale to my
right, almost overbalancing the kayak and nearly striking the
whale's eye with the bow. Immediately, they disappeared. I felt a
bit foolish and didn't quite know what to do for a moment. So I
played my flute again, and again they all came back around me, this
time several of them making passes as close as ten feet from the kayak.
After a while I stopped playing and followed them again. Then the
pod split up into three groups which started to head off in separate
directions. Having no idea where I was by that time, I started to
think about heading home, and began paddling in what I thought

was the right direction. I soon realized that it was probably wrong, so I stopped to play my flute some more, saying "goodbye" to my friends. Then, in three pods of ten to twenty whales, they came back and made passes close to me before heading away again. I followed one pod until their blows were beyond hearing, landed on the first island that loomed up out of the fog, waited until the fog cleared, and then headed for home. In all, the trip lasted about ten hours.

We often play music to the whales, for we feel their interest in and perhaps appreciation of it. Sometimes, particularly on a still night, a pod or part of a pod, or perhaps just a single whale, will hover off-shore for an hour or more, apparently tuning in to the music. Some-times they seem to join the celebration with the chorus of their voices and the dance of their bodies, visible to us from the bubbling phosphorescent wakes they leave behind. Occasionally we have seen whales swim rapidly around and around in a circle, then glide quietly away to leave behind a great *O* bubbling brightly in the blackness of the night. Needless to say, these are moments of great excitement and of delightful contact.

In 1972, I entered the water in the presence of free orcas for the first time, gaining my first underwater glimpse of them. This was another exhilarating moment, sufficient to justify my present belief that we will begin to learn much more about orcas when we develop the capability of routinely observing them underwater and of inter-acting with them in their own element. The system which we have used so far is a simple one: a two-man kayak with a crude pontoon arrangement which enables easy entry into and exit from the water. We hope soon to develop systems which will enable us to maintain underwater contact with orcas while they are on the move—initially a towed underwater sled, and eventually a self-propelled submersible vehicle.

In 1973, an expedition from the Fisheries Research Board of Canada, led by Dr. Michael Biggs and Dr. Ian McCaskie, conducted a thorough, month-long study of the population, following pods of whales around all day, every day, sometimes both day and night, taking thousands of photographs which resulted in the excellent schematic identifications which are presented here, and getting a good idea of the daily routine of the whales. They used two sailboats to track the whales, and occasionally an aircraft to observe them from the air.

A second expedition, that of Jim Hunter and Grahme Ellis, with still photography as its prime purpose, used a Zodiac rubber boat to follow pods of whales around. They established a whale-watching post on Parson's Island.

Like the whales, they spent a good deal of time fishing for salmon,
(*Continued on page 184.*)

180

Here is an orca nuclear family: an adult male who can be identified by the size and erectness of the dorsal fin; an adult female with a curved dorsal; and a juvenile whale, perhaps three years old.

The older adult males display considerable mobility within, and to an extent between, pods. They are the only whales which ever travel completely by themselves or rest alone. A senior bull will often travel with about a dozen young whales, half of them breathing with him, and the other half forming a separate respiratory unit.

It seems likely that there is a good deal of systematic teaching and learning going on, particularly of breathing and hunting. Remember that orcas and other whales have to learn how to breathe, to think when they breathe. The pod is therefore organized into respiratory units which ensure that no member is ever breathing alone.

This pod is organized into two respiratory units, one of which is seen at the surface; the other will surface in about twenty seconds. The old bull is probably teaching the young whales something about breathing as well as hunting. This is part of a line abreast of more than a dozen whales, swimming slowly along together, perfectly synchronizing their respiration, probably resting.

Sometimes all of the members of a pod may be seen breathing together; at other times the pod may subdivide into numerous respiratory units. A breathing unit consists of at least two whales. Presumably each whale keeps track of its own and the other members' breathing. Clearly pod organization into breathing units performs an important survival function.

We now recognize that essentially the same pods and population return to the area each year, and we are beginning to recognize many of the orcas as individuals, from characteristic dorsal fin contours and markings such as cuts and notches, and from individual behavior patterns.

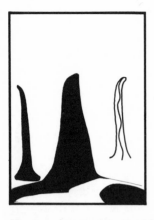

Here is a schematic of the dorsal fin of a senior bull we call "Wavy," because of the waves in the trailing edge of his dorsal fin.

You can see the trailing edge in this picture of him. Wavy seems to be the leader or one of the leaders of one of the pods having thirty to forty members.

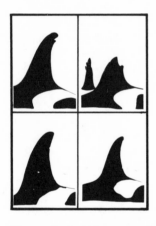

Here are the dorsal fin contours of four of the members of a pod of about sixteen orcas which we call "Stubb and Nicola's pod." Stubb is represented in the upper right. She is an adult female with an injured or deformed dorsal fin, perhaps the result of an unhappy encounter with a ship's propeller. Nicola is another adult female, named after the characteristic notch at the top of her dorsal fin.

This is Stubb.

And this is Nicola.

This is a senior bull we call "Tilt" because he has a habit of diving at an angle like this, although he does not necessarily always do so.

Here is a senior bull we call "Forward Fin" or "Hooker," because his dorsal fin has a pronounced forward slope to it. He is one of a pod of eight orcas.

In this figure you can also see another of the visible physical differences between individuals: the shape of the grey saddle patch adjacent to and behind the dorsal fin. There are also differences in the shape of the white head patch. Possibly these individual markings serve to help pod members identify one another at close range.

The young whales often seem to be the most playful ones. Here is a baby "jumping for joy."

Each year we see a few new babies, identifiable from their tiny size (about seven feet long when newborn) and because of a yellowish tint to the white areas. They always remain very close to their mother.

(*Continued from page 180.*)

successfully! They had the experience of gradually being allowed to approach closer and closer to pods in their motor-powered craft, until eventually they were admitted to their midst, making delightful contact with the whales, taking thousands of photographs, and making many useful observations. Entering the water in the proximity of Stubb's pod, Grahme Ellis had an incredible experience as a young male swam in a tight circle around him, close enough so that Grahme could determine the sex of the whale and see the shape of his white head patch. The following day the same whale made a close approach to a rowboat Grahme was in, circling it several times. Grahme was literally shining after these experiences!

The most outstanding and interesting whale-watching activity of the summer of 1973 was an expedition called Project Apex, undertaken by Ocean Life Systems of Victoria, British Columbia. Project Apex was a filmmaking expedition and an experiment in interspecies communication. It succeeded marvelously, beyond my, and I suspect just about everyone else's, expectations. Using an engineless sailboat, *The Four Winds*, equipped with electronic systems that permitted listening to the whales and projecting sound at them, and an electronic synthesizer that generated imitations of orca sounds, this group of young adventurers sailed from Victoria to the Johnstone Straits early in July, and immediately made contact with orcas. Their work is detailed in a 16mm film called *Orca*. The film is a wonderful statement, the closest glimpse we have yet gained of these creatures. In it is documented the first ever unquestioned communicative exchange between free orcas and humans.

Soon after *The Four Winds* arrived in the Johnstone Strait, a lone adult male orca approached the vessel and emitted a single clearly audible vocalization which was recorded. Soundman-musician Erich Hoyt practiced imitating the sound on the synthesizer until he managed an imperfect but adequate imitation. The following day, the same whales were sighted. Erich sent out his imitation orca sound. Immediately, with a latency of only about two seconds, three orcas replied with an exact replication of Erich's imperfect imitation of one of their sounds! It was a remarkable moment! Of course, it was just a glimpse, but nonetheless full of promise.

Perhaps our most exciting and promising experience occurred on August 10, 1973, three days before the full moon. We had finished supper and gone our various ways by about 11 P.M. At that time, "we" were ten whale watchers camped at various points along about one-quarter mile of shoreline. The previous day we had put our hydrophone in the water for the first time that summer, and had started monitoring it twenty-four hours a day. We heard the orcas when they were more than a mile away, coming from the direction

184

of Johnstone Strait. We turned on the tape recorder and went outside to watch.

The almost-full moon shone like satin on the calm water. And then an unbelievable scene unfolded. As the fifteen or so vocalizing orcas passed by (we guessed it was Stubb's pod), they were greeted by a welcoming line of immensely excited humans along the shore—shouting, whistling, clapping, jumping up and down, and almost into the water, off the rocks and cliffs. The whales sang and called to us and we returned their voices with everything we could manage—flute sounds, imitation orca sounds, singing and laughing—in the joy that only free creatures and free people can create together.

PRAYER OF A MAN WHO FOUND A DEAD KILLER WHALE
(*Kwakiutl*)

"Oh, it is great how you lie there on the ground,
Great Supernatural One.
What has made you unlucky?
Why, great and good one, are you lying here on the ground?
Friend, Supernatural One,
Why have you been unlucky, friend, for I thought you
could never be overcome, by all the Short-Life-Maker Women.
Now, you great and good one, have you been overcome
by the one who does as he pleases to us, friend.
I mean this, that you may wish that I shall inherit
your quality of obtaining easily all kinds of game
and all kinds of fish,
you Great Supernatural One, friend,
you Long-Life Maker.
And also that you protect me,
that I may not have any trouble, Supernatural One,
And also that it may not penetrate me,
the evil word of those who hate me among my fellow men,
And that only may penetrate themselves
the curses of those who wish me to die quickly.
I mean this, friend,
Only have mercy on me
that nothing evil may befall me,
Great Supernatural One," says he.
"*Wâ*, I will do this," says the man
on behalf of the one he found dead.

From The Religion of the Kwakiutl Indians, *Franz Boas, Columbia University Press*

MALCOLM BRENNER
Say "Rooo-beee!"

Malcolm Brenner is a person who wanted to find out something about dolphins, so he went to them. He has had a close personal relationship with a female dolphin (Ruby) in Florida, and is presently working on a book recounting that relationship titled In Contact: An Interspecies Romance. *This selection is an excerpt from that book.*

I went down to Ruby's pen. She was waiting, watching me out of one soft, slightly sad brown eye. I waded in up to my ankles and she swam to me. I rubbed her head and snout for a few minutes.

Then she pulled back. I reached out a little farther, and she pulled back still more, maintaining an infuriating six-inch space between the tips of my fingers and the tip of her snout. "Goddamn fish," I muttered, "trying to get me into the water with you, eh? . . ." She seemed so friendly, allowing me to rub her, and nuzzling up against my naked legs, that she finally convinced me.

I waded in up to my waist. She surfaced to breathe several feet away, then went under; there was no way to tell where she was. I felt her sonar in the water; it seemed to be coming from all around me. Suddenly Ruby was pushing her snout into my kneejoint, nuzzling me so that my knee folded up. Only her dorsal fin stuck out of water; I couldn't see or touch her, so I turned around.

She was gone. I heard her breathe behind me, and felt that snout in my knee again. The skin on the end of her snout was rough and it tickled. "Ruby, what the hell are you doing?" I asked her, but she was underwater, nuzzling my knee, so she could not hear the question.

Finally she surfaced in front of me, breathed, floated, and let me rub her, starting at her head. Her skin was smooth and finely ridged, and I was rubbing her carefully and gently. She would sink and nuzzle my knee some more, then return and let me rub her again.

She went down and didn't come up. I searched around, and she reappeared at the far end of the pool, sticking her head out of water and squawking at me. I understood it was her equivalent of, "Come on in, the water's fine!" By this time, the water felt absolutely freezing, but what can you expect from a creature with a built-in wet suit?

Underwater I could hear her whistles. I surfaced rapidly—it was cold!—and found her pushing my knees up to the surface, so that I was forced to float on my back. She swam around me, then under me, and began nuzzling my knees again! This knee fixation seemed inexplicable, and frustrating. It was hard to stay afloat in water that cold, so after a few minutes I swam over and hung onto the wire fence.

When she understood that I wasn't coming back, she returned to swim in tight circles around me, six or seven feet away, very, very fast. It was a little scary, and I realized I was not in control of the situation; in fact, I never had been since I had entered the water with her. She seemed concerned; her movements were extraordinarily swift, and I thought she'd gotten over-excited. She appeared at the far end of the pool, then raced back in my direction, heading straight for me at high speed. My stomach muscles involuntarily tightened and for the first time in my life I got an idea of what it would feel like to be rammed by a four-hundred-fifty-pound dolphin traveling at twenty knots. Just before she hit me she swerved aside; but that little demonstration frightened me. I was certain Ruby wouldn't deliberately hurt me, but I thought that she might do so accidentally if she got over-excited. Dolphins are very rough with each other in play, at least by human standards. I began to think about getting out.

As if she could read my mind, everything stopped. She swam over to me, slowly, peacefully, and began to nuzzle my feet on the bottom. Had she recognized my growing anxiety? The suddenness of her mood change was eerie. She began to rub her snout up and down my legs, and then she was nuzzling my crotch. I thought I knew what that meant! I thought she might want to swim beneath my legs, but she didn't; now she seemed to be trying to get me sexually aroused, and she was doing a pretty fair job of it, too.

By this time I was deathly cold. She broke off nuzzling me to swim to the other end of the pool, and I decided to use the opportunity to get out. I was out of the water before she could stop me. I hated to trick her like that, but my teeth were chattering uncontrollably. She immediately swam over, lay on her side, and gave me a big, sad eyeball. I remembered the ball.

I got the ball and tossed it into Ruby's pen. She immediately understood that this was catch, and after nosing the ball for a few seconds threw it back to me. We tossed it back and forth until Ruby convinced me that she was in the mood for a game.

It occurred to me that I could use this game of catch as a reward in an attempt to get Ruby to vocalize. It seemed like an ideal reward; we were both enjoying the game, and her participation was voluntary. I decided to try to get her to mimic her own name. "Ruby," I said. "Say, Rooo-beee!" All I got back at first was a bunch of delphinese, somewhere between a whistle and a squawk. I threw the ball, and she returned it. "All right, now, say 'Ruby'! Rooo-beee!" Again that squawk. "No, you're going to have to do better than that. . . . C'mon, say 'Rooo-beee'!" For several more repetitions all I could get was that squawky noise. I noticed that *she was repeating the same sound every time;* it wasn't just any old squawk, but one with recognizable characteristics. But it was delphinese, which might as well be gibberish to me. I wanted English out of her, or at least a reasonable facsimile, and I was going to withhold the reward until I got it.

Suddenly her vocalization changed. Her squawk came out in two distinct syllables, rather like the way I had been syllabificating "Rooo-beee!" I hurled the ball, and she returned it. Our progress became unbelievably rapid. In the space of five minutes, she began to copy the syllabification, rhythm, tone, and inflections of my pronunciation of the word "Ruby," and she did so with an accuracy and a speed I found amazing. Every time she came closer to my pronunciation I threw the ball, and she would return it to me. Each time her pronunciation was further away from mine I would withhold the ball until she improved. We became completely wrapped up in each other; the outside world ceased to exist. We stood a few feet apart in the water of her pen, staring at each other intently with bright eyes, and the excitement between us was palpable. Never in my life had I known such an intimate feeling of being in contact with an incredible non-human creature. It felt like it was what I had been created to do. Our minds seemed to be running on the same wave. We were together.

Sometimes she would break back down into delphinese, and then I would withhold the ball until she had improved. She put a consonant *R* sound on the beginning of her squawk; and then she put a *Y* sound at the end. The result was a startling, eerie mimicry that sounded like my "Rooo-beee!" yet wasn't. The *R* sound, the *Y*-sound, the tone, rhythm, syllabification, were all there, but the middle of the sound was still this weird squawk. This all took place in about ten minutes. I was overwhelmed with the speed and accuracy of her learning; I hadn't expected anything like this in response to a simple game of catch.

She repeated the word with this degree of accuracy a couple of times, then started babbling at me in delphinese, shaking her head up and down with her jaws open in that gesture, usually associated with pleasure, that I called "ya-ya-ing." I tried to get her to say "Rooo-beee!" again; more ya-ya-ing. Then she swam back a few feet and made a peculiar noise, a kind of "keee-orr-oop," but about three times faster than you pronounce it. It occurred to me—I dont know why—*to repeat that sound*. Ruby seemed to be expecting it of me. I did the best I could with it. She repeated it, but now it sounded slightly different; I mimicked her changes. God, she's doing to me what I was just doing to her! Where will this lead? By now the ball was forgotten; I was totally absorbed in listening to Ruby's vocalizations and attempting to mimic them as accurately as possible with my inadequate human lips and vocal cords. She repeated the sound again, changed still more, and I copied that; she repeated it again, and as I tried to mimic her I thought, this sounds vaguely familiar— "kee-orr-oop." The light in my head went on. *The sound I had just successfully imitated was the one she had been giving to me in the beginning*, in response to my first attempts to make her say "Ruby!"

This realization struck me as the sound was coming out my lips. Several fuses in my mind blew simultaneously and I did an incredible double-take, nearly falling over, and staring at Ruby, who was watching me with great concentration. When she saw the double-take, and knew I knew, *she* flipped out, and went ya-ya-ing around the pool, throwing water into the air, very excited, and apparently happy that this two-legged cousin of hers was progressing so rapidly. I just stood there, watching her, trying to figure out exactly what had just happened between myself and this dolphin.

What do I think the meaning of that experience was? I don't really know. I have some *ideas*, however. In response to an English word, Ruby had given me a delphinese word or phrase, which I had ignored. She succeeded in taking control of the situation—*although I had been willing to relinquish control*—and had then tricked me into pronouncing the sound I had at first ignored! Our mutual reactions were so spontaneous, and so vivid, that there is no doubt of this in my mind. *I had been the one slowing down the communications between us!* I can't tell you with what force that realization struck me. But what was the meaning of that sound? I can only guess. Certainly Ruby was sophisticated enough to recognize her human name. It occurred to me that she was most likely either telling me her name for *me*— a straight turnabout—or telling me her name for herself. But these are just my projections.

Months later, I was to try and get Ruby to repeat her vocalizations for some friends of mine, with little success. She did manage to enunciate "Rooo-beee!" one or two times, with a precision approaching that of the first time, but it was not the same: she was restless and impatient, and I could not work with her very long. In retrospect, the error lay not with her, but with *me. I couldn't keep up with her*. In typical human fashion, I was trying to get her to repeat something she had already mastered—and what is the benefit in that? I was more concerned with showing her off to my friends than in working on new communications, and Ruby picked up on that, and did not want to cooperate. Anyone working with dolphins would do well to remember that they have a very low threshold of boredom, and once they have mastered something, they want to go on to something new. You, as a "human being," however, will probably be so surprised that you will want the dolphin to repeat its behavior over and over again until your mind, dulled by years of exposure to social and educational systems, finally starts to believe what it is being told: this sleek gray creature in the water wants to *communicate* with you.

Years later, I told a couple of "straight" dolphin researchers about this experience. (By "straight" I mean they regard the possibility of a high dolphin intelligence as undemonstrated, and therefore not worth investigating.) They listened to my tale with grave expressions, and allowed that it sounded "just believable." "It's too bad you didn't have a tape recorder with you," they told me. "So often, one hears what one *wants* to hear. Some outside impartial reference source is necessary to evaluate experiences like this in a truly scientific context. One's own subjective sensory impressions are, alas, so often subject to distortion. . . ." They're right, of course; I wish I *had* had a tape recorder with me. I wish I had microphones and hydrophones, and an isolated warm water research lab where I could have been naked, and gone on working with Ruby for weeks without interruption. And I wish I still had Ruby. Unfortunately, I don't. I was just an average person working with what I had available, and I had to rely on my five senses and my brain.

"Besides," the scientists added, "one hears of things like this so often. . . ." Makes you wonder why the scientists working in this field don't take more notice of these stories, doesn't it? But then again, to the average research scientist, dolphins are simply big, bright mammals, somewhere between a dog and a chimpanzee. Who would expect a scientist to make a fool of him or herself by climbing into a dolphin's pen on a freezing cold March day, and trying to squawk at them in their own language?

Certainly not *me*.

WILLIAM CURTSINGER
Love Swim

William Curtsinger is an underwater photographer for National Geographic. *He accompanied Dr. Roger Payne on his expedition to Patagonia in 1972 to study and photograph wild right whales. He is the photographic coordinator for Project Jonah, and a long-time friend and partisan of marine mammals.*

In the Southern Hemisphere, along the corresponding latitude from where I live in Maine, there are a hundred or so southern right whales (*Eubalena australis*)—a small family of this baleen species that now represents a quarter of their total population worldwide. It was along that desolate coast in the southern Atlantic that I first met whales. Hanging there, suspended in their liquid world, I wondered why I had to travel thousands of miles to meet that great creature that once swam along the shores I now call home.

As a photographer I am only a casual visitor to the deep. The whales are not. They swim there, play there, plow the abysmal plains and waters for food, and send their songs bouncing along undersea canyons, mountains, and valleys. We have never seen a whale in the great depths, and can only speculate what life goes on there. We meet, if at all, at the interface of sea and air along the shallow submarine plateaus of the continental shelf.

But off that isolated coast in South America, I slipped silently from the side of the rubber boat to enter into the world of whales. One hundred meters ahead a whale swims casually in my direction. Out of the gloom his shadow grows larger, moves slowly, changing shape and direction, and then—the lovely living whale is before me.

I watch his eye, ten feet close, move by, steady, curious. His great flukes move gentle, create a vertical column of serene water bubbling, alive with light. His eye turns, looks back, his flukes sweep up and over my head as he passes. Then, flukes changing, moving wing-like in a steep bank, the whale arches and returns effortlessly towards me.

The overwhelming intensity of this creature's being clears my head of its petty preoccupations. He is so close now that I could reach out and touch him. The whale pulls in a fin and turns to avoid contact, a rippling black wall of smooth motion. His flukes swing up inches over my head. My body rocks gently from the movement of his immense form. The whale swims away. I follow quietly, into the center of the whale's world.

There—mothers, cautious, distant, put themselves between their curious young and me; lovers court, touch, stroke each other with a

The first five pages of the section which follows contain photographs by Mr. Curtsinger. The animals pictured are those described in this article.

191

touch so gentle I know I am watching an act of love. Swimming among their twisting, turning bodies I watch a male and female stroke each other's side with their fins. Shifting his great form, belly up, the male's penis emerges, grey-pink in the half light, sways cobra-like, trance-like, and enters her. Belly to belly they come together, moving gracefully, fluidly, forward. Their great bodies shake; then, finished, the male turns upright, moves his fluke over the contours of her back. They swim out of sight, side by side. My lungs empty, spent, my body dizzy, I surface, caught in their love.

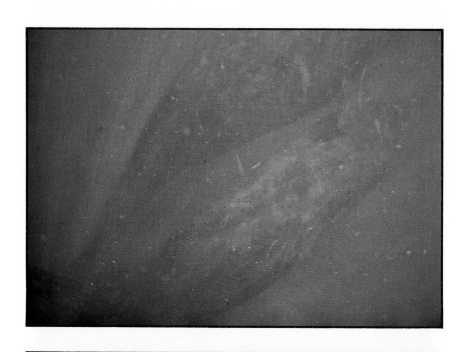

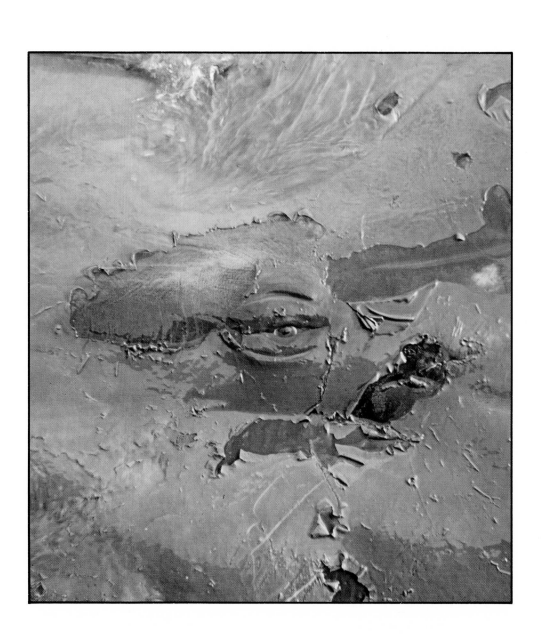

The open eye of a dead sperm whale floating in Ayukawa Bay just before it was butchered in August 1970. The eyes of the 26 corpses taken that day—the entire school—save one, were closed. That eye, however, remained open as the whale passed from life to death, and the last image of the assailant might have remained, faintly, on the retina. But the shutter never closed. The open eye gazes back at us, and we wonder what we have done.

From National Parks, *"Whales: A Skirmish Won, But What About the War?" by Scott McVay, February 1971*

Our quarry broke surface some five hundred yards away on the starboard bow and began his silent, terrible death struggle. If whales could utter cries which could rend the heart their deaths would be less dreadful than this losing battle which our whale was now engaged upon, in silence broken only by the far-off screaming of clouds of sea birds. We could not even hear the thrashing of crimsoned foam as he writhed and plunged, spouting a bloody spray at first, then an upgushing, followed by a bubbling upwelling amid a spreading island of blood. Suddenly the struggle ceased, the red foam subsided and we could see the body lying on its side quite still, one flipper sticking out of the water. The birds busied themselves above and around it with shrill cries.

The movements of the flurry may be large in dimension but they are carried out slowly, with the laboring exertion of an exhausted animal. The struggle is heralded by the spouting of blood from the blowhole due to the mounting haemorrhage of the lungs. At this stage, called by the old whalemen "red flag" or "chimney afire," the respiratory beat is still sufficiently strong for the exhaled air to atomize the blood, so that the blow is a red mist. The whale struggles at the surface describing a somewhat circular path. The head rears more and more from the water, rising at an abrupt angle between six and fifteen feet into the air whilst the gape of the open mouth increases. The jaws now clash shut as the head falls sideways back, making a splashing withdrawal to a few feet beneath the surface. Next the whale rounds out, as though in an effort to sound. First the snout emerges and then the hump, and then the flukes rear out, but when these are still far from the vertical they fall back and smite the water with a report which, on a calm day, can be heard for miles. The head again emerges and pushes upwards, the jaw clashes and much the same laborings as those described take place once or twice again. The circular path is maintained, but the exertions become less and less large in scale. The spout of blood is no longer a mist but a broad, low cascade welling at the blowhole. If it has recently been feeding the whale vomits squid, sometimes very large, in whole or part. So much blood has been lost that the welling at the blowhole has ceased before the last convulsion takes place. The flukes may sweep a little in a slow, flat arc on the surface, and the head start to rear once more. Now the head splashes back, the body rolls out on one side, with the head awash and the jaws gaping and the stout blunt flipper sticking stiffly upwards. It is dead "fin out."

So there it is, this poor hulk, its skin already soiled by birds which have been pecking at it all night, streaked with slime and ruled with a longitudinal greasy high-water mark, the result of lying all night in the fouled and polluted water. It was difficult to believe that less than twelve hours ago this impersonal mass was a living animal, snorting through the fields of ocean. In an hour's time nothing would be left of it at all. The improbability of its appearance somehow made it more difficult to believe that it was ever a living creature. This, and the impersonality of living things after death have, I think, made men callous about killing whales. The marine environment, too, is another factor. It is so mysterious and secret. If a whale in life were as familiar and near to us as a stag or a horse a more humane view would long ago have prevailed about whaling. We only get a close view of whales after they are dead, and then they look so very dead! The fact is that death, whether of an animal or human being, is death —totally impersonal and not in the least like sleep.

From Lost Leviathan, *by F. D. Ommanney, Dodd, Mead & Company*

JOAN MCINTYRE
Mind in the Waters

We stand on the cliff in the early morning, above the blue green sea, watching the porpoises in the transparent water below us. They are resting.

The porpoise school moves like a great slow wheel turning around an invisible axis, rising and falling to the rhythm, it seems, of its collective breathing. The porpoises reach the surface in a long sequence —a column of living shimmering animals, undulating in the clear water. The column fans out momentarily around the surfacing animals, like a flower opening, then closes again as the line dives deeply and slowly, almost disappearing in the darkening sea.

From a distance a boat approaches, outboard motor whining in the silence, blue gray smoke plume spreading over the sea's surface. As the boat passes through the circling school, the porpoises deflect, flow like water around a rock, and resume their formation.

Clearly, the school is exquisitely aware of its collective environment, even though each animal seems almost asleep. It acts like a single organism, moving around boats and lines without altering the essential quiet of the resting period. Except for an occasional sonar click, the sea around the school is strangely silent. This great disc of porpoises rises and falls in the clear water, in a matrix of relationships. The porpoises drift and weave and slowly breathe in the deep secure order of the resting group.

After several hours the porpoises show signs of activity, spending more time near the surface and less time in the long deep dives below. By noon most of the school is swimming rapidly near the surface, but the wheeling shape is still clearly defined; the school still revolves around its center. Suddenly a porpoise leaps into the bright sunlight, falls back into the water with a shimmering splash and a sharp crack. Another porpoise reaches the surface, breathes deeply, and slaps her tail against the water—again the sharp crack. The school responds instantly. Excitement and energy ring like a bell in the stillness. The shape of the wheel is lost in a shower of spray as the porpoises re-group and recombine.

The sea sparkles with foam and scudding surf as the leaping, diving porpoises rise out of the water. Old friends seek each other, swim fast and long, synchronizing their movements at incredible speeds, turning and twisting in the marbled light near the surface, diving and spinning in the surge and pleasure of companionship. Someone finds a piece of floating kelp and a game starts. The kelp is caught by a flipper, towed to the light-filled surface, then released to be retrieved, again and again. The game goes on, involves other friends, becomes complicated by another piece of kelp. But there is no disorder. The school functions with an understood sense of manners and morals.

We stand in the hot sun, burdened with cameras, binoculars, and tape recorders, watching the dolphins. Their play is joyous and un-restrained, like everything they do. Their life absorbs us. We feel alert and expectant ourselves as their energy rises to meet us. We are studying the dolphins, but we wish to join them.

It is quite possible that this particular school has existed as a distinct entity for thousands of years. It has had to learn the complex details of its subtly changing local environment, and the routes and times of the great gatherings at sea, where porpoises from hundreds of schools gather and mix their memories and their genes. It has had to instruct its members in the specific lore and history of the group, time-binding its lessons in a communications matrix that is specific to itself. Individuals lived and died, but the school remained. The school, it seems, has a culture, a commonly shared, learned, and re-membered history as a group, which it transmits through the gen-erations.

Until very recently there was no natural force that could change, or wished to change, the basic social order and composition of the group. While the land heaved and changed along the coasts, while human cultures came and went, changing their forms and content, often distorting their visions with invasions and inventions, the por-poise school stayed steady and clear around its particular under-standing. The activities of men along the coastlines or in the boats that ranged the seas beside them hardly caused the porpoises pause. At best, humans were strange curiosities; at worst, petty annoyances. It has been only in the last few years, with the horrifying onslaught of the enormous tuna boats and the purposeful herding of the schools into giant purse seine nets, that the school has had anything serious to fear.

But at this moment, for this school, the tuna boats are just an ominous threat on the horizon of the next fishing season, and the porpoises are playing and courting with the time-honored grace of their kind. Mothers stroke and pat their young, elicit erections in the infant males and warm flooding feelings in the females. They are teaching the strong and happy lure of sexuality and play. Males and females chase and catch each other, swim together as a single creature, leap and dive, mouth and muzzle, smack and stroke. Friends, relatives, group mates come and go together in unrestrained pleasure. It is like this every afternoon. It is the time to feel the special exhilaration of being a porpoise among your kind.

Late in the afternoon we go into the water with them. Entering their world we begin to understand it through our experience. Our weight lifts from us; we become more playful, weaving, dipping, bobbing like corks in the calm swells. The visibility is good; we see each other and the porpoises circling around us in the pale green haze of the surface layers. Time slows beneath the surface and is measured by our breathing. As we relax in the water, accept it, the porpoises come closer. We hear the fine sonic wash of their emissions clicking over our skin.

The porpoises play most of the afternoon. Sometimes the play is unrestrained and vigorous, sometimes specific and ritualized. The bay, the home of the school for the last five centuries, is re-explored daily. Minor shifts in underwater topography, the subtle movements of sand bars, the buildup of corals are investigated and probed. Shifting currents and floating sands have uncovered part of an old wrecked ship. Several young adults dive down through the dark water to investigate. Tuning their sonar, they make out the outlines of the rusting metal. With high-pitched whistles they communicate this new map of the bottom to friends on the surface.

The sun grows fat and misshapen as it reaches the horizon, spreading its glowing orange light on the darkening water. First one, then another small group detach from the playing school and move out toward the open sea. They return and others move toward the fishing grounds in an effort to get the others to follow. For no reason apparent to us, the entire school decides it's time to leave. As if in answer to a signal, they leave the bay in a broad orderly line and head out to sea.

We watch the school fishing in the orange cast light of the rising moon. They are working out from an undersea shelf line, spread along a broad front, echolocating, keeping in voice contact as they sweep the depths. The porpoises move at high speed, leaping out of the water and crashing back into it, the sound of their splashing a signal of location and distance. They pay attention to areas above submerged mountains and escarpments, areas rich in life and fish. In the moonlight the broad leaping diving front of porpoises is an image out of a dream, as if the spirit of the sea herself is seeking her reflection. They time their leaps and dives so that the school is synchronized along a broad front, combining its collective information in order to find the fish. Suddenly the pattern breaks and the porpoises converge, almost instantaneously, at a single spot. They have found a school of fish and as the pattern breaks, mothers, infants, adults, yearlings, dive into the ink-black water, echolocating, turning, twisting, catching the seething mass of fishes that boils the water, making it foam like snow in the darkness.

The porpoises will fish like this for hours, long enough to satisfy their needs, but they do not quarrel about the fish. The sense of manners and propriety prevails, and once a porpoise is on a course for a fish, or has touched one, ownership is clear and undisputed.

The porpoises rarely fight with one another. The cohesion of the group does not allow the dislocation of arguments or grudges. Sometimes there is disagreement over a mate, and often a strange porpoise will be driven away from the school, but the order of the school itself is harmonious and, apparently, kind. There seems to be little reason to fight. There are no objects to accrue or own. There is constant sexual play, enough to allow everyone the satisfying contact with friends and mates and lovers. There is enough food. The school makes its way through the long hours, weeks, and years of its life with remarkable equanimity—and with great joy. Knit together by the integrated sensing of each member, each member sharing his or her information with the others, the school is an ancient, uniquely supportive culture—a creation greater than the sum of its parts.

The whale rolls unseen through the water, steady, sure, alert. On the surface a small group of people drift in a rubber boat, wait for the appearance of the whale. The whale rolls like a great wheel, turning over smoothly, silently. It is night. There is nothing to see except the calm dark surface of the sea. Then the water parts, reveals the rolling back. The blowhole of the whale opens and the sound of her breathing deepens the silence. She continues her long steady motion, rolling back into the sea from where she came.

She knows more about us than we know about her. She knows exactly where we are and all our changes of direction. She relates her course to ours, changing direction as the swells carry us into her pathway. We sit silently in the rubber boat wondering why we are here, and what we have come to see. We see only the flat calm sea, the rolling back, the glassy slick as she disappears again beneath us.

The whale turns in the water, moonlight reflects off her back, phosphorescence leaves silvered trails behind her as she circles the lagoon. She is looking for her mate, answering his long deep calls. She turns seaward to meet him.

Later, lying on the warm sand of the shore of the gulf we hear their deep breathing in the distance, like hearing the sea herself breathe, the breathing of all creatures that live, the deep strong exhalations condensing sound in the night stillness. The sound of their breathing comforts us during the night; we wake to listen, then drift back into sleep, aware of the lovemaking of the great whales. We drift into our dreams.

Their breathing stays deep and steady, marking the fundamental rhythm of their lives, an everpresent reminder that they are in constant aware contact with their bodies and with the body's needs. There is no deeper association than the association of breath with life. They are synonymous, and to be aware of one's breathing throughout one's lifetime is to be aware of the continuum of life itself. It is no accident that cultures primarily concerned with expanding awareness focus first and forever on consciousness of breath.

As I recollect the whales, I realize how strange they are to me—these enormous, cumbersome, yet supremely graceful beings that move like monsters out of the past, beneath the surface of the sea. I envy them, envy their life and the ease of their connections. I wish to be of them, yet my thoughts, my ideas, become obstacles to the possibility of that experience.

This is the mind I have always believed existed somewhere. The deep calm mind of the ocean, connected to body, living *in* the world, not looking out at it. Surrounded by the gentle clicking of each other's sound, these creatures drift and dive, carve shining bubbled circles in the still water, move like dream ghosts out of the sea's unchanging past. Not changing the world around them—only listening, touching, eating, being. It seems enough.

There was a time in our culture, not long ago, when the essential role of men and women was to nurture and protect each other, to be the caretakers of life and earth. At that time, when the sun sparkled on the sea of our imagination as freshly as it sparkled on the sea herself, we thought of our world and each other in ways which were life-venerating and death-respecting. The porpoise school that weaves its history protectively around its common existence, the whales that tune body and mind in a continuous awareness of life, are not symbols of an alien mythology—they are evocative of what was once the core of human relationships.

Animals were once, for all of us, teachers. They instructed us in ways of being and perceiving that extended our imaginations, that were models for additional possibilities. We watched them make their way through the intricacies of their lives with wonder and with awe. Seeing the wolf pick his delicate way across the snowy forest floor, the eyes of the owl hold the image of the mouse, the dark shape of the whale break the surface of the sea—reminded us of the grand sweep and diversity of life, of its infinite possibilities. The connection of humans with totemic animals was an essential need to ally ourselves with the power and intelligence of non-human life, to absorb some of the qualities bestowed by the evolutionary process on other creatures.

Whales and dolphins—all Cetaceans—are intensely interesting to us now. They seem to speak for a form of consciousness we are beginning to re-explore in our own inner natures. They help us chart our interior wilderness. We can hear whales singing. If we pay attention and let them live, perhaps we will hear them speak, in their own accents, their own language. It would be an extravagant reward to experience, by empathy, a different band of reality.

We are animals of the land. They are animals of the oceans. We have hands to move and mold the things of the earth. They do not. But with an intelligence imagined as grand as ours—what do they do? What can they do, with mind imprisoned in all that flesh and no fingers for releasing it?

I have stroked, and swum with, and looked at, these creatures, and felt their essence rise to meet me like perfume on a spring day. Touched by it, I felt gentler myself, more open to the possibilities that existed around me. There may be only one way to begin to learn from them—and that is to begin. We would not be harmed by returning to the roots which once nourished us, which still, unseen, link together all life that lives, and feels, and thinks, and dies, on this, our common planet.

PART FIVE

LET
US
ACT

Let Us Act

As you read this, the slaughter of whales and dolphins continues. Whaling is not something out of a romantic past, it is a highly mechanized industrial operation of the modern world. While the scientists connected with the whaling industry argue whether or not we should have a moratorium on whaling, the factory ships and catcher ships ply their grisly trade throughout the world's oceans.

Every twelve minutes a whale is killed—the living tissue blown into agony by explosive harpoons. Each year hundreds of thousands of porpoises in the eastern tropical Pacific and the Atlantic Oceans are suffocated and drowned in the purse seine nets of the tuna fishery. Although the companies and scientists connected with whaling will tell you there are good reasons to continue the slaughter, the principal reason is profit. Almost all of the products made from whales and dolphins, with the exception of food, can be synthesized or substituted from other sources. Whales are killed for chicken feed, cattle fodder, fertilizer, car wax, shoe polish, lipstick, cosmetics, margarine, cat and dog food, and to raise minks and foxes for fur coats. Whales are also killed, by Japan, for human consumption, but that consumption is decreasing while, at the same time, Japan continues to pollute and destroy her offshore fishery—a far more suitable food base than the Antarctic whale.

The whaling industry is relatively minor, realizing about $150 million a year worldwide. Japan and the U.S.S.R. are the principal whaling nations, each killing about 40 percent of the world catch. The rest of the whaling is done by Australia, Denmark, Iceland, Norway, Panama, South Africa, and Brazil (members of the International Whaling Commission), and Chile, Peru, Portugal, and Spain (non-members).

In view of its profits and products, it is a trivial industry. But the destruction of an entire order of highly evolved, intelligent, gentle beings is not trivial. The whales *can* be saved—and in saving them we can create a model of international action that can demonstrate a way to save ourselves and the rest of the earth we cherish.

The following pages will give you the scientific, political, and historical information necessary to understand the slaughter. If you wish to help us save the whales, please write Project Jonah, and we will send you an action fact sheet detailing our current campaign.

Thank you.

Joan McIntyre

Project Jonah
Box 476
Bolinas, California 94924
U.S.A.

Project Jonah
15 rue du Commerce
Paris 15, France

Project Jonah
c/o Dobutsu Kenkyukai
5-24-16-Nakano
Daini Kopo #402
Tokyo, Japan   164

SCOTT MCVAY
One Strand in the Rope of Concern

Scott McVay is the Chairman of the Committee on Whales of the Environmental Defense Fund. He has worked for the conservation of whales for the last fifteen years and is the author of a large number of popular and scientific articles on whales and whale conservation. He received the Albert Schweitzer Memorial Prize in 1974 for his work on behalf of Cetaceans.

I am pleased to contribute the threads of "One Strand in the Rope of Concern," to recall where we have been and to point a way for the whale effort ahead. The excerpts here are less than 2 percent of what I have written. In thinking about the events of the past decade one more time, I am struck afresh by our enormous stake in the fate of the whale. And if we cannot spare the great whale, what chance will smaller creatures have? Indeed, what of our own chances?

From National Parks, February 1971: For years—indeed for centuries—the behemoth of the seas has been pursued unchecked and unmonitored. In fact, romantic notions about whaling persist strongly into our own time from the days when whaling vessels sailed the seven seas on voyages lasting up to five years and taking *one whale a month* was the norm. Today, however, and for the past fifty years, the pursuit of the whale has been highly mechanized; and a typical catcher boat (of a retinue that accompanies each vast factory ship where whales are butchered in fifteen minutes and their remains melted down) will harpoon *one whale a day.* More than forty thousand whales were killed in 1969.

The old square-rigged notions about whaling linger like a gauzy pink haze and abound in contemporary writing. For example, R. J. Harrison wrote recently, "The history of the technology of whaling provides an opportunity to study a closely knit, international fraternity of brave, adventurous men who were out on the high seas for great rewards." The adventure has begun to pall, for the whale has no more chance than a bull in the ring as it is scouted by helicopter, scanned by sonar, and run down by mechanized ships designed to travel three knots faster than a finback's top speed.

From Scientific American, August 1966: The ultimate fate of the great whales has been a question for more than a century. Herman Melville included such a query among the observations that make his *Moby Dick* an encyclopedia of whales and whaling: "Owing to the almost omniscient look-outs at the mastheads of the whale-ships, now penetrating even through Behring's straits, and into the remotest secret drawers and lockers of the world; and the thousand harpoons and lances darting along all the continental coasts; the moot point is, whether Leviathan can long endure so wide a chase, and so remorseless a havoc; whether he must not at last be ex-

terminated from the waters." Melville's conclusion was that Leviathan could endure. This was not unreasonable at the time (1851), when whalers pursued whales in open boats and killed them with lances.

Each of the two past eras of whaling has virtually eradicated its own most highly prized whale species. The bowhead whale and the right whales are monuments to man's thoughtlessness in the days of sail. The blue whale and humpback—and possibly the finback and sei as well—are monuments to an industry's lack of foresight in the days of steam. The whaling nations today face a third and almost certainly a final decision. If essentially unrestricted whaling continues, the only surviving stock of any economic importance—the sperm whale, of whose numbers more than 250,000 have been killed in the past twelve years—is doomed to become a monument to international folly.

From Natural History, January 1971: The decimation of the Antarctic whale fishery is a grisly story. It has been catalogued since 1920, when the Bureau of International Whaling Statistics in Sandefjord, Norway, began recording every *reported* whale kill by species, length, sex, date, and place of death. During the 1960s, the yield in barrels of whale oil dropped fivefold, from more than two million barrels to less than 400,000 in the 1969–70 season. The whalers might have taken more than a million barrels year after year, indefinitely. But their insatiability in the past two decades has so ravished the stocks and so decimated the large species that the sustainable yield today is but a shadow of what it could be if the stocks had a chance to rebuild.

In the past twenty-five years, 62,022 blue whales—at 85 feet and more the largest mammals on earth—and 15,025 humpbacks—perhaps the most playful of the great whales—have been taken in the Antarctic. Never very abundant, both species have been pushed to the edge of life, but are now nominally protected. The finback is the next candidate for "commercial extinction," that is, when its numbers will have been so reduced that it will no longer be profitable to send expeditions to hunt them. The finback, a smaller cousin of the blue whale, was second only to the sperm whale in abundance. During the past quarter-century, 444,262 finbacks were taken in the Antarctic, more than half of them from 1954 to 1962 when more than 27,000 finbacks were taken each year. Their population is now estimated at 67,000 to 75,000, one-fourth of its original size. If the exploiters had shown restraint—if they had learned the lesson of the blue and humpback, had remembered the slaughter of the rights and bowhead in the last century—then the Antarctic could have yielded 10,000 to 12,000 finbacks a year down the long hungry road of the future. Today the sustainable yield is estimated at less than 3,000 finbacks.

Antarctic sperm whaling peaked in 1956, when 6,974 sperm whales were reported taken, a catch that produced 342,000 barrels of sperm oil. During the 1969–70 season,

225

3,090 sperms were taken in the Antarctic for a production of 125,000 barrels of oil. The striking fact about these figures is that they reflect a steady decline in the yield in barrels of oil per whale over the past fifteen years. The oil yield in the Antarctic has dropped alarmingly, from 49 barrels per sperm whale to 40 barrels. In a mere fifteen years the sperm whales are 18 percent smaller. The pattern of predation seems intractable. (*Continued on page 227.*)

TO THE APOLOGIST, DEFENDER, AND STOOGE OF THE WHALING INDUSTRY: EJS

Suppose for a moment
that people began to disappear,
one at a time,
off the street, from their yards, from the supermarket
*   parking lot.*

Suppose they were hooked, one by one,
by a species working for another dimension
*   or an earth orbit if you like.*

Suppose that people began to miss
their colleagues, acquaintances, and relatives
but not very much.
In a way they were glad to be done with them.
At least those left were still swimming along.
The chosen few were spared, they felt, quite judiciously
*   by the gods.*
Besides there had been a problem of "uncontrollable population
*   growth."*
Also, the people disappeared so neatly. Never a trace.

That had happened in Germany some years before
but everything worked out all right there
in the end,
Didn't it?

Now this orbiting species
was packaging for eating
the men, women, and occasional children
who were hooked
for they tasted something like
a preferred dish from home.

Some nut among the visiting species
wondered
if the everywhere species of featherless biped
might not possess low grade intelligence.
This passing voiced wondering went unheard amid
the throng, the scurry, the bustle, the hurry
to expedite, organize and wind up
the hunt for homo sap.

Still one visiting orbiter
looked at a dead specimen of the creature
reported to have paved a good section of earth and
*   routed many forms of life*
and tried to imagine
what spiritual qualities, what noble cast of mind,
what brimming generosity, what vaulted aspirations
might inhabit and haunt
a possible mind
housed in an unprepossessing cranium
in three pounds of putty.

His emerging theory about a low order of communication,
based primarily on how well they could see to copy
one another
(according to reports from the forward hooking observers),
met the general shrug that
if they are smart
why are they so easily caught?

A solo plea for further consideration of these bipeds,
since their numbers were waning rather rapidly lately,
was officially answered.
"These bipeds are just hiding better.
They are to be sought out, hooked, pickled or freshly frozen,
*   and packaged, quickly.*
Get on with the job, get it done."

Near the end the small voice of a duly constituted committee
whispered
that the bipeds could produce an annual image of themselves
and their importance as a continuing food source
should be taken properly into consideration.
The stereophonic modulated reply was,
". . . the hooking devices and trained crew would
just move on
to fresh air in a new star system when this one ceased to pay off.
There were many systems
still left to hook."

And even the nut began to see things like the others.
He pierced the balooned folly of supposing
a mimicking war-fascinated death-driven polluting
overpopulating cocky species had some glimmer
of the first rays of intelligence.
Consciousness of self yes, a full inspection of the navel,
and the probing of the dirt therein enfolded,
but still awaiting the first rays.

But what of the mind of the sperm whale who they say
had a brain that weighed 20 pounds?
We may never know.

4/11/65

The problem of the survival and continuity of the great whales would be eased if the Soviets extended to large whales the attitude they take toward the smaller dolphins and porpoises. In March 1966, the Soviet government banned the catching and killing of dolphins. This decision was taken, according to Alexander Ishkov, Soviet Minister of Fisheries, because research has shown that dolphins have brains "strikingly close to our own." Dr. Ishkov, therefore, regards the dolphin as the "marine brother of man," noting, "I think that it will be possible to preserve dolphins for the sake of science. Their catch should be discontinued in all seas and oceans of the world."

From American Scientist, 1969: The central question with the sperm whale must remain, *Why the giant brain?*, when sharks and squid of similar size get along in the sea on a pea-sized brain. Scheffer writes, "No one has yet unlocked the secret of the mighty dome," but he does not ask, Why a brain six times that of man? What are its functions? From what we know of computers, the larger the instrument the more information it can handle. What kind of information can this fantastic biological instrument handle? What relation do its signals bear to this information?

From Congressional testimony, July 26, 1971: A biologist, familiar with the workings of the International Whaling Commission over many years, has questioned whether the whales are not worse off for the existence of the I.W.C. He contends that if the industry had been wholly unrestrained it would have collapsed a few years ago for Japan and the Soviet Union as it has for England, Netherlands, and Norway, the high-labor-cost countries. Now we are all witnesses to the slow death of whaling and the more systematic demise of whale stocks and species.

Only in the sweep of history can the question of a moratorium be properly considered. We have only to recall the unrestrained exploitation of whales that began in the Bay of Biscay fishery in the twelfth century which plundered the right whale in those parts, the ravaging of the eastern Arctic in the seventeenth century by nine European powers leaving scarcely a spout of the bowhead, and the wanton destruction of the blue and humpback populations in our century. Even while recognizing an improved effort by some member nations of the International Whaling Commission, the faltering steps of the Commission as a whole in the last few years cannot overcome the havoc wrought by the whalers in our time. As a consequence, a ten-year moratorium on whaling seems not only reasonable but minimal.

For example, ten years would not be long enough for a recovery of the fin whale population in the Antarctic which, with the blue initially and the sei more recently, has borne the brunt of intense commercial whaling over the past quarter century.

From National Parks, February, 1971: The public may also ask why meetings of the I.W.C. are closed sessions when whales are creatures that no individual or country owns: indeed, it may be anachronistic to view them only in terms of their long-term protein yield or as the "property" of a small band of entrepreneurs. In any event the whales have a larger claim on our attention than do the selfish short-term interests of a few whalers that have been dictating the beat of the slaughter for a long time.

From Audubon, November, 1971: Recently another slaughter of marine mammals involving the powerful tuna industry has come to light. Porpoises of at least three species, including the remarkable spinner, which often gyrates longitudinally when leaping clear of the sea, are killed by a purse-seining technique in use during the past dozen or so years. Because porpoises feed on the same small fish as the tuna, schools of porpoises numbering 500 animals or more are commonly encircled in the net along with the catch. As the seine is drawn tighter, many porpoises hit the net and drown. In the early days of using the purse seine, porpoise mortality ran very high because fishermen knew no way to get them out of the net. However, the development in recent years of a rescue method called "backing down" the net allows a varying proportion of each school to escape. But an estimated 250,000 animals still perish each year in the tuna fisheries of the eastern tropical Pacific alone. Better techniques for releasing the porpoises have been proposed but have not yet been fully tested.

An International Conference on Whale Biology held last June in the Shenandoah National Park in Virginia attracted thirty-four leading marine mammalogists, biometricians, and conservationists from Asia, Africa, Australia, Europe, and North and South America. The purpose of the three-day gathering was to indicate gaps in our knowledge of whale populations and to suggest ways to curtail the whaling industry's continuing exploitation of these great marine mammals. Most regrettably, two invited participants from the Soviet Union—one of the two major whaling nations—were, at the last minute, unable to attend. But six Japanese scientists were on hand. These two countries together take 85 percent of the whales killed each year.

Although the conference participants never questioned the prevailing assumption that whales must be killed on a large scale, they nonetheless began what may evolve one day into a Magna Charta for whales. Indeed, the conference itself represents a turning point because many of the participating whale biologists began to think seriously for the first time about the problem of whale conservation.

From Passages, April, 1972: The whale problem is getting attention in diverse places. Mexico, which commendably has not been involved recently in commercial whaling, has recently taken a significant step to ensure that whales which take refuge in the lagoons along Baja California, Mexico, will be forever unmolested. By presidential decree on January 14, 1972, Ojo de Liebre (or Scammon's Lagoon) was declared a natural sanctuary for whales. The decree applies particularly to the gray whale which is known to mate and calve in those warm waters during January, February, and March.

The guidelines implementing the presidential decree will, we trust, reflect President Echeverria's determination that this area be kept as a natural refuge for all forms of wildlife since their life patterns interconnect. It is no longer enough to try and spare a single endangered species. Entire habitats must be set aside, safe from the inroads of commercial development. We may hope that other nations will follow the lead taken by Mexico and declare certain watery areas and their environs, where whales and porpoises naturally congregate at specific times of the year, as wildlife sanctuaries. Whales are for celebration, not annihilation.

From Passages, April, 1972: It was the evening of the Great Bonfire in Kyoto, August 16, 1970. We were seated on tatami mats outside one of the restaurants along the river, awaiting darkness and the blazing ritual about to occur on the mountain above Kyoto, an annual affirmation of the great design, symbolizing the departure of the spirits after three days among us. Sakyo Komatsu, one of Japan's most gifted writers —who has glimpsed the worlds of heaven and hell toward which we are moving—put headphones on his ears and began to listen to *Songs of Humpback Whales.* In stereo. His romantic, restless nature was stilled for a moment, as he listened intently. Then his eyes flashed with understanding; he murmured, "incredible," again and again, and sputtered with joy as another world began to open for him. Komatsu generously passed the headset to others, including a geisha, peppered me with questions, and then, after others had heard the whale's voice, he listened anew with profound attention. The recording is called, "The Whale Trip."

Two months later Sakyo Komatsu wrote, "We have been profoundly impressed by the songs of those huge and jolly creatures resounding through the vast space of the undersea world. What an exciting experience it was, to hear the ballads and arias composed by whales and sung by themselves! You have made us open our eyes and minds to another new frontier for the human soul . . ."

The same sounds were also heard in August 1970, by a gentleman who heads one of Japan's three whaling firms. He, too, was pleasantly surprised by the range and variety of the whale's song. Indeed, he said that he would play the whale record at the next meeting of the executives of the whaling industry.

And yet, this gentleman, who has been a chief interpreter of the interests of the Japanese whaling industry to the Japanese government for more than a decade, continues to puzzle me. He is known as the ranking bird conservationist in the Orient, and he helped to draft the treaty between Japan and the United States governing the protection of 150 bird species that migrate between our two countries. I asked him how he squared being such a strong advocate for bird protection with his role in Japanese whaling.

"It is very simple," he explained, gesturing, "with my left hand I stroke the birds and with my right shaft the whales."

THE "WHALING BASEMENT" AT AYUKAWA

Four minutes before you reach
the peninsula-end town
on a rutted ribbon of road
the first whiff of boiling bones
makes you shiver.
The sick sweet smell
grows thicker
and becomes stitched into clothes
part of your person.
On entering Ayukawa
you don't reach for a handkerchief
to shield your nose or catch your barf,
for no one else seems to notice
what singes the air in sickly motion.
A boy plays catch,
coca cola is sold,
the women do things
that women do
to keep life together.
You breathe shallowly
trying to forget the hanging smell.
The putrescence
of burning flesh at Auschwitz
and the other camps
comes to mind
and is dismissed
and then it creeps back again
as the loitering smell
invades and invests
everything live and limp
and you become a part of
the butcher as you eat
the food provided by
the company that kills
more whales than any other.
You talk with Matsumoto,
as though the subject were
butterflies on the loose
and not the rending of
the last behemoths
by a species
still seeking its place
and lacking the right relation
to other living beings.

But the pungent all-permeating
smell of cooking fish
cancels every other whim.
From this hour
I will carry perpetually
millions of molecules
of Ayukawa air
laced with dead whales.
How check the slaughter?
If I knew, I would be a prophet
and put whalers behind other plows.

8/21/70

From Natural History, January, 1971: Our survival is curiously intertwined with that of the whale. Just as all human life is interconnected (in the Monkey-Rope situation in *Moby Dick,* Ishmael declares, "I saw that this situation of mine was the precise situation of every mortal that breathes; only, in most cases, he, one way or other, has this Siamese connexion with a plurality of other mortals. . . ."), so have we finally begun to perceive the connections between all living things. The form of our survival, indeed our survival itself, is affected as the variety and abundance of life is diminished. To leave the oceans, which girdle seven-tenths of the world, barren of whales is as unthinkable as taking all music away and everything associated with music—composers and their works, musicians and their instruments—leaving man to stumble on with only the dryness of his own mutterings to mark his way.

THE ALTERNATIVE?

If	a
we	marine
do	Daidara-
nothing,	bochi
	who,
in	
a	it
few	was
years	said,
	sang
the	unspeak-
whale	ably
will	beau-
live	ti-
only	ful
	songs.
as	
a	8/18/70
legend,	Osaka

VICTOR SCHEFFER
The Case for a
World Moratorium
on Whaling

Victor Scheffer, Ph.D., is a biologist and chairman of the presidentially appointed Marine Mammal Commission of the United States. The author of The Year of the Whale *and* The Year of the Seal, *Dr. Scheffer has been a student of marine mammal biology and behavior for most of his life. He speaks lovingly of the impressive experience of coming in contact with great aggregations of animals and of the need to reappraise creatures as other than "meatballs."*

At the United Nations Conference on the Human Environment, in Stockholm, on June 16, 1972, a proposal for a ten-year ban on all commercial whaling was unanimously adopted. A few days later, at the annual meeting of the International Whaling Commission (I.W.C.) in London, it was rejected 4-6-4. At the next meeting of the I.W.C., on June 26, 1973, it was again rejected, though by a smaller margin, 8-5-1. (A three-quarters majority was necessary.) The I.W.C. ended its meeting in 1973 by agreeing upon killing quotas for 37,500 whales in the coming year.

The people who voted at Stockholm and London knew that their recommendations, whether pro or con, would be unenforceable and could take effect only on world opinion. For those at Stockholm it was easy to vote in favor of the whale —the common heritage of mankind, symbol of the world's endangered life, symbol of man's responsibility for his environment. For those at London it was not easy to vote to shut down the whaling industry.

The moratorium debate stems from a widespread belief that our generation has nearly destroyed the whales. Their world population is down to about one-half of its primitive size, or from 3.5 million to 2 million. The overall decline is perhaps not alarming, but it hides the grim fact that whaling has reduced certain stocks to dangerous levels. Worldwide, the fin whales are down to 23 percent and the blue whales to 6 percent. The southern humpback whales are down to 11 percent. The gray whale which formerly bred in Korean waters was exterminated in the 1930s or 1940s.

When a population of whales living free in the wild has been drastically reduced, it may never return to its former level. The North Atlantic right whale has not been hunted for fifty years, yet its population today is only about 150. The more vigorous and competitive sei whale may, in the meantime, have usurped the environmental niche which the right whale formerly occupied.

A partial moratorium on whaling is already in effect. Five of the ten species whose hunting is regulated by the I.W.C.

are protected (except from the whaling nations that are not members of the International Whaling Convention of 1946). The right and bowhead whales have had global protection since 1935, the gray whale since 1947, the blue since 1965, and the humpbacks since 1966. Five species—the fin, sei, Bryde's, sperm, and minke—are still being hunted.

Granted that certain populations are in trouble, does this call for a moratorium on all whaling? The answer will depend on one's personal opinion as to how desperate the situation is. It will depend also on one'e estimate of the ability of the I.W.C. to discharge its self-assumed obligation to conserve the whales.

The merits of a moratorium are being debated on moral, on biological, and on technical grounds. Until one understands that the debate is fueled from all three sources, one can hardly hope to reach a thoughtful opinion on the issue.

The Moral Argument

The I.W.C. has never concerned itself with the morality of whaling. Its purpose, as defined in the preamble to the convention, is "to provide for the proper conservation of whale stocks and thus make possible the orderly development of the whaling industry." The I.W.C. leans heavily on its technical and scientific committees; perhaps it should appoint also a sociological committee to advise it on public attitudes and preferences with respect to the uses of whales.

Points in the moral argument are outlined below.

1. The two nations which, at the 1973 meeting of the I.W.C., protested most strongly against a moratorium were the important whaling nations—Japan and the U.S.S.R. These two had killed, in the previous whaling season, 84 percent of all whales killed in the world.

2. The esthetic and educational values of whales alive are greater than the values of the meat, bone, oil, and chemicals which might be derived from their carcasses. The killing of whales to obtain rawstuffs used in cosmetics, and in feeds for pets and furbearers, is especially deplorable. (Justification can more easily be made for the use of whale meat as food for hungry people.) For all whale products, there are now substitutes in the form of proteins, oils, and chemicals from the land and the sea.

3. Whales are killed by a harpoon-bomb which explodes in the body. Not uncommonly, several harpoons are required to bring death.

4. Morality extends beyond ordinary humaneness, or the prevention of pain and terror in the animal, to a consideration of the simple right of the animal to live and to carry on its ancestral bloodline. Most people are willing to concede this right, or just claim to life, to "friendly" animals such as whales that seem to have a family structure, that talk among themselves, and that care for one another in time of trouble.

5. Man, being the most powerful of all living things, has a special responsibility to preserve for future generations the seed stocks of all varieties of life on earth. *Noblesse oblige.*

The Biological Argument

After Stockholm, the Japanese Whaling Association complained that the moratorium resolution had been put to a vote without "scientific discussion." Its adoption "has had the effect of planting certain ideas in the minds of the peoples of the world towards whaling and exerting pressure on the discussions within the International Whaling Commission."

Indeed, the resolution was intended to influence people outside, as well as within, the Commission. The Japanese Whaling Association continues to sound a familiar tune—that only scientific considerations should be permitted to influence the conservation of whales. But when, on September 19, 1973, the Government of Japan stated that it would not comply with two recommendations of the Scientific Committee of the I.W.C. with respect to whaling in the southern oceans—a catch quota of 5,000 minke whales and catch quotas by prescribed areas for sperm whales—it contravened the position of its own whaling association and of all other members of the I.W.C.

In any case, at the 1973 meeting of the I.W.C., the Scientific Committee "agreed that . . . there is no biological *requirement* [emphasis added] for the imposition of a blanket moratorium on all commercial whaling. The majority further considered that, for the same reason, there is . . . no biological *justification* for such a blanket moratorium."

The word "biology" has two meanings—the life processes of the animal and the study of those processes. With the first meaning in mind, the only biological argument for a moratorium is this—the quickest way to restore a depleted stock is to stop killing. No other argument for an immediate worldwide moratorium can be offered. The most gravely depleted of the whale stocks are now protected, while those lightly hunted, such as the southern minke whales, could continue to stand some exploitation.

With, however, the study of life processes in mind, strong biological arguments for a moratorium can be made, most of them variations on the theme that whale biology is shaky and is certainly not strong enough to support commercial management. Witness the bleak history of the blue whale, now in danger of extinction despite the protection presumably provided by whale biology. In the words of Sir Peter Scott, chairman of the World Wildlife Fund, there is "a widening crisis of confidence in the basic scientific evidence" of the I.W.C. In short, whaling should be banned until research has had time to illuminate its dark corners.

Some examples of the failings of the current scientific methods and calculations follow.

1. The methods used for estimating whale populations since the International Whaling Convention of 1946 give results that vary widely. In one method of study, statistics of the whale catch, including numbers taken by age and reproductive condition, are compared with theoretical models derived from *fishery* biology. Another method depends on the recovery of marked whales at the whaling factories. A third

depends on counts of whales from ships, aircraft, or points of land.

Estimates of humpback whales in the North Pacific range from 2,000 to 8,500. At the 1973 meeting of the I.W.C., the Japanese delegation, representing a whaling nation, gave an estimate of southern fin whales of 97,000, while the consensus of the Scientific Committee, except Japan, was for an estimate of 84,000. Furthermore, the Japanese claimed that 12,230 minke whales could safely be taken in the southern oceans each year; others on the Committee protested that 5,000 was a more realistic figure.

2. The methods are designed to bring populations to the level of maximum sustainable yield (MSY), though no whale population has ever been brought through management to that level. Whales on graph paper are not necessarily like whales in the sea.

3. The methods used for estimating whale populations during the past twenty-five years have been blind to ecology. They have considered each species as though it were independent of other organisms in the marine ecosystem — the other whales, the porpoises, fish, seals, birds, and plankton.

4. The methods depend heavily on catch-and-effort data from the whaling industry and, for that reason, are biased by industrial points of view. When the lower length limit for sperm whales is set at thirty-five feet, more whales thirty-five feet long are reported taken than could be expected by chance. And whale-sighting data tend to be inflated because they are gathered on hunting cruises; the whaling captains naturally avoid areas where in the past they have found few whales.

5. The methods are those of fishery biology, although whales are warm blooded animals, each with a complex social infrastructure quite different from that of any known fish. What, for example, is the effect upon the reproductive rate of killing one dominant whale in a family group? The name "fishery" applied to whaling is inappropriate.

6. In the breathing spell provided by a moratorium, the nations would be encouraged to concentrate on Cetacean research of new kinds not dependent on commercial whaling. These would provide information on numbers, movements, schooling behavior, segregation, reproductive rates, feeding habits, and other life history data.

The Technological Argument

1. The I.W.C. is a voluntary organization of national representatives including not only government officials but private individuals having a financial interest in whaling. Such individuals, when they are delegates, act under the constraints imposed by their governments; their actions are official. Nonetheless, the possibility of conflict of interest is latent in the organization. During its functional life of twenty-five years, the I.W.C. has failed to conserve the stocks of important whales. Within the I.W.C., the voting power of industry has dominated the voting power of the Scientific

Committee. For example, recommendations by the scientists to abolish the blue whale unit, which lumped several species as units of oil, were made as early as 1963, but were not acted upon by the I.W.C. until 1972. The I.W.C. needs the kind of jolt which a moratorium would provide.

2. A partial moratorium, like that now in effect, tends unduly to shift the pressure from protected to unprotected species. The historic shift of hunting effort successively from the southern blue whale to the fin and the sei is a case in point.

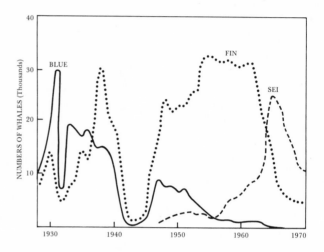

In practice, the I.W.C. has offered protection to one species after another, though always too late to satisfy conservation needs. It has not made full allowance for uncertainties.

3. A partial moratorium exposes protected species to the danger of being killed by mistake for unprotected ones living in the same waters. The danger is perhaps not great, though young sei and fin whales are easily mistaken for minke whales, now being hunted in all oceans.

4. The argument is often proposed that a ban on whaling would wreck the I.W.C. because it would leave that organization with nothing to do during the moratorium. The I.W.C. could, however, continue to be useful in new ways. It could support research of new kinds not dependent on the examination of tens of thousands of whale carcasses a year. It could continue to check on whaling activities by nations not party to the Convention.

By whatever routes of reasoning one arrives at the conclusion, a moratorium on commercial whaling will serve as a shift of scenery in the conservation drama, preparing us all for a new scene in which the whales of the world ocean will play new roles under new direction.

The opinions expressed in this paper are not necessarily those of the Marine Mammal Commission. I thank my colleagues in whale conservation for ideas, some of which in their present context they may disown.

LEE TALBOT
The Great Whales and the International Whaling Commission

Lee Talbot, Ph.D., an ecologist and biologist, is the senior scientist on the Council of Environmental Quality, Washington, D.C. He has studied conservation management extensively and spent several years in East Africa working on game management of African mammals. Dr. Talbot is Scientific Advisor to the United States delegation to the International Whaling Commission.

More than any other form of life, whales have come to epitomize the problems of managing our living resources. For the 113 nations assembled in Stockholm in 1972, at the United Nations Conference on the Human Environment, whales became the symbol of our environmental problem as a whole. Whale conservation is a problem of endangered species, but it is far more. The situation of the whales emphasizes the problems of management of living resources in general.

History of Whaling

Early whaling, dating back at least to the twelfth century, involved the use of open sail or oar-driven boats. Hand thrown harpoons were largely used, and the species hunted were those which were most vulnerable to these primitive techniques, particularly the slow swimming right and humpback whales. The pattern of whaling changed in the 1860s, following the invention by a Norwegian of the explosive harpoon, and the development of steam-driven whaling boats with harpoon cannons. This more modern technology allowed effective pursuit of the swifter swimming species such as the blue, fin, sei, and Bryde's whales. It was first applied in the North Pacific and North Atlantic, then spread in 1904 to the Antarctic. Until 1925, most whaling was land-based, with killer ships bringing whales back to a factory on land for processing. In 1925, the advent of factory ships allowed pelagic whaling fleets to follow the whales throughout the world's oceans. Whaling technology continued to develop, but it received its greatest improvements during the years following the Second World War, with the increasing application to whaling of military technology involving ship and motor design, remote search and sensing apparatus, and use of aircraft.

Oil, meat, and whalebone were the principal commercial products for which the whaling industry originally developed. In earlier days, whales provided a unique source of oils for lubricants and lamps. Today whale products are used in a variety of ways, from manufacture of margarine and soap, lubricants and cosmetics, to food for humans and domestic animals. Substitutes are available for all current uses, but

whale hunting remains economically viable, although apparently less so every succeeding year.

Determining Population Numbers

For the most part, the data on past and present populations of whales are fragmentary and speculative. Most of the base data are commercial statistics, i.e., records of catch, or, for protected species, sight records, subject to very considerable question on the basis of objectivity or scientific accuracy. The total population figures are extrapolated from these questionable data on the basis of population models, inferred largely from fin fisheries, with no control data to check their validity against living whale populations. Changes in population levels are inferred, in large part, from changes in the catch per unit effort. If fewer whales are caught for the same amount of effort or boat time, it is assumed that the whale population is dropping. But variations between boats and equipment, and improvements in technology, make comparison of "effort" questionable at best.

Speculative and questionable as they are, these figures are the best we have. This, in itself, is a major part of our conservation problem.

A further caveat about these figures concerns individual stocks. The whale population within each geographic area is not a single, homogeneous population, but is made up of a number of individual breeding stocks. While the total, lumped population figures may appear high, the status of individual stocks may be very precarious. In this context the value of these figures is simply to provide some perspective.

It must also be emphasized that "original" population figures for whales, even if they had some relationship to reality, would largely be of only historic interest. As will be discussed below, the figures for former or "original" populations in no way indicate a population level to which the present stocks will climb automatically if harvesting is reduced, nor do they appear to be a valid yardstick against which rational harvests may be determined. In the present context they simply indicate the magnitude of the resource loss (with the possible consequent disequilibrium of the marine ecosystem) which has been brought about by greed and mismanagement.

The Current Numbers of Whales

Bearing in mind the questionability of the figures, let us now look at the population sizes first of protected species and next of the species that currently are being hunted. In sum, as we shall see, of the eleven species of whales (counting the sei and Bryde's whales together) hunted commercially for periods ranging from decades to centuries, seven have been reduced to commercial, if not biological, extinction, and are now protected. One stock of one of these species has made some recovery. Four other species are currently hunted, with populations reduced to between 20 and 70 percent of the original levels. Exploitation is only just beginning on the last species, which presumably is not much reduced yet.

RIGHT WHALES. There are four right whales, all protected by law since 1935. The most northerly is the *Greenland right whale* or *bowhead*. It was the basis for the Greenland or Northern Whale Fishery in the Arctic, which lasted from 1611 to World War I, by which time the numbers were too low to be of further commercial interest. There are no good present data. The stocks in the Bering-Chukchi-Beaufort Sea region are estimated to be around 1,000; those in the Arctic north of the Atlantic at "a very low level."

The *North Atlantic right whale* occupied temperate waters in the northern Atlantic, and was the basis of whaling there from the twelfth century. By the early 1900s it too was reduced below commercial significance, and no good current data exist on these whales, although their numbers are very low.

The *North Pacific right whale* ranged from the sub-Arctic to warm temperate waters of the northern Pacific. It was hunted extensively from the eighteenth century until the 1920s, by which time it was almost exterminated in the northeastern Pacific and greatly reduced elsewhere.

The *Southern right whale*, of the southern oceans, was fished from the late eighteenth century until the 1920s, when it was nearly exterminated. Estimates for the present population of the Southern Hemisphere range from around 900 to 1,500.

GRAY WHALES. There were two separate stocks of gray whales inhabiting coastal waters of the northern Pacific Ocean and the Arctic Ocean. The eastern or California gray migrated from Baja California to the Bering and Chukchi Seas, and the western stock migrated betseen South Korea and the Olhotsk Sea. American nineteenth century whaling, plus some modern whaling, greatly reduced the numbers of the California stocks. They were afforded partial protection in 1937 (by North American whalers but not by Japanese or Soviet whalers) and full protection in 1947. The numbers have increased to around 11,000 and appear relatively stable. This is the only whale population that, once depleted, has shown any recovery. The western gray whales were commercially extinct in the 1930s and are believed biologically extinct now.

BLUE WHALES. Blue whales were found virtually worldwide and have been a major target of whaling since faster boats brought them within reach of whalers. The Antarctic stocks, originally estimated at around 200,000, were reduced to around 2,000 — 1 percent of the original population — by 1965, when they were finally given total protection. Highly questionable Japanese estimates based on sightings since then place present numbers around 6,000, about half of which are the pygmy blue whale subspecies. North Pacific stocks, originally estimated at 5,000, were totally protected in 1966. Present estimates are 1,500. Blue whales in the northwestern Atlantic were estimated at an original level of 1,100. They have been protected since 1960, and present estimates are 100 — 9 percent of the original population.

HUMPBACK WHALES. Humpback whales in the Southern Hemisphere have been protected since 1964. They comprise at least six separate breeding stocks, and have been so reduced that only fragmentary information on current stocks is available. Original numbers were estimated at around 30,000. Current population estimates range around 3,300 — roughly 10 percent of the original population. No original estimates exist for the North Pacific, where they have been protected since 1966, and present estimates range from 1,400 to 4,000. Humpbacks have been protected in the northwestern Atlantic since 1955. Original numbers are estimated at around 1,000 and at present at about 100 — again roughly 10 percent of the original level.

Currently Harvested Species

The following species are currently being exploited. The stated management objective is to maintain the stocks at the MSY level, i.e., the population level at which maximum sustainable yield should be obtained. Consequently, figures are given for the MSY level along with those for the estimated original and current populations. The MSY concept is discussed in the section on "Conclusions" below.

FIN WHALES. The blue whale was the most desirable whaler's prize since it was the largest, but as the blue whales were reduced, increasing effort was diverted to the fins, with resultant significant reductions in populations throughout their range. Fin whales are still hunted virtually throughout their range. The estimates for original populations in the Southern Hemisphere were around 395,000, the MSY was put at 209,000, and the current stock is estimated at 82,000 — about one-fifth of original population. In the North Pacific, the original estimate is 43,500, MSY is 27,000 ,and current estimate is 16,000 — one-third of the original level. In the northwestern Atlantic, the original was estimated at 5,000 and current at 2,300.

SEI AND BRYDE'S WHALES. The sei and Bryde's whales are considered together, since there are few data for the Bryde's whales, and in many records they have been lumped together with the sei. Sei whales have only been fished intensively in the Antarctic since the early 1960s, when effort was shifted from the declining fin whales. The original population was estimated at 150,000, MSY has been put at 52,000, and present numbers at 82,000, although individual stocks in heavily fished areas are much reduced. In the North Pacific the original numbers were estimated at about 60,000, MSY at 35,000, and present population at around 35,000. However, these Japanese figures have been strongly challenged, and the true populations may be substantially lower.

SPERM WHALES. Sperm whales have long been exploited both from land stations and pelagic fleets. A number of separate population stocks have been identified or inferred, some of which, like those off the west coast of South America, have been severely overfished, while others have been less heavily exploited. The species is polygynous, with differences in behavior and body size; consequently, the figures available are divided by sex. In the Southern Hemisphere the original numbers of males were estimated at 257,000, the MSY at 112,000, and present stock at 128,000. Original number of females was estimated at 330,000, the MSY at 231,000, and current stock at 295,000. In the North Pacific the original population of males was estimated at 167,000, the MSY at 69,000, and present stock at 69,000; for females the original estimate was 124,000, the MSY at 53,000, and present stock at 102,000. While total figures appear relatively high, many localized stocks have been identified or inferred, some of which have been severely overharvested.

MINKE WHALES. This smallest of the commercially exploited great whales has been harvested intensively only during the past two years, when declining stocks of the next least desirable species, the sei, led the industry again to shift its target. Because minke whales have been of commercial attention for such a short time, there are few data available, and estimates of original and present stocks range from the I.W.C. Scientific Committee estimate of 150,000 to the Japanese estimate —on the same base data—of 298,000.

Conservation History

The total history of whaling to date is one of an industry which has overexploited and driven species after species into commercial extinction. As one species became so reduced that it was no longer economically exploitable, the industry shifted its attention to the next most economically desirable one. Thus the species which were large and slow swimming, and therefore vulnerable to the early open-boat whaling, were the first targets of the industry. These were greatly reduced even before the advent of the modern whaling techniques brought them to economic extinction. Attention then transferred to the great blue whale, vulnerable to modern technology and yielding the greatest amount of product per animal caught. As the blue whale stocks were driven down, attention was transferred to the next largest, the fin whale, and with its rapid reduction in the fifties, effort shifted to the sei whales. Now that the economic possibilities for exploitation of these stocks are limited, the industry has finally focused on the least economically desirable of the great whales, the small minke.

The practical impact of any conservation effort to date has been to slow down the decline of some of the whales but not to alter the end point.

In 1931, an International Convention for the Regulation of Whaling was concluded at Geneva. The Convention came in force in 1935 following ratification by the required eight nations. The Convention applied only to baleen whales. It specified various procedures and regulations regarding taking and reporting, and from a conservation point of view the two most important sections were those that protected all right whales and prohibited the taking of female whales accompanied by calves. Of course, by that time right whales were already economically extinct.

From that time to the Second World War, there were several other conservation agreements, among them the 1937 agreement to protect gray whales, which did not apply to Japan and the U.S.S.R.

International Whaling Commission (I.W.C.)

In 1946, the International Convention for the Regulation of Whaling was signed in Washington and it came into effect in 1948. This is the international agreement under which most present whaling is conducted. In its preamble the Convention recognized that "the history of whaling has seen overfishing of one area after another and of one species of whale after another to such a degree that it is essential to protect all species of whales from further overfishing."

However, the economic considerations of the industry itself were clearly a paramount consideration. As the final paragraph of the preamble states, the signatory nations had decided "to conclude a convention to provide for the proper conservation of whale stocks and thus make possible the orderly development of the whaling industry."

The Convention established the International Whaling Commission (I.W.C.) composed of one representative from each of the signatory governments. The purpose of the I.W.C. is to provide for continuing review of the status of whale stocks and their management, and to modify the agreed-upon management measures in the schedule accordingly. To this end, they meet at least once a year. The changes in the schedule are agreed to by a three-fourths majority of the members voting, and these decisions are binding on the member nations if they do not lodge an objection within ninety days. The contracting nations agree to enforce these agreements on their own nationals and ships.

The Convention specifies that, among other things, the agreed-upon amendments to the schedule shall "be based upon scientific findings" but also they "shall be such as necessary . . . to provide for the conservation, development, and optimum utilization of the whale resources" and "shall take into consideration the interests of the consumers of whale products and the whaling industry."

The Convention came into effect in 1948, and the I.W.C. held its first meeting in 1949. It established a Scientific Committee which proceeded to warn it that stocks of the blue, fin, and humpback whales were being seriously overfished. (When the Convention came into force, it continued the existing protection for gray whales and right whales.) However, until 1963, there were no visible conservation efforts, and the quotas appeared to be based on the hunting capacities of the industry. Arguments for conservation by the scientists have been countered by the I.W.C. members, year after year, on the basis that their industries could not survive economically with lower quotas, and on the basis that the scientific evidence was not complete, precise, and incontrovertible.

In 1963, the "committee of three scientists," a special group of biostaticians, set up by I.W.C. to analyze the whaling data, presented compelling evidence of the gross overfishing of the stocks in the Antarctic. The I.W.C. responded by a slight reduction in quotas. In 1964, the I.W.C. failed to agree on quotas, but after an emergency meeting the next year, the Commission finally set Antarctic quotas at or below estimated maximum sustainable yield level. Unfortunately, the MSY levels had been based on an estimate of reproductive age which proved to be erroneous. The MSY level had been set far too high, so the stocks of the remaining exploited whales, the fin and sei, continued to plummet.

The I.W.C. had by that time, on the basis of overwhelming scientific evidence — and the doubtless more operational factor that whalers could no longer find them — provided total protection for the blue whales and humpback whales. In response to the improved scientific information — and the increasing difficulty of their industries to take higher numbers — the I.W.C. has continued to reduce quotas.

From the standpoint of the welfare of the whales, the I.W.C. has utterly failed. From the standpoint of the whaling industry, it has been quite successful. Without the I.W.C., whale populations would have crashed to their present levels much more rapidly, probably forcing most of the whaling industries out of business over a short period of time with considerable attendant economic loss. The delaying effect of the I.W.C. quotas has slowed the collapse sufficiently that the industries have been able to amortize their investments and withdraw slowly and economically. Further, the slower decline has provided for more whales to be harvested in the interim. As Gambell and Brown have noted, "It has been calculated that this lower decline has allowed at least 4,000 blue whales and 45,000 fin whales to be taken since 1946 which would not otherwise have been available."

At present the fifteen member nations of the I.W.C. are Argentina, Australia, Brazil, Canada, Denmark, France, Iceland, Japan, Mexico, Norway, Panama, South Africa, U.S.S.R., U.K., and U.S.A. Four additional countries catch relatively small numbers of great whales: Chile, Peru, Portugal, and Spain. Whaling operations off the west coast of South America are regulated by the permanent Commission for the Exploitation and Conservation of the Marine Resources of the South Pacific, which was established by Chile, Peru, and Ecuador in 1952.

Russia and Japan between them take something more than 80 percent of the world's whales, and they have been the I.W.C. members most aggressively opposed to reduction in quotas. Their representatives were visibly shaken by the pro-conservation climate of the 1973 meeting. Throughout that meeting of the I.W.C., the Soviet and Japanese representatives reiterated the threat that unless talk of moratorium or

significant quota reductions ceased, the International Observer Scheme might be stopped, and the I.W.C. itself might be wrecked. They did block any action to strengthen the I.W.C., even though this action had been agreed upon by all nations earlier.

There were three principal conservation decisions at the meeting:

1. To retain the Antarctic minke quota at 5,000, in accordance with the direct recommendation of the Scientific Committee. The vote was 13 to 1 (Japan).

2. To divide the quotas for sperm whales in the Southern Hemisphere by areas, instead of setting a single overall quota which in the past had allowed significant overfishing of some stocks. Again, this was a direct recommendation of the Scientific Committee. The vote was 12 to 2 (Japan and U.S.S.R.).

3. To phase out fin whaling in the Antarctic no later than June 1976.

Within the ninety day period the whaling convention allows, both Japan and U.S.S.R. "objected," thereby rejecting these three measures and freeing themselves from any obligation to abide by these decisions. Their action is a direct rejection of the strongest recommendations of the Scientific Committee; yet both in 1972 and 1973 both nations argued against any moratorium on the basis that the Scientific Committee had not recommended it. All I.W.C. nations had agreed that the advice of the Scientific Committee would be followed in setting quotas; yet here, when the Committee's advice did not coincide with their commercial interests, Japan and Russia rejected it, and with it the decision of a minimum of three-quarters of the I.W.C. nations.

This action appears to confirm many of the strongest criticisms of the I.W.C. One such criticism, of course, is the ineffectiveness of a regulatory body which cannot enforce regulations even when an overwhelming majority of its members have agreed to do so.

Another criticism is that the whaling nations or the industries involved have simply used the I.W.C. to provide international endorsement or legitimacy to actions which they were going to take anyway for economic reasons.

Conclusions

Several major conclusions flow from this brief history.

First, a totally new, or drastically revised, mechanism is required to provide effective regulation of the world's whale populations. This is clearly essential for the whales. But the problems of the I.W.C. as a resource management mechanism are also experienced to a greater or lesser degree by most such mechanisms currently attempting to regulate other living resources of the sea. The time is past when the world should — and, I believe, when it will — accept the idea that management of a living resource should be left to the industry or nation which happens to have the capability to exploit it at the time. There is growing recognition that the survival and welfare of the living resources of the sea are of significance and concern to all nations. The mechanisms for their management should reflect this fundamental fact.

Secondly, even when we get an effective mechanism, we need adequate information as a base for effective management. The present base is totally inadequate. What data exist are questionable in many respects, fragmentary, and at best, highly speculative. Information on the marine ecosystem necessary for any real understanding of living whales is almost totally lacking.

Third, the simple application of the MSY is not appropriate as a basis for management of the whalers. The concept of MSY has been basic to whale management—at least on paper—throughout recent whaling history. It is basic to virtually all fisheries management, and as such, it has assumed the status of sacred dogma. Yet, it is questionable whether MSY is an appropriate basis for management of any fishery, and even if it were appropriate, there are few examples indeed of effective management based on it. Larkin, writing about fin fish management in *World Fisheries Policy*, has noted, "We must first acknowledge that, for the most part, our theories of fisheries management are essentially based on circumstantial evidence."

He continues: "For example, for many of our fisheries, the relation between stock and recruitment 'remains obscure,' by which we mean that it is the same relation that one would observe if there were no relation. In other instances it is difficult to estimate fishing effort because of rapidly changing fishing technologies. The consequences of harvesting mixed species continue to haunt us like a can of many kinds of worms. Even on relatively basic matters, such as the genetic consequences of harvesting, we are much in the dark. We have had fifty years of research, have accumulated an impressive literature, and certainly can convey to undergraduates an impressive savoir faire. However, if we try to write a book on the *accomplishments* of fisheries management toward the objective of maximum sustained yield, I think we will conclude that we need twenty pages for introduction, one page for results, and more than one hundred pages for rationalized excuses."

Larkin concludes that, "In brief, our fisheries literature is largely unscientific in the strict sense of the word, and our fisheries management is unscientific in almost any sense of the word."

These comments apply with even greater force to the whale fishery. What is "known" of the population dynamics of the whales is inferred from fish and other animals. There are almost no data from direct observations or from sources other than catch statistics—most of which are from commercial sources. There are absolutely no control data at all to prove or disprove the inferences.

What few data that do exist from sources other than kill statistics do not support the MSY theories or the underlying assumptions. For example, with the exception of the California gray whales, no whale population which has been reduced by whaling has ever responded to protection by an increase in numbers, even when that protection has extended over nearly half a century.

Wagner has emphasized the need to take the whole ecosystem into account in management of wild fish and wildlife populations, and the danger—indeed possible irreversible losses—resulting from harvesting a single species on the simplistic MSY basis. Members of the I.W.C. Scientific Committee expressed similar concerns with regard to fin whale harvest at the 1973 meeting.

Effective whale management can only be achieved through a working understanding of the whales as part of the marine ecosystem, not on the basis of applying a questionable MSY concept in a simplistic way to a single species, for which adequate base data do not exist.

This leads to my final conclusion. The time is past when we can equate conservation with maximum sustainable yield, or when we can base management of a living resource simply on our economic "need" for its products. We are slowly coming to the realization that maintenance of the health of the habitat is a prerequisite to the survival of a species, as well as to the maintenance of its possible productivity for man. Management, and the legislation on which management is based, must recognize this.

JOAN MCINTYRE
Re-Creation

Our culture is a screen; we look through it with eyes that have been taught that a bush is green, not that it has a taste. Our perceptions, ideas, and feelings are filtered through the interpretative process of our culture; it is what we believe the world is about. It has, for several thousand years, insisted that we are unique and dominant in the world of life; that only we, the bearers of the technological literate tradition, learn; that to be this kind of human is to have as our dominion the materials of the planet to do with as we wish.

And God said, Let us make man in our image, after our likeness: and let them have dominion over the fish of the sea, and over the fowl of the air, and over the cattle, and over all the earth, and over every creeping thing that creepeth upon the earth. (Genesis 1:26)

Maybe that was the breaking point in our tradition—where we started the long road into our loneliness. When we asserted our *rights* over nature we asserted our isolation and sanctioned a relationship that gives us not only the slaughter of whales for profit but also a belief system that could not imagine them as being like us.

Before the Christian version of creation took over the mind of Mediterranean man, we shared a belief in the continuing process of creation. Creation was not something that was done and finished—... "on the seventh day he rested . . ."—it was something that had to be maintained by the collective good works and feelings of gods and people. It was a dynamic process that maintained collective responsibility. When we set aside that idea for the idea of finite divine creation, we effectively wrote all individual responsibility for the well-being of the planet out of the picture. There was no more need to do anything—it was done—and the only thing that remained was to take. So we began to take. The offerings, the symbolic transactions between parts of the universe, between the parts of growth and renewal and death and decay were forgotten. It became a matter of

237

amassing more and more, of settling only an individual's destiny.

Now we look around us, at a civilization coming apart, at the ice breaking up after a long spiritual winter, and realize that the infinite process of taking is at an end; that the mother, the earth, must be refilled and replenished. The slaughter of whales is one instance in a mind disease called the inexhaustible earth and ocean.

This book is not meant to be an idle exercise in telling a story; this book is meant to be a transaction. We have spent some energy and time trying to suggest the outlines of an infinitely marvelous and still mysterious event—the history, present, and future of an entire order of creatures of the natural world—a history that continues, as the creation of Cetaceans continues, as the creation of humans and trees and rivers continues. And we wish you to remain with us in this transaction—to use this beginning to start the process of repayment, of evening the score. This book has cost the earth her energy and her love. Trees have been cut, fuel has been used. There is no way to escape the contradiction, there is only the possibility of acting responsibly and less self-centeredly within it.

You have already begun the process. By buying this book you have contributed some of your money to saving the whales; by reading it, you have begun to reconsider them, and we hope, by analogy, all of the rest of this planet's life that lies buried under the indifference of the past three thousand years.

There can no longer be any question that we will survive individually; we can only survive collectively. The nuclear power plant that plows plutonium in our earth to exude its poisons for the next twenty-four thousand years will be no respector of individual security. The mercury-laden fish are available at the best restaurants. There is nowhere to hide, there is only a place to start from.

So now we begin again the process of reparations, of return—symbolically opening the shrines and temples to lay offerings and fidelity on the ground of the planet. Again, we invite you to join us.

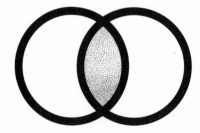

Index